Worth

Father of Haute Couture

By the same author

The History of Haute Couture 1850–1950

Worth

Father of Haute Couture

Diana de Marly

1980
ELM TREE BOOKS
LONDON

HOLMES & MEIER PUBLISHERS, INC.
IMPORT DIVISION
30 Irving Place, New York, N.Y. 10003

First published in Great Britain 1980
By Elm Tree Books, Garden House
57–59 Long Acre, London WC2E 9JZ

Copyright © 1980 by Diana de Marly

British Library Cataloguing in Publication Data

De Marly, Diana
  Worth
  1.   Worth, Charles Frederick
  2.   Costume designers – Biography
  746.9'2'0924   TT505.W6

ISBN 0-241-10304-5

Printed and bound in Great Britain at
The Camelot Press Ltd, Southampton

Contents

Acknowledgements	vii
List of Illustrations	ix
Author's Preface	xiii
Foreword	xv
Worth Family Tree	
1. The English Years 1825–45	1
2. Parisian Changes	12
3. First Successes	23
4. The Great Gamble	34
5. The Court Couturier	44
6. Masquerade	60
7. Worth and Fashion during the Second Empire	75
8. Maison Worth and Worth's Attitude to Dress	98
9. Disaster and Survival	121
10. A King among Queens	149
11. Leading Ladies	171
12. Le Grand Doyen	187
Appendix: Some surviving examples of Worth Gowns	212
Index	218

Acknowledgements

The author is much indebted to the following for their assistance: my dear friend Maurice Worth for his unfailing co-operation and hospitality; Sir John Gielgud for information on his family; Prince and Princess von Metternich for information on their records and Lady Cobbold for material from her grandmother's diary and her grandfather's letters.

I am grateful, too, to the staff of the museums and collections mentioned below and especially to: Jean-Marie Moulin, Directeur of the Musée National du Château de Compiègne for allowing me to roam through the Second Empire; Mme H. Vanier and her successor Mlle Delpierre of the Musée Carnavalet, Paris; Mme Yvonne Deslandres of the Centre d'Enseignement et de Documentation du Costume, Paris; Mme Sylvie Chevalley, Archiviste-Bibliothécaire of the Comédie Française; Jane Low of the Print Room, Royal Library, Windsor Castle; Valerie Cumming, formerly of the Museum of London; Anthea James of Merseyside County Museums; Elizabeth Anne Coleman of Brooklyn Museum; Paul Ettesvold of the Costume Institute, Metropolitan Museum of Art, New York; Matthew Kiernan of the Museum of Fine Arts, Boston; Joan Severa of the State Historical Society of Wisconsin and to C. Fellens, Conseiller pour Affaires Culturelles of the Belgian Embassy, for his detective work, and the Cultural Department of the Royal Swedish Embassy for translating some Swedish for me.

I should also like to thank the following inhabitants of Bourne, Lincolnshire: Canon G. Lanham, Dr Galletly, Mr J. Goode, and Mr H. Stanton, as well as the following libraries: the British Library, the London Library, the Victoria & Albert Museum Library, the Courtauld Institute of Art, the Senate House Library of the University of London, and Westminster City Libraries.

The author and publisher would like to gratefully acknowledge all those who gave their kind permission to reproduce copyright photographs in this volume: Her Majesty the Queen (11, 69, 73): Bourne United Charities (1); Guildhall Library (2); Museum of London (3, 5); *An Autobiography*, Kate Terry Gielgud, Max Reinhardt (4); British Museum (6, 7, 12, 12a, 56); Bowes Museum (8); Musée Ingres (9); Jean-Loup Charmet, Musée Carnavalet, Paris (13, 15, 17,

41); *Lady's Realm*, Victoria & Albert Museum Library (14, 100); Prince von Metternich (16); Jean Dubout, Centre de Documentation du Costume, Paris (18, 25); *A Century of Fashion*, J.-P. Worth, British Library (19, 28, 29, 30, 35, 36, 40, 57, 80, 84, 85); *L'Illustration*, Victoria & Albert Museum Library (20, 21, 22, 23, 27, 31); Giraudon (24); Musée National du Château de Compiègne (26); Victoria & Albert Museum (32, 33, 34, 37, 43, 52) *Un Siècle d'Elégance Française*, Nicole Vedrès, Les Editions du Chêne (38); Burrell Collection (39); *Les Elégances de Second Empire*, Henri Bouchot, British Library (42, 44, 79); Musée du Arts Décoratifs (46, 47); British Library (48, 49, 62, 102); Hermitage Museum, Leningrad (51); *Victorian Fashions & Costumes From Harpers Bazar: 1867–1898*, Dover (53, 64, 65, 66, 67, 93, 95); *Illustrated London News*, Victoria & Albert Museum Library (54, 59, 60, 71); Science Museum (55); Nadar, Arch. Phot., Paris/S.P.A.D.E.M. (58, 63), Worth Parfums, Paris (61, 97, 98, 101); *Punch* (68); Radio Times Hulton Picture Library (70, 72); *The Sunny Side of Diplomatic Life*, L. de Hegermann-Lindencrone, British Library (74); Georg Schafer Collection, Schweinfurt (75); State Historical Society of Wisconsin (76); Madame Tussaud's Archive (77); British Theatre Museum (78, 81, 82, 83, 86); *Harpers Bazar*, Victoria & Albert Museum Library (87, 88, 89, 90, 91, 92, 94); Duke of Marlborough, Blenheim Palace, Oxon (96); National Portrait Gallery, London (99).

The following photographs belong to the author's private collection: 10, 45 and 50.

List of Illustrations

1. View of Bourne, Lincs.   1
2. Lithograph by E. Walker – The Quadrant, Regent Street   6
3. Regent Street in 1849   7
4. Arthur James Lewis   7
5. Lithograph by Sands after Allan – The new National Gallery, London   8
6. Plan of Paris in 1850   13
7. Lithograph by V. Adam and J. Arnout – The Proclamation of the French Second Republic   15
8. J. de Vignon after Winterhalter – Emperor Napoleon III   17
9. Winterhalter – Eugénie, Empress of the French   20
10. Worth as a young man   25
11. Joseph Nash gouache – The French Stands at the Great Exhibition of 1851   27
12. Two of Worth's first dress designs to be published: a hand-painted gown and his first experiment with wider skirts   28
13. Lithograph by Charpentier – The Closing of the Paris Exposition Universelle   29
14. Maison Worth at No. 7, rue de la Paix   31
15. Guiseppe Canella – La rue de la Paix   32
16. Engraving after Winterhalter – Princess Pauline von Metternich   36
17. Lithograph by G. Bargu after H. de Montaret – A Reception at the Palais des Tuileries   38
18. The original label of the world's first haute couture House   39
19. Worth, the businessman   42
20. The first state ball of the 1860 season   47
21. One of Empress Eugénie's intimate Monday parties   48
22. Czar Alexander II receives Napoleon III and Empress Eugénie   50
23. The Prince Imperial presenting a grand prix to his father, Napoleon III   51
24. T. Couture – Princess Mathilde Bonaparte   53
25. The earliest illustrated advertisement   55

26. Winterhalter – The Duchesse de Morny   57
27. *Bal costumé* given by Empress Eugénie's sister, the Duchess
    of Alba, at the Hôtel d'Albe, 1860   62
28. Worth's peacock dress for the Princesse de Sagan in 1864   66
29. Miss Van Wart as Marie Antoinette   70
30. Mme de Benardaki in fancy dress   71
31. Bertall cartoon on the problems of the crinoline   79
32. The crinoline at its widest   81
33. Worth design for a swept-back dress, *c.* 1864   82
34. The swept-back look in a lace skirt   83
35. One of Worth's experiments with dress construction:
    Marie Worth in a prototype princess dress   84
36. The Duchesse de Morny in 1863   85
37. Worth's design for a dress and cape, 1865   86
38. Princess von Metternich   87
39. E. Boudin – Empress Eugénie and her ladies wearing the
    shorter skirt, 1863   88
40. Marie Worth, in a short walking skirt, with her sons,
    Gaston and Jean-Philippe, 1863   88
41. T. van Elven – Empress Eugénie in a Worth tunic dress
    with Czar Alexander II and Napoleon III at the Palais des
    Tuileries, 1867   92
42. Princess von Metternich in Worth's flat-fronted dress   93
43. The bustle in 1696. A. Trouvain – Charlotte Landgravine
    of Hesse Cassel, Queen of Denmark   94
44. The bustle as revived by Worth in 1869, and worn by the
    Comtesse de Pourtalès   95
45. The imperial couturier at forty   98
46. Lyon silk with feather pattern used by Worth for Empress
    Eugénie   104
47. Black satin with design of tulips made for Worth by
    Gourd, Payen et Cie in 1889   106
48. Worth supervising a fitting in 1880   107
49. G. C. Hellawell – Overcome by her first Worth dress. An
    incident in Frances Hodgson Burnett's novel *Louisiana*,
    1880   110
50. Méaulle after Nadar – Worth the artist in 1892   111
51. Winterhalter – T. A. Iocynosou, 1858   114
52. Worth evening dress design   115
53. A Worth tea gown, 1891   117
54. The steamship *Europe*, 1871   118
55. The 4-4-0 locomotive 1814, in 1888   118
56. Napoleon III surrenders to Bismarck   122
57. The Marquise de Manzanedo   125

x

58. The artist Camille Corot, photograph by Nadar   127
59. Prussian troops in the gardens of the Palais des Tuileries   127
60. The burning of the Palais des Tuileries   129
61. Worth's British passport   132
62. Empress Eugénie in exile   138
63. Nadar – Edmond de Goncourt with his brother, Jules   139
64. Worth's fan train of 1873   142
65. Narrowing the line, Worth's export model sold to Lord & Taylor of New York, 1874   143
66. The princess gown of 1875   144
67. An evening gown of 1876, obtaining fit without a waist-seam, using sections   145
68. Worth brings back the bustle, 1881   147
69. Frith – The Marriage of the Prince of Wales to Princess Alexandra of Denmark, 10 March 1863   150
70. Grand Duchess Marie Feodorovna, with her husband, Grand Duke Alexander and their son, Nicholas, c. 1872   155
71. Alexander III crowning Marie Feodorovna as his empress, 1883   155
72. Princess Alexandra of Hesse, 1894   156
73. V. Princeps – The Viceroy of India proclaiming Queen Victoria Empress   162
74. Queen Margherita of Italy   165
75. A. von Menzel – Im Weissen Saal, 1888   167
76. Mrs Julius Fairchild of Wisconsin   168
77. The British Court. Madame Tussaud's waxwork display about the time of Queen Victoria's Golden Jubilee, 1887   169
78. Hortense Schneider in Offenbach's La Grande Duchesse de Gerolstein, 1867   173
79. Sarah Bernhardt, 1867   175
80. Marie Louise Marsy in Le Misanthrope, 1890   177
81. Lillie Langtry in The School for Scandal, 1885   178
82. Adelina Patti in Romeo and Juliet at Covent Garden, 11 July 1867   180
83. Emma Albani at Covent Garden, April 1872   181
84. Nellie Melba in La Traviata, 1888   183
85. The cloak for Melba to wear in Lohengrin, 1891   183
86. Emma Eames in The Lady of Longford, Covent Garden, 21 July 1894   184
87. Worth at-home toilette in grey-green damask   188
88. Worth's afternoon tea gown, Cleopatra, 1891   189
89. Worth spring costume, 1891   190
90. Worth summer cape, July 1891   191

91. Worth tailored suit showing late eighteenth-century influence, October 1891   192
92. Worth's seamless princess gown, October 1891   192
93. Worth's bias cut seamless dress, 1892   193
94. Worth autumn cloak, 1891   194
95. Worth evening gown, 1894   195
96. Carolus-Duran – Consuelo Vanderbilt, 1894   197
97. Worth's château   199
98. The gateway to Worth's château   199
99. Watts – The first Earl of Lytton, 1884   202
100. Empress Eugénie, 1896   205
101. Friand – Worth at sixty-seven in 1893   207
102. Marie Worth as a widow, 1895   208

Author's Preface

Any biographer tackling the subject of Worth faces a surprising dearth of original material. Worth himself did not keep a diary, nor was he a great letter writer, so his only statements are those recorded by journalists or those in other people's memoirs. In addition, his couture house did not keep an archive on its founder, and on several occasions in its history what records they did have were lost or discarded. Material disappeared, for example, when the House changed its premises in 1935, and again when the whole business was bought up by Paquin in 1954 – only to be closed down in 1956. So, there is no information on what the customers bought, who all the customers were or what regulations the master laid down to run his establishment.

One cannot look to Worth's clients for information either. Prince Napoléon, Prince Paul von Metternich, Prince Napoléon Murat and the Duchesse de Mouchy all regret that time and war have destroyed whatever records their ancestors may have possessed, while the Pierpoint Morgans doubt if their predecessors kept very much in the first place. The nineteenth century was probably the start of the 'throw-away' society because the period before that is certainly richer in wardrobe accounts. Consequently, this examination of Worth can only be based on what there is available and not on comprehensive archives.

All translations from the French are by the author except where otherwise stated.

Foreword

Anyone who works in the sphere of fashion knows the name of Worth, but what we don't know are the details of his extraordinary career. His name is surrounded by legend, but in Diana de Marly's book we can, at last, discover the real facts.

There are two reasons why I was delighted to be asked to write this Foreword: firstly because I find it fascinating that the first great couturier in the capital of French fashion should have been an Englishman, and secondly because during my own career I have been involved with Maison Worth in London. In the war the army allowed me to work for short periods over a three-year span at Maison Worth, and when I opened my own business in 1946, two vendeuses, two tailors and two cutters came to me from Worth. Consequently, I am intrigued to learn about the founder of that great House and this book will become a companion which I shall often consult.

It is only since the war that dress designers have become socially acceptable. I once said to Charles, Vicomte de Noailles, at a fashionable dinner party, that I knew my place: after the actors and before the hairdressers. '*Pas du tout*,' said the vicomte, 'at a luncheon the other day in Paris, I looked round the very distinguished table and remarked to my neighbour that the guests were mostly relatives or friends but I did not know the gentleman on my hostess's right.' The reply was that it was Monsieur Alexandre, the famous hairdresser. That it is how far we have come today and it is amazing to learn from Diana de Marly just how much Worth got away with in the nineteenth century. He was autocratic in a way which no dress designer today would dare to be. My maxim is the customer is always right, but Worth ignored his customers' own opinions completely – dictating exactly what they should wear.

It is a unique and incredible story and the author is to be congratulated on telling it with such authority, and for presenting her wide knowledge with both elegance and humour.

HARDY AMIES

Worth Family Tree

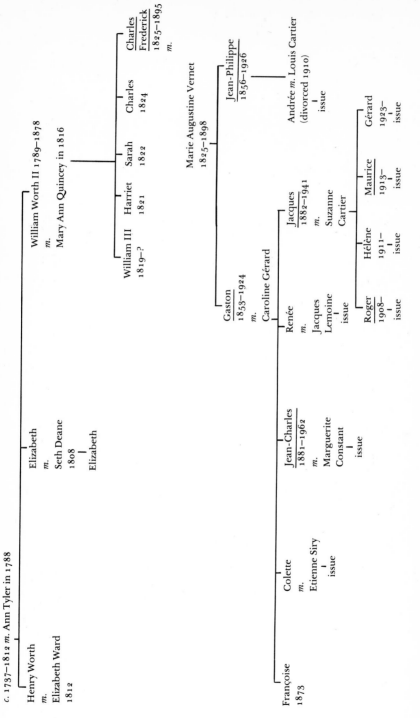

Worth family tree was compiled with the assistance of Maurice Worth.
Names underlined are those of the couturiers.

Chapter 1

The English Years 1825–45

'. . . The men believe in the Bourse, and the women in Worth', so wrote the journalist Felix Whitehurst about Paris under the Second Empire, where a former English shop-assistant called Charles Frederick Worth was all powerful in the capital city of international high fashion, as the first haute couturier and the first world-wide fashion dictator.

Worth was born at Wake House, North Street, in the small market town of Bourne in south Lincolnshire, on 13 October 1825. He was christened at the Abbey Church of Saints Peter and Paul on 10 November.[1] The Worths were a family of solicitors who had no connections with the dress trade whatsoever. Charles Frederick's

1. View of Bourne, Lincs., with the Old Mill, and the Abbey Church where Worth was christened.

grandfather, William I, who had died in 1812, had been a partner in a firm of solicitors in the nearby village of Horbling and his son William II, who was born in 1789, established his own legal practice in Bourne, where he married Mary Anne Quincey from Threckingham in 1816.

Five children were born to William and Mary Worth during the six years between 1819 and 1825. Their first-born, William III, was followed by two girls and a boy – all of whom died in infancy. Their last child was Charles Frederick himself. The eldest son followed in his father's footsteps and pursued a legal career, and young Charles Frederick would also have expected his life to follow a similar course towards a professional occupation. In his early years he was surrounded by comfort and respectability, for he lived at a time when the local solicitor, along with the doctor and the vicar, formed a highly respected trio in the hierarchy of many a small town where society was full of the niceties of correct position – as readers of Jane Austen will be aware. His home was only a few paces from the Market Place and the Town Hall, so the Worths lived at the very centre of town activity, but in 1836 disaster and shame overwhelmed them. William Worth (II) became bankrupt and deserted his family.

There are conflicting accounts as to the cause of his downfall. Charles Frederick's own son Jean-Philippe Worth thought his grandfather lost all his money gambling; *The Times* in its obituary on Charles Frederick in 1895 stated that the family's financial collapse had been due to bad speculation; while local tradition in Bourne believes that Worth's disgrace was brought about by drink. A combination of all three factors may have been the reason for his flight. William II left the district and did not return for thirty years. His practice was not sold, however, until 1852, when it was purchased by a Mr Andrews, whose firm, Andrews, Stanton & Ringrose still exists today.[2] After this disgrace in 1836, Charles Frederick never saw his father again. Years later, when William II made overtures to his son, he was met with icy refusal to ever meet him again, for Charles Frederick never forgave the man who had abandoned his wife and son to shame and humiliation. In rejecting his father's behaviour and divorcing himself from him thereafter, Charles Frederick was merely reflecting the attitudes of an era when drinking and gambling were looked on as signs of moral turpitude and depravity, and not the psychological illnesses they might be considered today.

Whatever hopes the child may have had for the future were all now dashed by his father's failure, and his bitter resentment is understandable. It fell to Mary Worth to try to build what she could from the ruins – in the full view of a small town which knew every detail of the family disgrace. In order to escape comment and the obvious drop in social status, she moved to the village of Billingborough, taking Charles Frederick, who was now eleven years old, with her. The elder boy William III had already left home to start his legal training, so Mary Worth's main concern was to feed herself and the younger boy. It is possible that her marriage had been breaking down for some time, as her husband's gambling and drinking had slowly built up to the crisis of 1836, and she may have been struggling for years to maintain a façade of respectability and to conceal her husband's failings. It is noticeable that no more children were born to the couple after 1825, although they had appeared almost annually before then, so personal relations may have been growing increasingly cool during the following period.

In Billingborough, Mary Worth was befriended by the Blason family as she struggled to find work. What indeed could a middle-class woman, accustomed to a few servants of her own, do? Eventually her Quincey cousins agreed to take her on as their housekeeper, which was the only occupation Mary knew anything about, although her cousins do not appear to have given her any more than her keep by way of payment. Certainly she could not afford to support her son – Charles Frederick's childhood and formal education were over; he would have to go out to work. It would be surprising indeed if the boy did not resent this change in his circumstances very deeply; his brother William had embarked safely on a professional career, but he himself would have to accept whatever menial job his mother could find.

Mary Worth's first concern was to identify the kind of job which would give her son a secure future and some sort of training; she took him along to a printer's shop. There was a small printing office named Sang just opposite the Town Hall in Bourne, so this may well have been the printer concerned, for there cannot have been many such businesses in this country area. For the next twelve months young Charles Frederick spent his time cleaning inky plates and scrubbing out the premises, but he grew increasingly bored and dissatisfied with the dirty work. Even at the age of eleven he wanted something that required some mental challenge. He endured the job for one year and then begged his mother to try to find him something better. There is a tradition in Billingborough that at this stage in his life young Worth expressed the desire to become a couturier – this is a nice idea but completely impossible. There was no such career for men in the 1830s, when dressmaking was virtually a female monopoly. Moreover, what would a boy in a country town know about international high fashion? What is more likely is that Mary Worth thought of haberdashery as the sort of post which might suit her son. In view of her middle-class background she would not want

3

to send the boy into a factory, or to make him into a common soldier or a servant. Being a clerk would probably bore him just as much as printing, so what other alternative was there for an impecunious twelve-year-old but an apprenticeship in a shop? It is possible that Mary Worth had some fashion plates from magazines, and if her son had liked the idea of dealing with fabrics and elegant customers it could have clinched the matter. Charles Frederick could work for a London draper.

Local legend maintains that young Worth raised his fare to London by making ladies' Easter bonnets, but the huge bonnets of the late 1830s seem too big a job for a boy to tackle single-handed, and, if there is any truth in the story, Mary Worth probably obtained some basic hoods which she and her son decorated with lace and artificial flowers. They would certainly have needed to raise the money somehow. The reference to Easter provides a date for the time when Worth left Lincolnshire; after Easter 1838. It is likely that his mother went with him on the coach, as a parent's signature would have been necessary on the indenture.

There is some confusion as to which shop Worth went to, because Jean-Philippe claimed that his father started at Lewis & Allenby, but this is countered by W. F. Lonergan who interviewed Charles Frederick himself in the 1890s and recorded that he served his apprenticeship at Swan & Edgar from 1838. Moreover, *The Times* obituary agrees with this.[3] Lonergan's account does seem more reasonable, for Lewis & Allenby was the most exclusive silk mercers in town – by appointment mercers to the new queen Victoria – and would have had little use for a raw country lad. On the other hand, Swan & Edgar was not too grand to train apprentices from scratch and, while no staff records survive from the era, it does seem reasonable to accept as the true story the House's tradition that Worth trained there. The probable explanation for Jean-Philippe's mistake is that Mr Allenby was a buyer who made regular visits to Paris. He may have been staying there in 1867 as Charles Frederick's guest, when young Jean-Philippe would have met him, so that the name of this shopkeeper stuck in Jean-Philippe's memory rather than that of Swan & Edgar.

What greater contrast could be imagined for young Charles Frederick, than this translation from a quiet country environment to one of the biggest shops in that bustling new thoroughfare of Regent Street and Piccadilly Circus? In fact Regent Street was not much older than Worth himself, having recently been laid out by John Nash to form a grand route from Regent's Park in the north, to the Prince Regent's residence at Carlton House in the south – neatly dividing smart Mayfair from the Soho slums. From the 1820s Regent Steet flourished, and rapidly became the smartest shopping area in London, outclassing the traditional locations of high-class trade along the Strand and in the City.

It was the centre of the fashionable world in Britain, particularly where male fashion was concerned. Paris might have suzerainty over female modes, but London had acquired dominance in male dress thanks to the emergence of the Dandy. The sons of Regency bucks, Corinthians and Bond Street beaux now had a new parade ground in Regent Street down which to strut with arrogant splendour; the whole area catered for their needs, with smart tailors like Henry Creed, smoking divans, gambling dens, drinking and eating houses, clubs, ballrooms, and bordellos. Yet, despite this emphasis upon the Peacock male, Regent Street also became the new home of the leading English milliners, as dressmakers were then termed, and of mercers and drapers.

Very few ready-made clothes were sold at this time, apart from loose garments like cloaks and mantles. A lady desirous of a new dress would go first to select the material at a haberdasher's or mercer's, and then take it to her milliner to have it made up into a gown in the latest style. These milliners were open for very long hours, particularly during the Season, and customers who wanted a ballgown in a hurry would expect an order placed in the morning to be ready by that evening. The working conditions endured by the seamstresses who had to make these dresses, sometimes labouring from 8 a.m. until midnight and beyond, and by the sewing women who supplied the trimmings and accessories on outside contract, have since become notorious in the history of labour. The ladies who could not afford the prices of metropolitan milliners, went to the myriads of small milliners elsewhere, or made their own clothes, while the poor had to rely on street markets like Seven Dials and the old clothes shops.

Swan & Edgar, which was to be Worth's home for the next seven years, had grown out of the street trade. John Swan and William Edgar had both sold haberdashery from stalls, and when the area began to be redeveloped they teamed up to open a shop at 10 Piccadilly in 1812.[4] In 1821 they took larger premises at the Quadrant, Regent Street (now called Piccadilly Circus), where the firm remains to this day. William Edgar died in that year, so during Worth's time the head of the House was John Swan. Worth grew up in this establishment, for the whole of his adolescence, from the age of twelve to nineteen, was spent there. Apprentices still lived on the premises, and it is Worth family tradition that the great Charles Frederick used to sleep under the counter. Shops were open from 8 a.m. to 8 p.m. six days a week, and staff holidays were few. Swan &

2. Lithograph by E. Walker – The Quadrant, Regent Street, with Swan & Edgar's shop on the left.

Edgar sold materials, which is what young Worth had to study above all. He had to learn to identify the different kinds of textiles, and to understand their individual characteristics, before he could graduate to selling the fabrics to customers as a fully fledged shop assistant.

At a fashionable establishment, all the shop assistants were young men, as smartly turned out as any Dandy, with large cravats, starched shirt fronts, waistcoats sporting watch chains, well-cut coats and fashionable hairstyles and sideboards. Every lady customer was greeted at the door and then conducted to a chair so that she might peruse the materials in comfort. Behind the shop assistants, the apprentices replenished the shelves and fetched and carried. The few ready-made garments on sale were displayed in the windows, and there was a footman on duty at the door to admit customers and to drive off beggars. The accent was very much on gentility, and it gave Worth invaluable training in polite address and the courteous way to handle clients. By the time he had completed his training in 1845, Worth had gained sufficient sophistication to move on to even more distinguished establishments, and this was when he joined Lewis & Allenby.

The royal silk mercers was founded at the end of the eighteenth century by a Welsh draper, Stephen Lewis, and his wife Jane, in the Upper Regent Street area. They worked hard and prospered, and when they wanted to expand they took their buyer, Mr Allenby, into partnership, so that the firm became Lewis & Allenby. They moved to 195–197 Regent Street where Worth joined them when he was nineteen. The Lewises had two sons – Stephen II took over as head of

3. Regent Street in 1849 with the royal mercers Lewis & Allenby at Nos. 193–7.

the firm when his parents retired, and Arthur James acted as the courier and assisted Mr Allenby on his buying trips abroad. Indeed, Mr Allenby and Arthur James Lewis would have been the most knowledgeable experts on Continental textiles that Worth had yet encountered, for they made regular visits to Lyon, Paris, Brussels, Mechlin and Geneva, purchasing silks, velvets and brocades. Arthur

4. Arthur James Lewis, courier and textile buyer at Lewis & Allenby.

James Lewis also mixed in artistic and theatrical circles, and in 1867 he became engaged to the actress, Kate Terry, and subsequently became grandfather to another doyen of the stage, Sir John Gielgud.[5] Having such personalities as these as his bosses must have helped to widen Worth's outlook considerably.

Worth was determined to overcome the social downfall caused by his father. While his formal schooling was over at the age of eleven, he still tried to maintain some educational standards and sought to improve himself by reading contemporary novelists and visiting art galleries. One building in particular attracted his interest, the National Gallery in nearby Trafalgar Square, which had moved to those premises in 1838, the very year that Worth had come to London.

5. Lithograph by Sands after Allan – The new National Gallery, London, with a projected design for a memorial to Lord Nelson, which was not chosen.

It was, however, closed on Sundays and two other days a week were reserved for art students, so the galleries were only open to the general public on four days a week. Nevertheless, Worth managed to go there, either when out delivering goods or carrying messages, or he may have sacrificed some lunchtimes. To Worth the National Gallery proved a palace of delights, and art was to become a constant inspiration to him later in his life. Never before had he seen so many pictures or so many variations in colour range, such differences of artistic style and diversity of subject matter – a whole new continent was revealed, compelling him to explore. Working as he was in a field where a sense of colour and a sharp visual awareness were essentials in appreciating the texture and design of textiles, he already possessed those faculties necessary for some sort of appreciation of art.

The National Gallery collection from 1838 to 1845, when Worth was living in Regent Street and Piccadilly, consisted of the union of two private collections – that of Sir John Beaumont, which was presented by the owner, and that of John Angerstein, which was bought for the nation. It included works by Titian, Rubens, Rembrandt, Claude, Poussin, Hogarth and Reynolds. Worth's eye was attracted most of all by what he was already familiar with, and he became fascinated by the depiction of fabrics and costumes in art. The complete cycle of Hogarth's 'Marriage à la Mode' presented a wide survey of English dress in 1743, while a work the Gallery acquired in 1842, Jan van Eyck's 'The Marriage of Giovanni Arnolfini and Giovanna Cenami', preserved the clothes of 1434. Here was the history of dress laid out for him to see. He was also much impressed by a work in a private collection, the Rainbow portrait of Elizabeth I at Hatfield, although he may only have known it in reproduction. What fascinated him about the picture was the use of symbolism in the textile, the 'eyes and ears' on the queen's mantle, signifying that she saw and heard all. Years later he was to have that pattern copied in a fabric for himself.

To Worth the art of the past was to be the inspiration for the future. In particular it was the catalyst for costume design, with the clothes of one period of portraiture sparking off ideas for clothes of his own times. He must have noticed how certain elements in dress recur, such as low necklines and large sleeves, although reinterpreted in different ways over the centuries. The very big sleeves worn by women in his own 1830s were a reflection of the Romantic period's interest in the early sixteenth century, while the current vogue for wide lace collars showed a similar interest in the dress of the early seventeenth century. When he had realized this Worth could begin to see that the creation of fashions for the present age was not such a mystery after all, when there were examples from previous periods to act as guides. These visits to the National Gallery must have considerably reinforced any interest Worth then had in dress, and they were a valuable introduction to a treasure house of information. The knowledge gained here was to be of immense importance in the future, when Worth was faced with the need to design hundreds of historical costumes for the masquerades and the theatre in Paris. It could be argued that Worth showed little appreciation of works of art in their own right, but he had never received any education or guidance in the fine arts. His training was in selling textiles to be made into clothes, and consequently this conditioned his appreciation. His preference was of course for portraits, for they were the most informative and useful where dress was concerned; a noble landscape could not help him here, but at least his imagination was excited, his eyes were opened, and he learnt from what he saw.

9

Worth's appetite had been aroused, and as he approached his twentieth year he became increasingly restless with the desire to satisfy it. Valuable as a post at Lewis & Allenby was, it was still a silk mercer's and not a temple from which new fashions were proclaimed. The magazines displaying coloured prints of the latest modes made it very clear that the seat of invention for female fashion lay in Paris. As his interest in dress increased, Worth realized that if he wanted to be at the centre of the dress trade he would have to cross the Channel. But how could he go to France without knowing the French language? What could give him the confidence to strike out on his own? The answer, it seems, was a novel. Years later in 1873 Worth met Robert, first Earl of Lytton, son of the novelist Edward Bulwer-Lytton, for the first time. The earl wrote of that meeting:

> On hearing who I was he rushed up to me, and after an infinite number of compliments and fine speeches, said he owed everything in life to my father. 'As how?' I asked. Whilst yet a youth struggling with fortune he had read *Night and Morning*. The book had made a profound impression on him, had awakened his genius, aroused his courage, kindled his hopes, directed his aims, etc.[6]

Although little read today, this three-volume work taught that heroes must overcome disappointment and learn to be masters of themselves and of their destinies. It suggested to Worth that he might arrange his own future. It gave him the courage to pursue his own interests and ambitions, to dare to go it alone. In resolving to do this, Worth was embarking on that policy of self-help which was to become established as one of the virtues of the new Victorian society.

No doubt he discussed his plans with Mr Allenby and Arthur James Lewis, because they could tell him where to aim for, and which were the best French silk mercers in Paris who might eventually give him a job. And as references were extremely important when seeking employment in those days, Worth would hardly have taken such a step if his employers had not approved. At this stage Worth's plans were probably rather vague, and he may not have intended to settle in France on a permanent basis. A few years working in Parisian shops and then perhaps back to London as a buyer for an English store, or making valuable contacts in the French textile trade prior to opening his own silk mercer's one day; these may have been the thoughts at the back of his mind, rather than any plan to emigrate. In addition he had his mother to think of; the time would come when her working life would be over and then her sons would have to support her, for her husband had vanished. Because of this, Worth probably did not mean to leave England for ever.

Deciding to go to Paris was one problem; finding the means to do so was another. During his apprenticeship he had been maintained by Swan & Edgar, and his few months at Lewis & Allenby were the first time he had been paid a living wage. What little he could save was insufficient to pay for a trip to Paris and keep him while he looked for a job, so once again Worth had to appeal for help to his mother. As she had no income apart from what she received for her board and lodging, she in turn had to beg for money from her relations, and the sum thus raised was enough to pay Worth's fare and to leave him with £5 to maintain him while he looked for employment. Thus equipped, with youthful optimism in greater supply than assets, and knowing no French beyond the vocabulary of fashion, Charles Frederick Worth caught the steamer from London Bridge in the winter of 1845, just after his twentieth birthday. He was embarking on an adventure that was to sweep him to unimagined heights.

Notes

1. Baptismal Records, Abbey Church of Sts Peter and Paul, Bourne, Lincs., courtesy of Canon G. J. Lanham, Rural Dean. There is some confusion about the exact date of birth, as Jean-Philippe Worth stated in his book, *A Century of Fashion* (1928), ch. 1, that Worth was born in November 1826, and this has been copied by other writers since, but the church records show that it was in fact in 1825. Jean-Philippe Worth's book was published two years after his own death, and consists of his rambling memories and not of definitive research.
2. I am grateful to Mr Horace Stanton, to Mr J. E. Goode of Andrews, Stanton & Ringrose, and to Dr J. A. Galletly – all of Bourne – for their help in providing information on the local traditions about Worth.
3. W. F. Lonergan, *Forty Years of Paris* (1907), Fisher Unwin, p. 198; *The Times*, 12 March 1895.
4. A. Adburgham, *Shops and Shopping* (1964), Allen & Unwin, p. 15.
5. Kate Terry Gielgud, *An Autobiography* (1953), Max Reinhardt, p. 14; I am indebted to Sir John Gielgud for his advice.
6. *Personal and Literary Letters of Robert, First Earl of Lytton*, ed. Lady Betty Balfour (1906), vol. I, p. 307, letter dated 8 November 1873.

Chapter 2

Parisian Changes

Worth's first couple of years in Paris were fraught with difficulties: he came close to starvation and found the whole period too unpleasant to wish to remember it later. It was a subject on which he refused to be drawn, so the precise details will never be known. He had enough money to exist for a few months at subsistence level, but if he had hoped to master the language and find secure employment in that time, his aspirations were to be disappointed. For an immigrant things are rarely that easy.

No doubt there were two places of interest to which he took himself as soon as he arrived in Paris. First there was the Louvre, with its great galleries full of paintings, where he could see scores of examples of historical costume in both portraits and subject works. Immediately to the north of the Louvre, and to the west of the Palais Royal, ran the rue Richelieu, stretching as far as the Grands Boulevards. Situated here were the most prestigious establishments in the world of high fashion, whose names he would already have known from the magazines and from Mr Allenby, who was a regular visitor to these parts. Worth would have paid particular attention to No. 83, Gagelin, the most exclusive and luxurious silk mercers, more renowned than even Lewis & Allenby in London. Nearby were the foremost tailors and dressmakers who obtained many of their materials from Gagelin. The French king Louis-Philippe had his clothes made here by Ebeling, while his queen Marie-Amélie ordered hers from Mme Delatour. Other monarchs such as Queen Victoria had their clothes made in this street. But what use would such distinguished Houses have had for a newly qualified Englishman with little knowledge of the French language?

Confronted by the reality of his predicament Worth's hopes may well have sagged. He could not walk straight into the textile trade, but must prepare himself for a laborious climb. Every meal he ate reduced his supply of money, every franc spent removed the reserves that could have gone towards his home fare. If at any time during this difficult period he mused about going home, he knew that it would

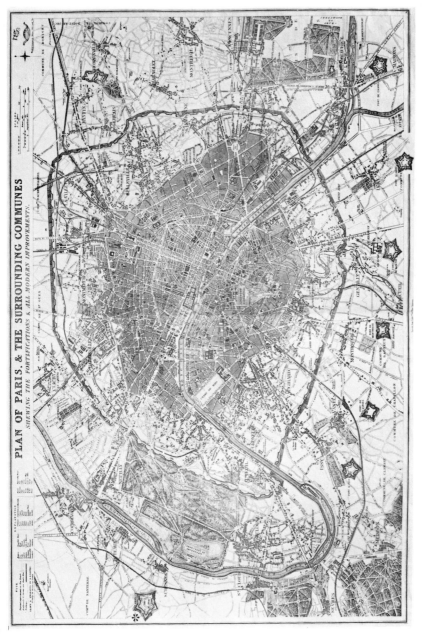

6. Plan of Paris in 1850, showing the ring of fortifications. Worth's working life was in the very centre of the city, and the country estate he acquired at Suresnes is on the far left near the fort (*).

mean defeat. It would mean that he was a failure like his father, and this he was determined to avoid. He had to stay and struggle on.

There may have been a score or more of casual jobs. He had to lower his sights and take whatever unskilled work he could find, for he could hope for no higher form of employment which would have involved talking to customers. Of course he must have equipped himself with a French phrase book, and tried learning new sections every day, but this was not enough. With labour being so cheap, few employers would have had much patience with a worker who could not speak the language. Menial jobs, where no vocabulary was involved, were the most one could imagine for him at this time. He was not the first young hopeful to come to Paris to find that his only bed was under the bridges and that he could not afford a proper meal every day.

Eventually Worth did find work in a shop again, but it could have been more than a year before he did so. He was engaged by a dry goods store where he worked the normal twelve-hour day. This suggests that he had mastered enough French to reply to customers, and the twelve months he spent here were invaluable in giving him some experience in selling and dealing in French. No matter how humble the work, or how long it took him to get there, he was in an area that he knew something about. After one year in dry goods, Worth decided that he was sufficiently fluent in the language to try for higher things. After all, he was speaking French and living French every single day – the very best way to learn a language. So he went back to the rue Richelieu, and presented himself at Gagelin. At this stage a testimonial or a good word from Arthur James Lewis or Mr Allenby would have been essential, for Gagelin was too grand a shop to take anyone without references. Thus Worth obtained his entrée into the very centre of French high fashion, doing what he was trained to do – selling materials.

He was in. Now the two years of struggle would have seemed worth the effort. He could begin to hope for greater things, such as becoming a partner in the firm, or opening his own fabric house. For all his interest in dress, there was no question of his thinking of himself as a prospective dressmaker. That was a female profession; men were haberdashers, mercers, or tailors. The boutique of the most famous dressmaker until that time was still standing in the rue Richelieu. It had belonged to Rose Bertin, who had dressed Marie Antoinette, and a very elegant neo-classical façade it had too, but Worth at twenty-two would hardly have considered any step so outrageous and provocative as trying to break into a female trade. He was a shop-assistant who supplied the materials which the dressmakers came to choose, and no more.

14

Gagelin was to be the centre of Worth's life for the next eleven years – from late 1847 to 1858 – and here he sold fabrics, cashmere shawls and a few ready-made garments, just as he had done in London. It cannot be said, however, that he had arrived on the scene at a very scintillating moment in the sphere of high fashion: the fashionable look of the 1840s was for ladies to appear demure, in sombre colours and with downcast heads. Poke bonnets meant that their vision was severely restricted, the sloping shoulder line prevented wide arm movements, and the heavy skirts made walking fatiguing. In fact their clothes imposed on them that limited and unenergetic role which society demanded of them; even queens were looking modestly domestic.

In the following year, 1848, Worth must have wondered whether he had not made a great mistake in coming to France at all. It was the year of revolutions, sparked off by events in Paris and spreading across the Continent. The French monarchy may have seemed relatively secure from England, for Louis-Philippe had been on the throne for eighteen years and had a numerous family to ensure the succession. Yet there had been revolts and attempted coups in that time, and the king's refusal to reform electoral law was the final match which lit the fuse and caused the powder to explode. The French royal family fled to England, as was usual in such crises, the Paris mob burned the French throne on 24 February, and by May the Second

7. Lithograph by V. Adam and J. Arnout – The Proclamation of the French Second Republic outside the Chamber of Deputies, 4 May 1848.

Republic had been proclaimed. Business of course came to a stand-still, and the outlook for the world of fashion suddenly appeared quite bleak. How would they fare without court receptions to clothe and debutantes to dress?

More fantastic events were to follow. The head of the Bonapartist party intervened, Prince Charles-Louis Napoleon, son of Napoleon I's brother Louis, former King of Holland, and his queen Hortense de Beauharnais. In 1835 at the age of twenty-seven Prince Louis Napoleon became engaged to his seventeen-year-old cousin, Princesse Mathilde, daughter of another of Napoleon I's brothers, Jérôme, King of Westphalia, and he then set about trying to oust Louis-Philippe from France in order to restore the Bonaparte dynasty. In 1836 Louis Napoleon attempted a coup d'état at Strasbourg, but was captured and King Louis-Philippe had him packed off to the USA to avoid the creation of a Bonapartist martyr by having him shot. At this failure, uncle Jérôme cancelled the engagement to Princesse Mathilde. Louis Napoleon came back to Europe when his mother was dying and then took up residence in London between 1838 and 1840, becoming one of the lions of society. From there he embarked on yet another attempted coup, trying to organize a rising at Boulogne, which was such an incompetent business that he was recaptured and spent the next six years locked up in the fortress at Ham. In 1846 he managed to escape, disguised as a workman, and returned to London. The revolution of 1848 and the deposition of King Louis-Philippe gave Prince Louis Napoleon sudden new hope. He offered himself as a candidate for the new National Assembly and was elected – which enabled him to return to France without this time being arrested. With the approach of the first presidential elections at the end of 1848, Louis Napoleon put himself forward as a candidate, promising the restoration of Napoleonic glory, peace and social order. His policy and the surname Bonaparte worked wonders, for he achieved a landslide victory and took office as Prince-President early in 1849.

The next two years saw severe strains between the National Assembly and the imperial president, culminating in Louis Napoleon mounting his third coup d'état on 2 December 1851. This time he was successful; he arrested his leading republican and royalist opponents, and emerged with dictatorial powers. It was now only a question of time before he turned the Second Republic into the Second Napoleonic Empire and when a plebiscite approved his actions, he proclaimed the empire restored in 1852. The Second Empire had begun. Little could Worth have realized as he watched these amazing events – the transformation of France from Bourbon monarchy, to republic, to Napoleonic empire in the space of only four years – how much the new emperor's policies would affect his own life before the decade was out, and how one word from this man would take his career to the very top.

Paris was now granted the status of an imperial capital, with all the ceremony and display which that entailed. The scale of official receptions was greatly increased to outshine the bourgeois splendour of the Bourbons with all the glory and glamour of the Napoleonic dynasty. The new emperor, who called himself Napoleon III

8. J. de Vignon after Winterhalter – Emperor Napoleon III, whose single word took Worth to the top.

(Napoleon I's son, Napoleon II, King of Rome, having died in 1832), was only too well aware that his rise to power was far from orthodox. He confessed to Princess von Metternich: '*N'oubliez pas, princesse, que je suis un parvenu dans la véritable acception du mot.*'[1] Consequently he tried to dazzle his critics with success. Paris was to see a spate of state openings, state visits, court receptions, lavish social seasons, grand military reviews, and universal exhibitions which were even more numerous and glittering than those held under Napoleon himself fifty years before.

The capital was to be replanned and rebuilt on an unprecedented scale, and the new prefect Baron Haussmann was to be granted wide powers to carry out the emperor's schemes to create a city worthy of a Bonaparte. The historic jumble of palaces, tenements and alleys was cut through by wide avenues and boulevards; vistas were opened up, government buildings and new churches were sited at dominant points, and a uniform architectural vocabulary was enforced for street façades. Paris was increased in size, incorporating the surrounding countryside into the city region so that avenues could be extended and new suburbs created. Vienna was to replace its ramparts with the Ringstrasse and London was to undertake some metropolitan improvements, but no other capital in Europe embarked on such a mammoth reconstruction, giving the whole city a completely new look and forming another Paris in the eyes of posterity.

Inevitably all this reorganization and rebuilding caused some degree of hardship; cheap accommodation in the city centre was demolished to make room for elegant town houses and apartments. Worth was only one among many of the working and lower middle classes who now found themselves obliged to live a considerable distance from their places of employment, because they could not afford the rents in the new centre. The *Daily Telegraph*'s reporter commented wryly: 'We are, you know, knocking down old Paris and building new Boulevards. When you go out, you leave your key with the *concierge* and your compliments for M Haussmann, and "if he does not particularly wish to pull down your house today, perhaps he will kindly leave it standing till tomorrow".'[2] There were some who resented these changes strongly. François Guizot, a former minister under Louis-Philippe, who had been greatly opposed to reform, was equally hostile to the Parisian alterations. He complained in 1858 that the growth of the city was horrible in scale, population and traffic. It was no longer a comfortable size with everywhere reachable on foot.[3]

Not content with changing Paris, Napoleon III also set about changing France. Taking his example from the industrial and commercial power he had seen in Britain, he set in train a quantity of public works, new factories, new industries, new institutions for commercial credit, new housing for workers, and the modernization of agriculture. The railway system was expanded rapidly following England's lead, and this improvement in communications was of vital importance to Worth's future success.

While Worth may have fumed at some of the difficulties the rebuilding of Paris had put in his path, he could also see that the Second Empire and its glittering new metropolis were attracting the attention of the world. Bourbon royalists might look down their noses and decline to participate, and republicans might scowl, but for the rest, Paris was becoming a mecca. The Bonapartist aristocracy, those whose fathers had owed their titles to Napoleon I, came back in force, opening up town mansions and embarking on lavish entertaining to add to the imperial display. Court life in London might be becoming more staid as the queen approached middle age, but Paris was acquiring the reputation of the brightest city in Europe, and foreigners flocked from far and near.

All this expenditure on grandeur, magnificence and luxury was to benefit the purveyors of such goods considerably: jewellers, dressmakers, mercers, hairdressers, producers of accessories, restaurateurs, musicians, entertainers and designers were all to be swamped with orders. If in 1848 Worth's gamble had seemed on the brink of disaster, by the mid-1850s it was becoming clear that he was living in the most exciting city on the globe.

The new emperor was particularly anxious to win the formal recognition of other monarchs, and of Britain above all. He sent his cousin, Count Colonna Walewski, son of Napoleon I and the Polish countess, Marie Walewska, as ambassador to London, in an effort to persuade the British government that the new Napoleonic empire had no intention of behaving towards Great Britain as the first one had done. In this he succeeded, the two countries became allies in the Crimean War, and state visits were exchanged in 1855. One outcome was a fashion for things English and Scottish in France, which Worth was to exploit later. Napoleon III also saw himself as the arbiter of Europe, as shown in his support for the reunification of Italy, and to some extent he succeeded. The Second Empire was to become a legendary epoch, mulled over with backward sighs in scores of memoirs thereafter. The brilliance and gaiety were remembered, the mistakes faded, and the principal contributor to this myth was the emperor's wife.

Napoleon III would have liked a royal bride, but the crowned heads of Europe were uncooperative and refused to bestow any of their daughters on a Bonaparte upstart; so he was forced to look elsewhere. He had already had numerous liaisons, and continued to do so during marriage. His English mistress, Elizabeth Howard, had followed him to Paris, and was making herself too obvious, so he pensioned her off with a title, a château and £20,000 a year. He was still hoping for someone with more style and his eye alighted on a countess of mixed Scottish-Spanish descent, Eugénie de Montijo de Guzmán, whose sister had married the eighth Duke of Berwick y Alba. The emperor became infatuated with her and would have liked to have made her his latest mistress, but the countess and her mother would consider no proposition which did not include a wedding ring. Gossip ran rife, the countess was subjected to speculation and innuendo until she could stand the uncertainty no more and resolved to return to Madrid. At this ultimatum Napoleon III came to a decision; he gave up hoping for a royal wife and proposed to Eugénie. The imperial marriage took place in January 1853 and France gained an empress. This brought about Worth's first involvement with the new court, because the materials for the empress's trousseau were supplied by Gagelin and the details were published in the fashion journals. Eugénie's dressmakers were mesdames Vignon and Palmyre, and no doubt the whole of Gagelin put itself out to satisfy their requirements, but one assistant in particular had made a mark in appreciating the suitability of certain textiles for dressmaking – this was Monsieur Worth. At Gagelin, it had become established procedure to discuss the finer points with him, so when the imperial dressmakers delivered their creations to the bride there was something of Worth in them.

9. Winterhalter – Eugénie, Empress of the French.

The arrival of an empress in her mid-twenties brought grace and beauty to the summit of society – in contrast to the maternal charms of the previous queen. Eugénie had an elegance and enchantment which proved powerful weapons in giving the new regime an aura of glamour. Georges Sand in *Impressions et Souvenirs* vowed that all the men were in love with her, while the English journalist George Augustus Sala wrote '. . . the beauty and grace of her form seem but the reflex, patent to all men, of the kindness and tenderness of her heart'.[4] Eugénie had auburn hair and a rose complexion with a skin of almost transparent clarity. Her long slender neck and sloping shoulders were often described as swan-like and looked their best in the décolleté of evening dress. Her eyes were bright blue and she wore just a suggestion of eye-liner; her mouth was small, outlined with a hint of lipstick. She had all the elegance of a dancer and was surprisingly athletic for her day, as she was fond of riding and cross-country walks. The tastes of this woman, her fads and fancies, were now extremely important to all those in the clothing and textile industries, for it was the empress who set the style at court.

Eugénie had her critics. To the pure monarchist she was a commoner unworthy to occupy a throne; and not every member of the Bonaparte family considered her suitable. Napoleon III's former fiancée Princess Mathilde moved to Paris together with some of her other relations. Her father had married her to a wealthy but dissolute Russian nobleman, but Mathilde appealed to the Czar and was granted a divorce. As a result she arrived in Paris with a large settlement, and established the most important literary salon that the city saw in the nineteenth century. To the serious Mathilde, Eugénie was a shallow and flirtatious creature who could think of nothing but clothes, but Queen Victoria was charmed by her when they met in 1855 and remained Eugénie's friend and sympathizer thereafter. It is true that Eugénie was not schooled in that royal dignity and restraint which never behaves incorrectly whatever the circumstances: she could be impulsive and be persuaded to join in pranks, as when she and Princess von Metternich dressed as men and rode round Paris on the top of a horse-drawn omnibus, but nevertheless it was felt that these little lapses added to her charms and made her adherents the more fiercely devoted to her. Whatever her faults, Worth and the rest of the Paris fashion trade were compelled to take their lead from her.

If the emperor was a *parvenu* and his empress a commoner, their court was little different. While it was attended by some members of old houses, many of its dukes and princes were modern creations, and it was even open to the *nouveaux riches*: the bankers and industrialists. In this the court was more attuned to the rise of industrial wealth than the more rigid courts in Europe where hereditary landed wealth was still the only qualification. Some of the beauties Empress Eugénie gathered about her came from these new backgrounds: the Comtesse de Pourtalès was the daughter of an Alsatian manufacturer who had married a Swiss banker, while a frequent visitor to court festivities, Mrs Charles Moulton, was the wife of an American millionaire. The privilege of wealth, from whatever source, was beginning to oust aristocratic prestige, and the newcomers were particularly anxious to advertise their arrival in high places by extravagant entertaining. Thanks to their efforts the Second Empire became synonymous with luxury and pleasure. Lavish spending was the order of the day, and without it Worth would never have made his fortune in the years that followed.

As he surveyed his circumstances, Worth could see where the best opportunity lay. After the disorder and confusion there was now a period of political certainty. Social activity expanded, money flowed and all eyes were on Paris. It was definitely not the time to leave, for an empire had been created in France and the new empress was a positive guarantee that mercers and dressmakers would prosper.

Notes

1. *Souvenirs de la Princesse Pauline de Metternich 1859–71*, notes by M. Dunan (1922), Librairie Plon, p. 86.
2. F. Whitehurst, *Court and Social Life in France under Napoleon III* (1873), vol. I, p. 56.
3. N. W. Senior, *Conversations with M. Thiers, M. Guizot, and other distinguished persons during the Second Empire*, ed. M. C. M. Simpson (1878), vol. II, p. 192.
4. G. A. Sala, *Notes and Sketches on the Paris Exhibition*, Tinsley Bros. (1868), p. 295.

Chapter 3

First Successes

Worth's career at Gagelin went through three phases. Initially he was simply a shop-assistant selling across the counter, unrolling lengths of silk, satin and brocade, and persuasively enlarging on their superior qualities. In this position he was at the service of the most fashionable ladies of the day as they called, and of the most famous dressmakers, mesdames Vignon, Palmyre and Rodger. He had to be an authority on which colours and patterns were coming into favour, and something of a psychologist – able to persuade customers to buy more expensively than was their original intention. In this position he gained an insight into the personalities and tastes of the court, albeit from a distance, and thereby improved on the experience he had gained in London.

As his French vocabulary expanded and he acquired more style, Worth was ready for promotion to more sophisticated work. Gagelin engaged a number of *demoiselles de magasin* – these were girls who were apprenticed at the age of sixteen (their parents paid for their training), whose duty it was to model shawls, mantles and cloaks so that customers might appreciate the beauty of such articles in motion. Worth was appointed to do the sales talk as the mannequins paraded, which called for a further development in his persuasive powers, for he had to wax lyrical and be able to charm countesses and duchesses into believing that a particular shawl was only right for them. The model with whom Worth worked most was Marie Augustine Vernet, from Clermont-Ferrand in the Auvergne. Born in August 1825 she was two months older than he, and her personal history was not unlike his own. Her father was a tax-official who had fallen on hard times; he had married his elder daughter to an architect with a respectable dowry but there was no money for a dowry for Marie. She was forced to go out to work, and what money could be spared was invested in giving her a training so that she could become self-sufficient. The working relationship between Worth and Marie was to be the foundation of a long partnership, and it changed the nature of

Worth's career completely. Marie was the catalyst which turned Worth from a textile salesman into a dressmaker.

As he had to sell what she was wearing, Worth became more and more concerned about Marie's overall appearance. It was necessary to consider the right sort of dress for modelling shawls; one that would always appear elegant no matter how different the wraps and mantles draped over it. Fashionable dresses around 1850 were very fussy, with layers of frills and flounces, and were not suitable as a neutral background for the display of cashmere finery. The only solution was for Worth to make Marie something much simpler.

During his life in London he must have been aware of the importance of English tailoring techniques which gave both men's suits and women's riding-habits an excellence of fit unequalled in the rest of the world. While at Swan & Edgar and Lewis & Allenby he would have seen mantles and wraps being made, and may have done some of this simple making himself. He had no formal education in tailoring, but he had been observing clothes and their construction for years, and he had been playing with textiles since he was twelve. It was not an enormous step for him to put this observation into practice. Once he had got Marie's pattern worked out, he could produce any number of dresses from it; the important consideration was to make that pattern perfect.

The first dresses Worth made for Marie were of white muslin and utterly plain. Nevertheless the fit was so good, and the line so elegant that customers began to take note. So many ladies expressed a desire to order copies that Worth approached his employers with the suggestion that Gagelin might open a department for women's dresses. After all it was impossible for Worth to take on any orders himself when his only day off was a Sunday, and he worked too late to have any spare time during the evenings. Gagelin, however, were absolutely horrified at the very idea. They were the most distinguished silk mercers in the whole of Paris and not a common dressmakers! Worth tried to change their minds by pointing to the example of the dressmaker Mme Rodger in the rue Nationale Saint Martin. She had recently started to sell materials alongside her clothes, which made it possible for customers to both select their fabric and have it made up on the same premises. This saved the chore of first having to go to a mercer's to choose a textile, and then taking it to the dressmaker's. Surely it would be convenient for Gagelin's customers if they could do the same? His employers refused. Worth had to explain to ladies who asked for copies of Marie's dresses that Gagelin would not allow him to sell such items. This of course only made them the more determined to have the dresses; after all, titled ladies were not used to having their wishes ignored. The directors of

Gagelin were pressurized until they gave in. Worth was permitted to open a small dressmaking department, although he was initially restricted to summer gowns only. However, he had got his way and thus Worth became a professional dressmaker – a man in a female trade.

It was only a small beginning and went unobserved by the international press; the outcry was to come in the 1860s. But from 1850 Worth was gradually evolving his own type of dressmaking firm, and

10. Worth as a young man, determined to succeed.

it was to be very different from those of his female competitors. The major difference was that Worth's department was in a textile house; not even Mme Rodger could equal the quantity of fabrics which Worth had at his disposal. The choice he could offer his customers was enormous, for a Worth dress could be ordered in any of the materials which Gagelin stocked. What is more, Worth was in a position to meet the sales representatives from the silk mills in Lyon because he was in a textile house. The dressmaker never encountered such salesmen, and had no influence on the types of materials they offered. Worth on the other hand could deal direct with such men, and could tell them which fabrics he favoured and which colours and patterns he thought should be produced. This sort of link with industry was unprecedented.

Another difference was Worth's obsession with exact fit. No other term could express his determination to improve dressmaking techniques. Because he appreciated tailoring, he was infuriated by the careless and unimaginative approach of dressmakers with their rigid traditions. To Worth, invention and experiment were dominating principles where dress construction was concerned. Never mind what dressmakers usually did – was there a better way to achieve it? He was like an engineer or an architect for whom the soundness of the construction was the fundamental consideration. No amount of decoration could make a house or a dress right if the foundations were wrong. From 1850, until the day he died, Worth never stopped experimenting with new ways to obtain old results by simplifying the process, and evolving new styles of dress by changing the technique. He created a new craft, nothing less, where fit and construction were the governing factors, the absolute principles, founded on superb cut. Because the cut and finish of Worth's gowns were so unparalleled in quality, his approach came to have another name. It was not dressmaking; it was haute couture.

Worth married his inspiration, his model, his pattern, Marie, on 21 June 1851, which suggests that he had made a little money by this time. The big event of 1851, however, as far as the outside world was concerned, was the Great Exhibition of the Works of Industry of All Nations, housed in Paxton's revolutionary Crystal Palace in London's Hyde Park. Countries around the globe sent examples of their produce and manufacture, and France had no intention of being outshone. Gagelin had been bought by new owners, but they were just as concerned as their predecessors to maintain the reputation of the house. How far they appreciated what Worth was doing is debatable, but they did decide to include some of his dresses in their display. The official exhibition catalogue lists them as follows: 'France No. 336: OPIGEZ & CHAZELLE, late GAGELIN, 83 Rue Richelieu, Paris, – Ready-made articles for ladies: – Rich Lyons silk embroidered fabrics, shawls, &C.'[1]

Jean-Philippe Worth thought his father won France's only gold medal at the exhibition, and that his dresses were criticized for not being exactly the same as the current mode, but this is untrue. France won dozens of first prizes, seriously challenging Britain on her own doorstep, and the Jury Reports praise Opigez & Chazelle's entry 'for

11. Joseph Nash gouache – The French Stands at the Great Exhibition of
1851, with a display of silks and brocades from Lyon in the centre.

very excellent embroidered silk, wrought up in dresses of elegant
style'.[2] The prize was of course awarded to Worth's employers and not
to him as an individual.

In view of this success his employers started to advertise their
clothing department in such fashion magazines as *Le Moniteur de la
Mode*, with fashion plates of Worth creations showing pelisses and
shawls of the sort modelled by Marie Worth, hand-painted dresses,
and his earliest experiment with the crinoline in 1852–3, which he
called a great novelty. Moreover, when France and the Second
Empire launched their answer to Britain's Great Exhibition with the
Exposition Universelle of 1855, Worth's employers again entered his
dresses, so it is clear that their earlier objections had been overcome
by pride in the quality of his creations.

The firm entered the display in Class 25, '*Confection des Articles de
Vêtement; Fabrication des Objets de Mode et de Fantasie*', with a selection
of fashionable novelties, court trains, and designs for reproduction –
while its expensive embroidered shawls and silks were exhibited in
Class 23.[3] Of these it was Worth's court train, or *manteau de cour*, which
attracted the most attention. Whereas the usual court train of 1855
was suspended from the waist, Worth had attached his to the
shoulders. He was probably thinking of the court trains of the first
Napoleonic empire, which had hung from a high waistline, and had

12. Two of Worth's first dress designs to be published – a hand-painted gown (top right), and his first experiment with wider skirts (bottom).

been commemorated by such artists as Gros, Gérard and Régnault. There was no high waistline in 1855, so by attaching the train to the shoulders, Worth came as close as he could to complimenting the Second Empire by recalling the first. The advantage of this position was that there was a greater sweep of material on which to display large-scale embroidery, as Worth showed by making the train of watered silk embroidered in gold. The international jury considered the effect so magnificent that they awarded the train a first-class medal. Once again Worth had triumphed, and once again his employers collected the award.

13. Lithograph by Charpentier – The Closing of the Paris Exposition Universelle, with Napoleon III presenting the awards to the prize winners in the Palace of Industry on 15 November 1855.

One striking fact about both the 1851 and 1855 exhibitions which Worth could not have failed to notice, was the huge number of foreigners who visited them. Thanks to the new railways and steamships, it was now possible for far greater numbers of people to travel than ever before. Not only did French, Germans, Italians, Spanish and Russians come to London; so did Americans. Communications had been speeded up, and, whereas American colonials in the eighteenth century would have had to wait months for an order of clothes to be shipped out from England, by the 1850s such orders could be received within weeks. Apart from the wealthy sightseers, the steamers brought American buyers to reconnoitre on behalf of American stores, and the observant tradesmen could see the possibility of increased exports to the USA opening up.

While one-sixth of French clothing manufactures was exported, the garments were mainly loose articles like mantles and wraps, and the finish was not high. Worth was quick to see that foreign buyers should be given the same opportunity to purchase model gowns as French customers. He offered them quality, and of course variety. What a delightful surprise it must have been to weary travellers to discover that here was a silk mercer's which made dresses on the spot, thus saving them the need to trail all over Paris looking for fabrics and then for dressmakers. Monsieur Worth could offer them beautiful clothes in whatever material they fancied; if they were tired of silk, then that same dress could be had in velvet, muslin, brocade or wool. Worth sold them model gowns and patterns to be copied, and from this beginning came forty years of American custom for himself, and ninety years for his family.

Having achieved all this, Worth felt that it was about time his employers showed him more respect. He was never more than a *premier commis* – a leading salesman – and the more his dress department flourished, the more he came to resent his humble position. Moreover, Gagelin was never considerate to Marie Worth. She worked at her husband's side and continued to do so during her pregnancies, but the work was arduous. When she was not on her feet all day modelling, she was helping to sell dresses; but the twelve-hour day, the long journey to and from work, wore her down. Worth therefore asked if he might not rent some empty rooms in the building to make life easier for Marie, but Gagelin refused.

Two sons were born to the couple: Gaston Lucien arrived on 5 November 1853, and Jean-Philippe in July 1856. He was named Philip after the hero of Bulwer-Lytton's novel which had inspired Worth when he was young. It has been thought that this un-sympathetic treatment of Marie was the reason why Worth left Gagelin, but as he did not break with them until two years after Jean-Philippe's birth, there was more to it than that; after all, the firm had seen three changes of ownership in the early 1850s, from Gagelin, to Opigez & Chazelle in 1851 and to Opigez & Gagelin by 1855. Considering all the good he had done them with his profitable department and international prizes for dress design, Worth must have felt that the house should be known as Gagelin & Worth. According to *The Times* obituary, Worth applied for a share in the business and was refused – it was that sort of insult to his pride which made Worth conclude that there was no promotion for him at Gagelin.

However, Worth lacked the money to go into business on his own, so he had to seek a partner. He knew of another *premier commis* who was dissatisfied with his employers, a Swede, Otto Bobergh, and the two agreed to pool their resources and raise a loan. Otto Gustaf Bobergh deserves some consideration. He is usually thought of as Worth's financial partner and no more, but he was not without talent.

Born in Sweden in 1821 he studied art in Stockholm before embarking on a career in the clothing trade.[4] In his early thirties he worked in London stores, and then moved to Paris shops in about 1855, so that he had had four more years' experience of clothing than Worth and his artistic training meant that he could sketch and design on paper – something that Worth could not do. The two men set about looking for suitable accommodation for Worth's dressmaking business, with living-quarters attached, so that the Worth family did not have to travel. They settled on a first-floor apartment at No. 7, rue de la Paix. This was further west than the most fashionable shopping street and primarily a residential area for the rich, but it was not very much further west; there were some shops in the street, and it was only minutes from the Jardin des Tuileries and the imperial palace. Moreover it was the western part of Paris that was seeing the erection of new mansions and luxury apartments, while the eastern end was left to the artisan classes, as in London. Thus the area was a

14. Maison Worth at No. 7, rue de la Paix.

promising one, with more trade likely to be attracted to it in the future.

Worth et Bobergh opened in 1858. It had a staff of twenty seamstresses, at least one of whom, Albertine Debechaux, had followed Worth from Gagelin, and she recalls this in a letter she wrote when Worth died.[5] A small advertisement was placed in the trade press announcing that a new firm of superior dressmakers had started

15. Guiseppe Canella – La rue de la Paix, looking towards the Place Vendôme with its column, and the gardens of the Tuileries at the far end.

up and noble custom was invited. The great gamble had begun. Would Worth's name and reputation be enough to sustain his own family, Bobergh, and their loyal team of seamstresses? More than his own fate rested on his shoulders.

Notes

1. *Official Catalogue of the Great Exhibition of the Works of Industry of All Nations* (1851), p. 226.
2. *Jury Reports, Great Exhibition* (1851), vol. III, p. 482.

3. *Catalogue Officiel de l'Exposition Universelle*, Paris (1855), Part II Empire Français, pp. 165, 176; *Exposition Universelle 1855 Liste Générale des Récompenses Décérnées par le Jury International*, p. 289.
4. *Svenskt Konstnärslexikon* (1952), Allhems Förlag, Malmö.
5. *Letters of Condolence* (1895), coll. Worth Parfums.

Chapter 4

The Great Gamble

While some customers followed Worth from Opigez & Gagelin, the new dressmaker's was very domestic in character to begin with and far from being a stately salon. A description of it in these early days was given by the wife of the novelist Octave Feuillet. She had been invited to an imperial reception, but when her dressmaker delivered her gown the evening before, it proved so dowager in style that Mme Feuillet decided it would not do. In desperation she resolved to try the new house of Worth et Bobergh, and dashed along to the rue de la Paix at dawn on the day of the reception. The Worths were still in bed and the door was opened, not by a porter or butler, but by a Burgundian nursemaid carrying a very plump Jean-Philippe. Mme Feuillet sent in her card, and in a quarter of an hour Worth emerged in his dressing-gown, and suggested that she should come into the bedroom to discuss her problem with his wife as well. Marie Worth was still in bed, enveloped in layers of lace, and perfumed with iris; the bed itself had a canopy and a satin cover which gave it a royal air. Perhaps the bedroom was the best room in the apartment. Once Mme Feuillet had explained her problem, Worth leant against one of the bedposts and dreamed up the solution in his mind's eye, seeing a gown of lilac silk covered with puffed-out lilac tulle caught by knots of lilies-of-the-valley, the whole ensemble softened by a final veil of white tulle. Mme Feuillet loved the idea, installed herself at Worth's for the rest of the day, the dress was made on her, and to her surprise she was given some make-up – powder on her shoulders and rouge on the face. Monsieur Feuillet was sent for, marvelled at the creation, and carried her off to the palace. At the reception the Empress Eugénie stopped in front of Mme Feuillet and complimented her on her toilette.

'Tell me the name of your *couturière*.'

'Madame, it's a man, an Englishman.'

'Good heavens! And what is he called?'

'Worth, madame.'[1]

The empress moved on, astonished, amused, appalled. The very idea of a man making women's dresses and supervising the fittings was outrageous, not to say indecent, and far too sensational for royalty to have anything to do with it. The gown was nice, but too dangerous to touch. As a matter of fact the empress did have a male tailor, Henry Creed, who made her riding habits, but that was different. Creed had been appointed Napoleon III's tailor because Prince Albert had told Napoleon in 1855 that his suits were so bad that he must have an English tailor, and Creed had opened a branch in Paris. Tailors, however, did not make ladies' toilettes and confections, as more fashionable clothes were termed, but restricted themselves to tailored sportswear. It was unheard of for a man to be a dressmaker, a *couturière*.

Thus a Worth creation was worn at the Palais des Tuileries, and others may have been in 1858 and 1859, but there was no hope of imperial patronage. Every fashionable dressmaker needed her own particular client; one of the leaders of society, a lady of wealth and rank whose regular attendance at court functions would ensure that her clothes were admired in the highest circles. Worth et Bobergh needed such a *grande dame* desperately, but it had to be a very special lady, one who could afford to ignore public opinion and who was not afraid to be avant-garde in her choice of dressmaker. Whom could they approach? Fate then very kindly introduced an important new face to Parisian high society.

France and Austria had been at war over the question of Italian reunification; indeed it had been such a bloody war that it inspired the foundation of the International Red Cross. France and Italy had been victorious and the terms for peace were due to be arranged. Austria sent Prince Richard von Metternich, who had been secretary at their Paris embassy in 1856, to bring about the ratification of the Treaty of Leipzig with Napoleon III in 1859. In September that year the prince and his wife were guests of the emperor and empress at their villa in Biarritz. The visit was such a success that, in December 1859, Austria appointed Prince von Metternich ambassador to the French Empire, and he and the princess moved into their Paris town house in the rue de Varennes in that same month. Prince Richard was the son of the famous Austrian chancellor, Prince Clement von Metternich, one of the architects of Europe after the defeat of Napoleon I. His marriage was most unusual, for his wife was also his niece. Prince Richard's half-sister Leontine married the dashing Hungarian count, Moritz Sandor, and they had a daughter Pauline, whom her uncle Richard had come to love. The marriage was arranged by papal dispensation and took place in June 1856. This alone was enough to make the Metternichs a talking point in Paris, but Princess Pauline was such an energetic character in her own right that she dominated that society for the next decade.

Princess Pauline was no beauty and called herself '*le singe à la mode*'. She was deeply interested in dress and had no inhibitions about wearing anything that might be considered by others to be too daring. Indeed she took a positive delight in being somewhat reckless and sensational. As the possessor of one of the most famous names in European aristocracy, she could afford to do exactly as she pleased and she had inherited all her father's Hungarian high spirits. To the society journalists her arrival was a blessing, for the variety of her dresses, her free and easy manner, and her enthusiasm for pranks, were all excellent copy.

16. Engraving after Winterhalter – Princess Pauline von Metternich, Paris 1861.

Empress Eugénie fell under the spell of this tempestuous personality, and Princess von Metternich rapidly became established as one of the most influential figures at court. With her great energy for organization she soon took over the arranging of all the amateur activities such as charades and comedies, disciplining the noble participants into producing performances of almost professional standard. For example, for the empress's birthday on 15 November the princess and three other court ladies performed a ballet, *Diable à quatre*, but only after weeks of arduous lessons from a ballet master from the Paris Opéra. Within two years of her arrival Princess von Metternich had Napoleon III, who was no lover of music, commanding a special performance of Wagner's *Tannhauser* just to please her. The opera was much too advanced for Parisian taste and caused a furore, but it illustrates how far the French court would go to satisfy her requirements.

It was this *grande dame*, of the highest birth and diplomatic importance, whom Worth and Bobergh decided to approach. As it would have been too unorthodox for men to raise so personal a matter as her wardrobe with the ambassadress, poor Marie Worth was dispatched, very nervously, to request an interview early in 1860. The princess describes the approach in her *Souvenirs*:

> One morning I was quietly installed in my salon reading when my *femme de chambre* appeared, holding an album in her hand. I asked her what she was carrying, when she replied: 'There is a young woman in my room who requests that Your Highness may deign to glance at the designs contained in this book. They are sketches of toilettes which her husband makes. He would be very desirous of making a dress for you, no matter at what price, provided that he may make one for you.'
>
> I asked the name of the individual: 'He is English, and is called Worth.' An Englishman who dares to claim that he makes toilettes for ladies in Paris, that is a strange idea, I cried, I don't want anything to do with it, under any pretext.

The suggestion was too startling even for Princess von Metternich, but her waiting woman said that the designs were charming, and eventually with an air of exasperation the princess did glance at them. The sketches, probably by Otto Bobergh, proved so delightful that the princess changed her mind and sent for Mme Worth at once. Blushing shyly Marie Worth explained her husband's career, and requested the privilege of making something for the princess, for which she could name her own price. Pauline von Metternich decided to give the new House a try and ordered a morning dress and an evening gown, neither of them to cost more than 300 francs each. Marie Worth rushed home with the good news.

Worth sent his staff to measure the princess at her residence, and the dresses were ready by the end of the week. To the princess's surprise there was only one fitting, instead of the usual half-dozen, for a Worth pattern was precise. She was delighted by the gowns which she considered masterpieces and sent Worth her congratulations. She considered the evening dress the prettiest and best made she had ever seen and resolved to wear it the following Wednesday at the state ball in the Salle des Maréchaux at the Tuileries, one of the most prestigious events in the social calendar.

It was in white tulle spangled with silver (which was completely new) and garnished with daisies with pink hearts, placed in bunches of wild grass. These flowers were veiled with white tulle. A wide sash in white satin encircled my waist; I had pinned diamonds all over . . . and Worth had his first success.

Before the ball the Corps Diplomatique used to assemble in the throne room *'pour le cercle'* when the emperor and empress would circle round the company, greeting each ambassador in turn. Empress Eugénie noticed Princess von Metternich's dress at once.

> When she came to me she asked me straight out who had made this evening dress, so marvellously pretty in its simplicity and elegance. 'An Englishman, madame, a rising star in the firmament of fashion!' – And what is his name? – Worth. 'Very well,' the Empress replied, 'the star must have some satellites, please instruct him to report to me tomorrow morning at ten o'clock!'
>
> Worth was launched and I was lost, for from that moment on dresses at 300 francs no longer saw the light of day.[2]

The empress's resistance had been overcome. Worth et Bobergh had gambled on pleasing a princess and won. They had risked money too, for silver spangled tulle cost more than 300 francs, but the result was astonishing.

17. Lithograph by G. Bargu after H. de Montaret – A Reception at the Palais des Tuileries, with Napoleon III and Empress Eugénie making the circle of their distinguished guests.

Worth was actually in bed while the palace danced all through the night, and did not learn of his good fortune until the morning, but the summons to the Tuileries caused consternation. Worth had no court costume – black evening dress with knee breeches, black silk stockings and buckled pumps – so he had to rush there just as he was in his frock coat, the normal wear for businessmen. Fortunately an imperial command could not be ignored, even by palace chamberlains, and Worth was grudgingly granted admission. Empress Eugénie told him that she would order one evening dress to begin with; if that proved satisfactory, further orders could follow. She left him free to choose the style and material – let him surprise her with the excellence of his invention.

Needless to say Maison Worth et Bobergh was a flurry of excited activity for days. Worth contacted the silk mills in Lyon; he must have the very best fabric they had. Lyon replied that there was a drop in brocade sales, and couldn't Monsieur Worth do something to redress the situation by promoting brocade at court? The two came to an agreement and Worth selected a biege Lyon brocade, with a pattern taken from a Chinese fan. Although the gowns the empress had admired, those of Mme Feuillet and the princess, had both been of tulle, Worth and Bobergh felt that brocade was more sumptuous and

18. The original label of the world's first haute couture House, with the imperial coat-of-arms which it was awarded from 1860 to 1870.

thus better suited to an empress. They were wrong. When Worth unpacked their precious creation, heavy with magnificence, the empress frowned. 'We don't like brocade. It looks like curtain material.' The fate of Worth et Bobergh teetered on the edge of disaster. Gathering his wits Worth entreated the empress to consider that she had only to wear the dress once to start a fashion for Lyon brocade, for there were a dozen fashionable ladies waiting at his salon agog to be the first to learn what the empress had chosen. Empress Eugénie said No.

All would have been lost but for the entry of Napoleon III himself at that very moment. The emperor was mildly interested – after all, he had an English tailor, so wouldn't it be amusing if his wife were to choose an English dressmaker, and a male one at that? With brilliant versatility Worth took advantage of the emperor's entry and tried a political approach. Lyon, he said, was a very republican city, hostile to the emperor's policies, but that attitude could be changed significantly if the empress would only wear more products from its factories. Moreover, their majesties were to visit Lyon later that year so a gesture towards the silk industry would be very wise. Napoleon III agreed. He told the empress that she had a duty to support his industrial policy, and that she was to wear the brocade dress once or twice because he wanted her to. The empress was obliged to yield. Thus it was that a new kind of dress came into being, as was summed up by one of the empress's ladies-in-waiting, Mme Carette:

> . . . the Empress often wore thick material of Lyon manufacture in order to encourage commerce in silks, *passementeries* and lace, thus leading fashions, to feed the different industries. These were what the Empress used to call her 'political toilettes'.[3]

Worth had risked a great deal for the sake of Lyon brocade, but no doubt the silk mills would be generous in recognition of his achievement. He had, however, gained a double advantage, where he might have hoped for only one: not only was he to dress the empress, but the emperor's decision gave Worth the authority to tell her to wear something which she did not like, if he felt that it would be good for a particular product. This meant that Worth now had enormous patronage at his disposal: he could decide which fabrics were to be promoted at court. To the *chambres de commerce* in Lyon for its silks and lace, to Rheims, Elbeuf, Sedan and Roubaix for their light fabrics, and to Sedan for heavier stuffs; altogether, Monsieur Worth was going to be an extremely important person. There was for example a shortage of hand-made lace, but machine-made lace was still frowned on as too inelegant.[4] Worth asked the lacemakers in Paris, St Etienne and Lyon to produce gossamer fine laces, used several layers at a time in the empress's evening dresses, and so made machine-made lace fashionable and respectable. He even came to exercise control over the names for new dyes. A new tone of green he dubbed Metternich green, and a very unpleasant tone of brown he named after someone equally unpleasant in French eyes, Bismarck. None of the empress's other dressmakers had attained such authority – it took a Worth to fully understand the complexities of textile production, for he had started as a textile man.

So from 1860 Worth et Bobergh became one of the empress's dressmaking houses; men were making dresses for the Empress of France, the most fashionable lady in all Europe! Only now did the realization dawn that there were a couple of couturiers in Paris; males working in the most intimate area of the female wardrobe. It caused not only surprise but moral outrage. The scandal crossed the Channel and Charles Dickens reported it in 1863:

> But would you believe that, in the latter half of the nineteenth century, there are bearded milliners – man-milliners, authentic men, like Zouaves – who, with their solid fingers, take the exact dimensions of the highest titled women in Paris – robe them, unrobe them, and make them turn backward and forward before them.[5]

The English had a problem in that they had no term to describe the phenomenon. The French could use the masculine form of *couturière*, *couturier*, but in England dressmakers were called milliners, so Worth had to be called a man-milliner. Even John Ruskin came to use the term, in an obvious reference to Worth: 'You hear of me, among others, as a respectable architectural man-milliner; and you send for me that I may tell you the leading fashion.'[6]

What caused the outrage was the idea of men seeing ladies in a state of undress, and actually fitting garments on them, touching their bodies, ordering them to move around and parade up and down in various stages of déshabillé. To the dressmakers of Paris, Worth was now a mortal enemy, a man trespassing in their imperium, and vicious rumours were sent scurrying through the city that Maison Worth et Bobergh was a brothel, a bordello where the most outrageous indecencies were perpetrated.

The period was very sensitive about when and where full dress and undress were worn. It was a social rule that no lady should show a centimetre of bare skin, beyond her face and hands, during the day-time, but it was in order for her to wear a plunging neckline in the evening. No gentleman should show a glimpse of chest in town, but they still went swimming in the nude. It was a question of what people were used to, rather than a question of morality or common sense.

41

Marie Worth was most upset by the tales of indecent behaviour, but Charles Frederick could afford to shrug his shoulders and smile. Where the empress dressed, everyone else of note would follow, no matter what the gossips might say.

19. Worth, the businessman.

The news of Worth's appointment in 1860 raced round the capitals of Europe and crossed the Atlantic. Before the year was out Worth gowns were being ordered from New York, where the visit of the Prince of Wales made the best dresses to be had an absolute necessity. The New York socialite Mrs Hewitt ordered a Worth ballgown of turquoise blue silk moiré, with a bertha of silk velvet, trimmed with lace, and with thirty yards of Valenciennes lace in the petticoat, to wear at the dance held in the prince's honour at the Academy of Music. In London old Lady Jersey, aged eighty but looking fifty, started wearing Worth's latest creations straightaway. From Germany, Countess Annie de Moltke sent Walburga Lady Paget some Worth gowns as a present, to show her what masterpieces they were.

When the Empress of France changed her dressmaker, the civilized world took note.

Notes

1. Mme Valerie Feuillet, *Quelques Années de ma Vie* (1894), pp. 200–6.
2. *Souvenirs de la Princesse Pauline de Metternich 1859–71*, notes by M. Dunan (1922), Librairie Plon, pp. 135–8.
3. Mme Carette, *My Mistress, the Empress Eugénie; or, Court Life at the Tuileries* (1889), p. 178.
4. Machine-made lace was to be much cheaper than hand-made. Nottingham machine-made lace was mostly of flax. Examples of Alençon, Brussels and Malta hand-made lace cost £200 for handkerchiefs, and £800 to £1,000 for skirts. At the 1862 London Exhibition, Nottingham machine-made lace was considered to rival hand-made in quality. 'Textile products at the Exhibition', *The Exchange*, November 1862, p. 99.
5. C. Dickens, *All the Year Round*, vol. IX, 28 February 1863, p. 9.
6. J. Ruskin, 'Traffic', *The Crown of Wild Olive*.

Chapter 5

The Court Couturier

It was the Empress Eugénie's custom to receive her purveyors at the start of each season, when they would bring their materials and dresses to the court. She would then select the number of dresses she thought she would need, try them on, and think no more about them. For Worth, however, this pattern did not apply. He was on call all the time, for the quality of his evening creations and day gowns was so high that the empress wanted new ones every day. She required a new gown for every official occasion, from state visits down to dinner parties, and she never wore such dresses twice. Consequently she had an enormous wardrobe which had to be cleared out at regular intervals, as her lady-in-waiting explained:

> Twice a year the Empress renewed the greater part of her robes, giving the discarded ones to her ladies. This was a great source of profit to them, because they sold them generally to people in America and elsewhere, where it is customary to lend toilettes on hire.[1]

There was nothing unusual about this. For centuries officials and servants at court had the right to acquire a monarch's clothes and linen when the wardrobe was renewed. In fact there could be trouble when servants felt that their rights in this area were not being respected. The same pattern also occurred in stately homes and bourgeois residences, anywhere where servants were employed.

Because the empress only wore a gown once, it was made a rule of court that no lady could appear in the same dress twice, and this also applied to guests at the imperial seats, as *Punch*'s correspondent observed in 1856:

> The guests are all expected to change their costume twice a day; and no lady is allowed to appear at the Château twice in the same dress; the Empress setting the example by giving every robe once worn to her attendants. As these are of course sold again, all Paris overflows with the Imperial *défroque*, and a few nights ago on the

boards of one of the theatres was recognized a brocade that had lately figured on the throne.[2]

This too was customary. The donation of unwanted robes and royal birthday gowns to the public theatres was a regular part of theatrical costuming in the seventeenth and eighteenth centuries, so the nineteenth century was merely continuing an established procedure. What was so different about the Second Empire was the frequency of the festivities, the scale of entertaining. Every court insisted on new garments for important events, and royalty felt insulted if they recognized a gown from a previous occasion, but the number of such celebrations was fairly modest. The French court rivalled the Czarist court in St Petersburg in the size and lavishness of its entertaining and this was why Empress Eugénie had to have so many new clothes, which caused people to marvel. As a result she acquired a reputation for extravagance in dress which became part of the legend of the luxurious frivolity and *gaieté parisienne* of the Second Empire. She was criticized in her own day for such excess, but Mme Carette insisted that it was her mistress's duty:

> The *goût* of the Empress for luxury and toilette has often been the subject of much passionate exaggeration. Luxury is the necessary appendage of sovereigns; tastes in toilette the privilege of handsome and intelligent women. Elegance in dress is the first element in the consideration of a woman's appearance; and should a few persons find fault with a sovereign about the variety and luxury of her attire, by far the greater number would complain of that *parure* which failed to correspond with the tastes and requirements of our times.[3]

She claimed that the comforts of the poor lay in the luxury of the rich, for it provided them with work. The system certainly provided Worth et Bobergh with plenty of work, for the empress came to rely on them more and more.

Worth was never the empress's only supplier, although posterity has often regarded him as being just that. He was however her most important purveyor, for she ranked him as her first costumier. In 1864 the hierarchy of imperial dressmakers was as follows: Worth for grandes toilettes; Laferrière for ordinary clothes; Félicie for cloaks and mantles; Mme Virot and Mme Lebel for hats; Henry Creed for riding wear. In other words Worth held the monopoly for all the empress's state and evening wear, for court dress, for the *grandes toilettes de ville*, and for her masquerade costumes. Thus he controlled the most important part of her wardrobe. The unfortunate mesdames

Vignon and Palmyre faded from the scene; their heyday had been in the court of the 1850s; the court of the 1860s was Worth's.

He now became a regular visitor to the Palais des Tuileries, his domain being the wardrobe which was housed immediately over the empress's own apartments, and the imperial dressing-room. There was an ingenious system for supplying the empress with the clothes for each day, which was described by Anna Bicknell, governess of the daughters of the First Chamberlain, the Duc de Tascher de la Pagerie:

> Four lay-figures, exactly measured to fit the dresses worn by the Empress, were used to diminish the necessity of too much trying on, and also to prepare her toilette for the day. Orders were given through a speaking-pipe in the dressing-room and the figure came down on a sort of lift through an opening in the ceiling, dressed in all that the Empress was about to wear. The object of this arrangement was to save time, and also to avoid the necessity of crushing the voluminous dresses of the period in the narrow back-staircases.[4]

It was to these chambers that Worth would bring his choicest creations, and be on duty as the empress dressed before an important occasion to ensure that the ladies-in-waiting made no mistakes with his ensembles, for he became rapidly recognized as an arbiter of taste. With the empress requiring such a multitude of new gowns, the demand on Worth's imagination was enormous, and he needed every suggestion Bobergh could provide, as well as some from Marie. His life was now dominated by the imperial programme.

Between January and Lent every year the court held four grand official balls for four or five thousand guests, which were very colourful affairs. All the male members of the imperial households wore white breeches and white silk stockings, with different coloured coats. The emperor's chamberlains had scarlet coats with gold embroidery, his equerries green with gold or silver, his prefects of the palace amaranth and gold, his masters of ceremony violet and gold, while the orderly officers wore pale blue with silver. The empress's chamberlains and equerries wore blue and silver. All these officials were on duty for the state balls.

Those guests honoured with an invitation entered the palace by the Pavillon de l'Horloge in the centre of the building, and ascended the stairs to the Galerie de la Paix, passing the emperor's Centgardes in their uniforms of pale blue edged with crimson, and helmets and breastplates of shining steel. The dancing took place in the Salle des Maréchaux where the emperor and empress sat enthroned. The Corps Diplomatique had to arrive at 9 p.m. for *le cercle*, the ball opened at half past nine with a waltz, and a buffet supper was served at eleven.

20. The first state ball of the 1860 season, with the Quadrille of Honour being danced in the Hall of the Marshals of France, at the Palais des Tuileries.

Male guests not in uniform had to wear the black court dress with knee breeches, which was copied from the garments required at the British court. Princess von Metternich though that it was a pity the Austrian court did not also insist on such a simple but elegant costume. Lady guests were required to have trains three or four metres in length, which meant that everyone had to be very careful where they put their feet.

At these balls the empress and her ladies all wore court dress which was white, because the women of the court at the time of the First Napoleonic Empire had worn white, which had then been regarded as the neo-classical ideal. On full state occasions trains of purple or red velvet were added. This official use of white meant that Worth had to conjure up scores of dresses out of variations on white and silver – the only difference really being in the trimmings. A lesser designer would have collapsed before such a limited range but Worth conquered the challenge. White silk, white tulle, white velvet, white brocade, cloth of silver, white lace, and white gauze were all employed to create gowns of such beauty that contemporaries were dazzled, and recalled them years afterwards. Mme Carette remembered the empress in 1860 in white tulle and coiffured with a wreath of Parma violets looking bewitchingly beautiful. In 1863 Mrs Moulton saw her in a white tulle ballgown trimmed with red velvet bows and gold fringes. Felix Whitehurst of the *Daily Telegraph* observed the empress 'beautifully dressed in white trimmed with ivy' in 1866. In 1867 Princess von Metternich attended a ball at the Palais de Versailles, where the Empress Eugénie was attired in 'a white gown spangled with silver, and dressed with her most beautiful diamonds. . . . She had carelessly thrown over her shoulders a sort of burnous of white embroidered with gold, and the murmurs of admiration followed her like a powder train.' There was no limit to Worth's ingenuity.

The fact that the Empress Eugénie wore a Worth on such occasions meant of course that all her ladies-in-waiting had to have Worth gowns as well, and most of the female guests wanted the same. It was almost a rule that Worth dresses were worn at court. As the number of ladies at these balls could be between two and two and a half thousand, even if Worth only made half the gowns it still involved creating about one thousand new dresses, which all had to be ready on the same night, four times a season. In addition, he had to dress the empress's Monday parties. These were more intimate, attended by only about four hundred guests, and held in the Blue Salon. In 1863 Mrs Moulton estimated that the value of the Worth gowns present was $200,000 (£40,000). 1867 was the year which saw the court making its greatest demands on Worth's genius for invention, for the current Universal Exhibition attracted several crowned heads to Paris, including Czar Alexander II of Russia, Emperor Franz Josef of Austria with his brothers the Archdukes Charles Louis and Louis Victor, the

21. One of Empress Eugénie's intimate Monday parties, with the Prince and Princess of Wales and Archduke Louis Victor of Austria as chief guests.

King of Prussia, Queen Sophie of the Netherlands, Queen Isabella of Spain with her husband, King Ludwig of Bavaria, and numerous princes and royal dukes. Every reception, dinner and ball given at the Tuileries or Versailles, and at the embassies, required the most gorgeous gowns imaginable for the empress, for these too were political dresses in that they had to astound the imperial visitors with the richness and glory of France, and the beauty of its empress.

For the official opening on 1 April 1867 on the Champs de Mars, the empress and her ladies wore *grande toilettes de ville*, but as this was day-time, bonnets were allowed. In the imperial party there were Sultan Abdul Aziz of Turkey, Ishmail Pasha Viceroy of Egypt, and the Prince of Wales with his sister, Victoria, Princess Royal, and her husband, Crown Prince Frederick William of Prussia. Unforeseen circumstances forced Worth to make last-minute changes in the empress's clothes twice during the course of the exhibition. The *toilette de ville* or day dress which he made for her to wear at the opening was of pale lemon faille, with a pattern of pompadour blooms, and trimmed with Alençon lace and pale lavender satin bows. Eugénie cried out with delight when she saw it, but news arrived of the downfall of the Emperor Maximilian in Mexico and the empress regretfully decided that she would have to wear something plainer as a gesture of imperial sympathy. Worth prided himself on the ability of his house to cope with such emergencies:

> We can finish a costume in twenty-four hours. French ladies have ordered a dress in the morning and danced in it at night. I once made a gown for the Empress Eugénie in three hours and a half.[5]

This was for the second unforeseen event. A patriotic Pole tried to assassinate Czar Alexander II during a military review which Napoleon III had laid on in his honour. The Czar escaped unhurt but the incident was highly embarrassing for the emperor and empress of France. Worth had made the empress a sumptuous dinner gown, for she was due to dine at the Russian embassy that very evening, but in view of the attempt on her guest's life the empress again had to wear something simpler and, in desperation, she sent for Worth. There were just three-and-a-half hours to go before the dinner, but she had to have something new yet plain. This set Worth a real problem, for it was not possible to make a voluminous crinoline gown in that time, so he decided that they would have to adapt an existing dress. He took a plain court dress from her wardrobe, discarded the trimmings and covered the skirt with three layers of white tulle with a tracery of silver stitches – replacing display with expensive simplicity. The empress was able to go to the embassy attired in purest white alone. Fortunately there were no more emergencies of this sort, and Empress Eugénie was able to attend the prize-giving at the Universal Exhibition in the actual dress that Worth had designed for the occasion – a court dress of white tulle embroidered all over with ears of wheat in silver, the hem finished with silver scallops.

While the empress favoured simple black dresses when off duty, her public life was dominated by white. Many years later, in 1892, old Admiral Duperré told Baroness de Stoeckl of an evening under the Second Empire, with Empress Eugénie in white tulle with a black velvet sash, attended by Mélanie Comtesse de Pourtalès and Princess von Metternich, listening to Gounod playing the piano, although he suspected that the empress was wondering what Worth would be sending her to wear that night rather than paying much attention to the music.

22. Czar Alexander II receives Napoleon III and Empress Eugénie at the Russian Embassy in Paris.

The last gala of international proportions for which Worth had to provide quantities of spectacular gowns for the empress was in 1869. Empress Eugénie's distant cousin Ferdinand de Lesseps had just completed the Suez Canal, and the Empress of France was to open it, paying state visits to countries along the route. Such a programme with all the receptions, parades, and balls involved, made a large wardrobe essential. While it would not be essential to change clothes three times a day during the voyage, several changes would be necessary during trips ashore and receptions on board ship. The ladies-in-waiting ordered up to eighty gowns each, the empress over

23. The Prince Imperial presenting a grand prix to his father, Napoleon III, for his designs for workers' housing and model farms, at the end of the Paris Exposition Universelle of 1867.

one hundred. Here too the dresses had a political function, for they had to impress Near-Eastern potentates with the glory of imperial France. Accordingly Worth et Bobergh used gold and silver in abundance, both as embroidery and interwoven with other fabrics to create glittering tissues. Empress Eugénie was so delighted with these creations that she could talk of nothing else for days. Princess Mathilde commented dryly that the empress was still as mad about clothes as she was on her wedding day.

The empress travelled to Venice by train and there embarked on the imperial yacht *Aigle*. Her first port of call was Piraeus for Athens and a state visit to King George of Greece, and she then sailed on to Constantinople for a lavish reception by Sultan Abdul-Aziz from 13 to 18 October. She reached Egypt on 20 October for a month of festivities. At a reception for the French colony in Alexandria on 14 November, the empress wore a Worth *toilette de ville* of straw-coloured silk covered with white lace, and with a matching hat of straw silk with white plumes. She opened the canal on 17 November, the imperial yacht sailing ahead of a line of ships, which included Emperor Franz Josef in his yacht *Grief*, the Crown prince of Prussia, the Prince and Princess of the Netherlands, and Grand Duke Michael of Russia. Britain, rather sourly, as the canal was not a British venture, only sent an ambassador. On the 18th the Khedive of Egypt held a state ball in the empress's honour, at which she appeared in glittering full court dress and a bejewelled diadem.[6] Little did she or Worth know that the partnership between them would not last much longer.

Apart from the empress all the imperial circle were clamouring to be dressed by Worth. Princess Mathilde with her famous literary salon, numbering Sainte-Beuve, the Goncourts, Merimée, Gautier, Dumas, Sardou, and later Proust among its members, might be highly contemptuous of the pleasure-loving socialites who crowded round Napoleon III and Eugénie, but this did not stop her from going to the same dressmaker as the empress. The princess declared that she dressed to please herself and was no slave to fashion, but now that Worth had made the rue de la Paix the most fashionable street in Paris she was often to be found there, visiting jewellers and florists, and then dropping into Worth et Bobergh, for a sit down, to look at dresses, and to chat. She also attended imperial balls in the full panoply of Worth's latest creations, and she and Worth remained friends for thirty-five years.

Entertaining of course was not limited to the court. Balls and dinners were also given by ministers of state, ambassadors, generals, prefects and society leaders. It has been estimated that between Twelfth Night and Shrove Tuesday 1864 there were 130 balls in Paris, and that the costs involved were:

Coach hire	2,700,000 francs
Gloves	4,680,000
Dresses	29,250,000
Hairdressing	1,800,000
Satin shoes	2,304,000
Bouquets	1,800,000
Jewellery, etc.	17,500,000
Total	60,034,000 francs[7]

This came to over £2,000,000 without including the cost of food and wine. The biggest expense was the dresses at more than £1,000,000, there then being twenty-five francs to the pound sterling.

The most costly privilege for the guests was an invitation to stay at one of the imperial châteaux. The court moved to Fontainebleau for the summer, and to Compiègne in the autumn. Visits lasted a week or eight days, and as each lady was allowed to wear a dress only once, the invitation involved them in considerable expense. Prosper Merimée spoke of a friend, by no means rich, who went to Fontainebleau for a week and had to take fifteen dresses, two per day and one for accidents.[8] Princess von Metternich took eighteen dress cases to Compiègne – each dress was packed separately to avoid crushing –

24. T. Couture – Princess Mathilde Bonaparte, customer and friend to Worth for many years.

but some people took twenty-four. When another Worth customer, Mrs Charles Moulton, went to Compiègne for the first time in November 1866 she took twenty-one garments:

8 day costumes
1 green hunting habit
7 ball gowns
5 tea gowns

When she was invited for a second visit in November 1868 it caused an explosion in the family. Her millionaire father-in-law protested that another new wardrobe from Worth was more than they could afford, never mind the enormous tips which the imperial servants demanded. When Napoleon III heard of the tipping he put a stop to it, and Mrs Moulton was then allowed to go on the visit. In view of the fuss she recorded what she took:

MORNING COSTUMES   Dark-blue poplin, trimmed with plush of the same color, toque, muff to match.
Black velvet, trimmed with braid, sable hat, sable tippet and muff.
Brown cloth, trimmed with bands of sealskin, coat, hat, muff to match.
Purple plush, trimmed with bands of pheasant feathers, coat, hat to match.
Gray velvet, trimmed with chinchilla, hat, muff and coat.
Green cloth (hunting costume).
Traveling suit, dark-blue cloth cloak.

EVENING COSTUMES   Light green tulle, embroidered in silver, and for my locks, what they call *une fantaisie*.
White tulle, embroidered with gold wheat ears.
Light-gray satin, quite plain, with only Brussels lace flounces.
Deep pink tulle, with satin ruchings and a lovely sash of lilac ribbon.
Black lace over white tulle, with green velvet twisted bows.
Light-blue tulle with Valenciennes.

AFTERNOON GOWNS   Lilac faille.
Light *café au lait* with trimmings of the same.
Green faille faced with blue and a red Charlotte Corday sash (Worth's last gasp).

AFTERNOON GOWNS A red faille, quite plain.
(cont.) Gray faille with light-blue facings.[9]

It was customary for guests to write thank-you letters to the
emperor afterwards, which the less than rich must have found a
joyless duty. The emperor would then reply in his own hand
graciously accepting their thanks, as he did to the Marchioness of
Stafford who stayed at Compiègne in November 1859. Another
English guest was the Duchess of Manchester. The number of those
invited was around 100 at a time, so that fifty ladies would mean 1,000
dress cases arriving at the château simultaneously, transported on the
imperial train. This was the scale on which Worth operated: 50 ladies,
1,000 new gowns. As the 1860s is often criticized for its use of bright
new aniline dyes, Mrs Moulton's list shows that Worth's colour sense
was much more disciplined – avoiding garish effects with the morning
costumes all en suite. His clothes were popular among the rich not
only because they were well made, or because the empress wore them,
but because they also displayed good taste.

With the court as their publicity agent, Worth et Bobergh had no
need to advertise; the society press did that for them. The earliest
known advertisement which they condescended to publish, was for a
court costume in 1868. Princess Mathilde was still ordering court
dress from Worth in 1888. His other great publicist was of course
Princess Pauline von Metternich, whose demands on his services were
hardly less than Empress Eugénie's, for she was a great entertainer.

25. The earliest illustrated
advertisement by Worth
himself, with a court dress
showing his distinctive
shoulder-hung court train.
Paris Trade Journal, 1868.

On the Thursday of mid-Lent she would give a ridotto (a form of entertainment which mixed dancing and listening to music) at the embassy for 1,500 to 2,000 guests. It lasted until 3 or 4 a.m. and the ladies had to change their dominoes two or three times. Her most lavish ball was for the 1867 exhibition with décor by Alphand, director-in-chief of the works of the City of Paris, who built a huge room in the garden and filled it with flowers. The orchestra was conducted by Johann Strauss, introducing his new waltz 'The Blue Danube'. The next day the Press was full of descriptions of the splendour of the gowns and Worth himself praised the princess for her success, but added, 'And tell them that it is I who have invented you'. The princess was gracious enough to admit that perhaps he had, for a large part of her reputation rested on her being well dressed by Worth. Thanks to her relationship with him she was regarded as a judge of taste, as Whitehurst noted:

> In the corner is the *ne plus ultra* of Paris fashion, the Princesse de Metternich, Mesdames de Gallifet and de Pourtalès, and the Duchess de Saigon [sic]. They sit in judgment on society, and out of their lips comes the dreaded sentence.[10]

All four dressed *chez* Worth but he could pass very cutting remarks himself about some of the ladies who came to him expecting to be turned into goddesses overnight. A very short woman who wished to be dressed all in dark green was told that she would look like an ivy bush. Of one vain creature he remarked to Princess von Metternich that even if he put his most beautiful creation on her back, she would never be more than the *petite bourgeoise* that she was at heart. Of a certain marquise he declared; 'She is nothing. There is no foundation. I have to *reconstruct* her altogether,' while he said to another that he could supply her with a dress, but that he could not supply her with style.

One court beauty whom Worth never criticized was the Duchess de Morny, wife of the emperor's half-brother, for her ethereal beauty was an inspiration to him. Pale and fair, soft colours suited her best, so he dressed her in very simple gowns with a sash as the only decoration. As she looked almost fragile this suited her best. Another court lady was Princess Anna Murat, a close friend of Empress Eugénie, and descended from one of Napoleon I's most dashing marshals. In 1865 she became engaged to the Duc de Mouchy which was quite a social triumph for the Bonapartistes, as the duke was leader of the old royalist aristocracy which held the Napoleonic peerage in contempt. Of course the court couturier was called upon to make the dresses, which caused such a rush of orders that poor Worth was reported to be worn out with the responsibility. Marie Worth was invited to the wedding and wore a gown of silver grey faille. She at least could watch the proceedings; her husband was closeted with the bride until the very last moment, ensuring that every detail was perfect, and rarely got a chance to see the actual ceremony, which he had clothed.

Not all his customers at court were so gracious. Princess Rimsky-Korsakov was a vain and extravagant beauty fond of making impossible demands for creations both impractical and immodest. It was easier to dress her for a masquerade than for a ball. On the whole, however, most of the women at court knew how to behave, and how to wear his clothes well. The empress insisted that all the ladies about her should be elegant, and in this Worth satisfied her will.

> You walk up a glorious hall, and find yourself between two files of the best-dressed women in Paris – and, mark this, *they* are the best-dressed women in Europe.[11]

Sometimes Worth would smuggle his little sons into the palace and take them up to a gallery overlooking the ballroom, to feast their eyes on the glittering splendour below. Thousands of metres of silk and tulle waltzed down there, hundreds of dresses, each one of which had to look different. Contrast in fabrics, contrast in tone, flowers, fringes, loops, embroidery, lace, ruching, appliqué work, drapery, sequins, metal thread, tassels, beads, feathers, bows, ribbons – these

26. Winterhalter – The Duchesse de Morny, one of the many court beauties who flocked to Maison Worth.

were the variations which Worth employed as he plundered his imagination, striving to make each gown unique.

Colour was allowed for ordinary dances and dinners, for anything official it was white. The demands taxed Worth et Bobergh to the full, but the result was a beauty that would live on in people's minds. At a ball for 2,000 guests given by the British ambassador on Friday, 17 May 1867, attended by Napoleon III and Empress Eugénie, the Prince of Wales, the Duke of Edinburgh, Princess Mathilde, Prince Napoleon, the King and Queen of the Belgians, the Queen of Portugal, Prince Oscar of Sweden, Prince and Princess von Metternich, the Duc and Duchesse de Mouchy, the Duchess of Manchester, and la Rimsky-Korsakov: '. . . there was the prettiest picture – a Winterhalter it should have been – which I have ever seen in a ballroom. At the end, before a glass, and in a bower of flowers, sat the Empress, surrounded by her ladies-in-waiting, and some of the best specimens of London and Paris beauty'.[12]

It was a magnificence which was not to be seen again. France was to have no more royal or imperial courts after the Second Empire, and no presidential ball could ever rival such extravagance. Worth had been given a designer's dream, an empire of his own, where he could conjure forth unlimited numbers of spectacular gowns to his heart's content. Little wonder that he remained devoted to this period in his memory, for Paris was not to see the like again.

Even a critic of extravagance had to concede that it has its attractions, wrote Whitehurst:

> I confess that, opposed as I am to the 'unbridled extravagance of women', I look on with supreme pleasure at a luxury which, while reminding me of the decadence of Rome, now indicates only the wealth of France.[13]

Without it there would have been no Worth.

Notes

1. Mme Carette, *My Mistress, the Empress Eugénie; or Court Life at the Tuileries* (1889), p. 177.
2. A. Adburgham, *A Punch History of Manners and Modes* (1961), Hutchinson, p. 54.
3. Carette, op. cit., p. 170.
4. A. L. Bicknell, *Life in the Tuileries under the Second Empire* (1895), p. 40.
5. W. F. Lonergan, *Forty Years of Paris* (1907), Fisher Unwin, p. 199.
6. F. Ribeyre, *Voyage de Sa Majesté l'Impèratrice en Corse et en Orient* (1870), Librairie Napoléonienne.

7. J. Stodart, *The Life of the Empress Eugénie* (1906), p. 184.
8. N. W. Senior, *Conversations with M. Thiers, M. Guizot, and Other Distinguished Persons during the Second Empire*, ed. M. C. M. Simpson (1878), vol. II, p. 115.
9. Lillie de Hegermann-Lindencrone, *In the Courts of Memory* (1912), p. 189.
10. F. Whitehurst, *Court and Social Life in France under Napoleon III* (1873), vol. II, p. 209.
11. ibid., p. 346.
12. ibid., vol. I, p. 289.
13. ibid., p. 165.

Chapter 6

Masquerade

The nineteenth century was very fond of dressing up. Masquerade parties had become a regular part of court life since the late seventeenth century when masques proper with their elaborate sets and costumes had grown too expensive to maintain. Initially such festivities had had a politico-allegorical purpose to flatter and idolize the monarchy, but from the eighteenth century the only theme of a masquerade was enjoyment. The anonymity of masks, the wearing of fantastic costumes, gave a release from a person's conventional role and allowed for the expression of traits in the character which might not have a showing in ordinary life. Thus a government minister could forgo responsibility and pretend he was an Italian brigand for one night. A virtuous lady could flirt dangerously behind her mask without ruining her reputation. Masquerades were naughty. The Second Empire, with its fondness for over-doing things, had masquerade parties by the score. The *Daily Telegraph*'s Paris correspondent came upon signs of masquerading on every side:

> Turning up the Rue des Ombres, for instance, on Saturday, I found myself face to face with a whole shop-front full of black, pink, red, and white masks. . . . Turning the next corner, into the Rue des Bonnes Femmes, a whole army of female disguises met my astonished view, from the early period of Boadicea. . . .[1]

Fancy dress was big business in Paris, for the court set the pace and society followed. The most extravagant masquerades were held at the Palais des Tuileries, but imperial ministers were also expected to hold such festivities. Princess von Metternich considered the following ministers to be the best hosts on these occasions: Count Walewski, Minister for Foreign Affairs; Marquis de Chasseloup-Laubat, Minister for the Navy; Duc de Morny, President of the Corps Législatif; General Fleury, Master of the Imperial Stables; M. Rouher, Minister of the Emperor's Household.[2]

Indeed ministers would throw a masquerade party to celebrate their own appointment. One of the most famous was that given by

Count Walewski in February 1856 to celebrate his creation as minister, following his good work as ambassador in London when he had persuaded the British government to recognize Napoleon III. His countess, Anne-Marie, an Italian by birth, had a passion for the eighteenth century, and insisted on guests looking to that period for their costumes. Indeed there was a rough similarity in size between eighteenth-century hoops and 1856 crinolines, so that fancy dress in that style would not look too outlandish, whereas clothes from a narrower period would have seemed too revealing and indecent. People's vision is conditioned by what they are used to. Lady guests respected the countess's tastes and mostly arrived dressed *à la* Louis XV, with costumes copied from leading eighteenth-century engravers and designers. General Fleury's wife came as a lady-in-waiting to Queen Marie Antoinette, after the engraving by Moreau le-Jeune. Princesses Mathilde, Murat and Poniatowska all had their hair powdered, while Countess Walewska herself was Diana the Huntress, her costume taken from a ballet design by Boquet. Lady Cowley, wife of the British ambassador, went as Queen Anne. When Count Walewski was made president of the Congress of Paris, his wife threw a masquerade ball every Wednesday during February and March.[3] Another influential party-giver with a passion for the previous century was Empress Eugénie herself, who was fascinated by the sad history of Marie Antoinette and often adopted that disguise at masquerades.

Thus before Worth's court appointment the vogue for dressing-up and the taste for the eighteenth century were firmly established. What he had to do was to follow this pattern and improve upon it. His love of art was now invaluable, for he knew which paintings to turn to for inspiration. Improvements in photography were a great assistance here, for it became increasingly easier to obtain photographs of portraits by famous painters, such as Holbein, Van Dyck and Gainsborough. In addition Worth built up a reference library of costume histories, to which he added over the years. The oldest work in it was an original eighteenth-century volume by Pierre Duclos, *Receuil des étampes, représentant les grades, les rangs, et les dignités, suivant le costume de toutes les nations existants* of 1779–80. Other books he purchased as they came out: *Costumes historiques de la France* by Paul Lacroix of 1852, *Album de coiffures historiques* by Henri de Bysterveld of 1865, *La France et les français à travers les siècles* by Augustin Challamel of 1882, and *Costume de l'Opéra aux 17e et 18e siècles* by Charles Nuitter of 1883. As the Second Empire often looked back to the First, Worth wisely included items from the Napoleonic period, such as *The Magazine of Female Fashions of London and Paris* 1798–1806, and *The Lady's Magazine* of 1806. Moreover, as people sometimes liked to dress up as their parents, he also gathered magazines from the earlier decades of his century, such as *The Ladies' Cabinet of Fashion*, 1832–8, *La Galérie Théâtrale* of *c.* 1825, *L'Aspic; journal artistique des modes*, 1838, *Le Caprice: journal de la lingerie*, 1841–2, and *The Court Magazine* of 1839–41. Thus equipped, he could face all the demands for fancy dress with some confidence.[4]

It is possible that Worth made some masquerade costumes while still at Gagelin, but the earliest recorded one is that worn by Mme Octave Feuillet. So pleased was she with the evening gown Worth had designed for her that she rushed back to the rue de la Paix for a masquerade costume, when she was invited to a fancy-dress ball given by the empress's sister the Duchess of Alba. He created a glittering costume of red and blue satin, covered with gold and silver lace, sparkling with spangles, and with golden fringes falling over the velvet bodice. It had a little hat of black velvet with a large rose, and the shoes were of blue satin with red heels.[5] Mme Feuillet loved it.

As might be expected, it was the lively Pauline von Metternich who was to make some of the greatest demands upon the inventive powers of Maison Worth et Bobergh, for she liked costumes that were sometimes witty, as well as those that were the epitome of taste and magnificence. To one masquerade ball at the Tuileries the princess went dressed as the Devil, in a black costume embroidered with silver

27. *Bal costumé* given by Empress Eugénie's sister, the Duchess of Alba, at the Hôtel d'Albe in 1860.

and spangled with diamonds, which Worth crowned with two little horns of diamonds. To a ball given by the Comtesse de Castellane, Princess von Metternich went as a milkmaid with silver buckets, to the great amusement of her friends. In 1863 she attended a court masquerade ball as Night, draped by Worth in quantities of dark blue tulle covered with diamond stars. Her husband, with rather heavy humour, kept remarking how pretty she looked in her nightgown. At another masquerade ball at the Tuileries in February 1866 the princess appeared as a shepherdess – Worth took the costume from a figure of Sèvres porcelain. The creation the princess admired most from his hands was copied from an eighteenth-century portrait, a Louis XV costume of yellow, garlanded with pompon roses and caught up by silver tassels. With it went a huge hat of yellow crepe surmounted by yellow plumes. As the princess was not very tall this outfit compensated for her lack of height by being very striking, and everyone agreed that it was a masterpiece.

It was Pauline von Metternich who was responsible for bringing redoubts or ridottos into fashion in the 1860s. The first one she gave was in honour of Empress Eugénie, and everyone had to be masked. Napoleon III wore a Venetian cloak and the empress came disguised as Juno. A special ballroom was erected in the embassy garden for the occasion, its walls decorated with large mirrors and covered in light blue satin. The princess's fondness for dressing-up did not stop there. Marquis Philippe de Massa, playwright to the emperor and director of the imperial private theatres at Fontainebleau and Compiègne, called the princess his muse because of her great love for amateur theatricals. She mounted, rehearsed, acted and sang in his topical comedy *Commentaires de César* in 1865, which was a salute to the emperor's own work on Julius Caesar. In Act 1 the princess appeared as an old woman dressed all in rags, which she threw off in Act 2 to reveal a ravishing toilette from Worth. As if this were not enough, Princess von Metternich was also the organizer of the *fêtes champêtres* at St Cloud, where the court played at being eighteenth century out in the open air. The inspiration here was the paintings of Watteau, Lancret and Pater, so Worth created gowns with Watteau pleats from the shoulder. On these occasions the princess insisted on all the ladies powdering their hair white. When Mme de Persigny refused, she rushed to the empress to complain. Empress Eugénie excused the lady by explaining that she was an unstable creature because her mother was mad. Princess von Metternich replied, 'My father is also mad, yet I am well powdered.' In her productions everyone had to look perfect, and she would bully them until they did. The indefatigable princess with her wild enthusiasm and unflagging energy was not easily resisted.

Worth's masquerade costume for the empress could omit comedy and wit, for beauty and grandeur were the primary concerns. For the carnival of 1863 he dressed her as the wife of the Doge of Venice, in a costume of black velvet caught up by diamond brooches to reveal an underskirt of scarlet satin. She was so *cuirassée* in diamonds that it was said she glittered like a sun goddess. Other guests included Princess Mathilde as Holbein's *Anne of Cleves*, wearing her famous emeralds, Countess Walewska was of course in a Louis XV costume of yellow as an equestrienne, and the Marquise de Gallifet appeared as the Archangel Gabriel with wings of swans' feathers.

At the court masquerade ball of Sunday, 11 February 1866, Worth dressed the empress as Marie Antoinette after the portrait by Vigée Le Brun, but copying from famous paintings did have its dangers.

> In a gorgeous costume of ruby velvet trimmed with fur – the period Louis XVI, the hair raised to a vast powdered 'tour' profusely decorated with diamonds – the Empress, looking splendidly, stood before us like an historical memory. . . . Soon she encountered a 'counterfeit presentment' of herself, in the fair person of Madame Rimsky-Korsakov; both costumes were unknowingly taken from the same picture, but the Korsakov had elaborated and hardly improved on the original.[6]

Mme Carette also remembered the empress in this dress as being particularly striking.

It will be observed that the empress's disguises usually reflected her own status. She was a Doge's wife, Juno, Queen of the Gods, and Queen Marie Antoinette, as if her own persona should never be in question, even when disguised. The same attitude was shown by Queen Victoria in the early days of her marriage, going to fancy-dress balls with Prince Albert, dressed as Edward III and Queen Philippa, or as Charles II and Catherine of Braganza. Royalty could not step down the ladder. The empress did act, however, in Octave Feuillet's *Portraits de la Marquise*.

The emperor himself rarely dressed up, considering it beneath his dignity. An exception was for a party given by his half-brother the Duc de Morny, when Napoleon III dressed as a Bedouin chief, but he usually wore a black domino. The men of the corps diplomatique also refused to wear fancy dress, and they would attend masquerades in evening dress with knee breeches, and venetian cloaks decorated with little masks. Prince Richard von Metternich's cloak was of red moiré, bordered with black and mauve velvet.

The ladies had no such inhibitions. The Duchess de Morny was attired by Worth as the Morning Star, in white tulle spangled with silver, a diamond star on her head, so that she could waltz as a vision of ethereal beauty. Princess Mathilde was not afraid to be more original:

> In the winter of 1864 she took a great interest in a fancy dress which she had designed to wear at a ball given by the Duc de Morny. She did not go as a *marquise* of the eighteenth century, nor yet as Diana the Huntress, but as a beggar, dressed in rags – studio rags – arranged for her by her own artist Giraud, and her face covered by a wire mask so disfiguring that she was totally unrecognizable.[7]

Usually, however, Worth's customers asked for glamour above all. The Princesse de Sagan – for whom Worth created a Turkish costume after a painting by Van Loo, and a costume of flowers for the Peasants' Ball – was a regular client for masquerade apparel. Worth's most famous creation for her was the peacock dress (fig. 28), worn at the Bal des Bêtes; this was one of the few occasions when such balls had a central theme. It had a headdress like a small peacock, and a train decorated with peacock plumes, while the skirt was covered with tiny stars and veiled with tulle caught up at the sides by hand-painted cherubs. Peacock dresses were to become something of a Maison Worth speciality, for in 1903 Jean-Philippe designed one for the Marchioness of Curzon, Vicereine of India.[8]

National dress was a popular costume for masquerades, and it had a double advantage in also being acceptable for state balls where it could be worn in an official capacity. Thus at a formal ball given by the Prefect of Paris, Baron Haussmann, at the Hôtel de Ville on 4 February 1866, there was:

> . . . a Polish princess in white tulle, dressed *en soufflé*, with a robe of black velvet reaching three of my paces; round her waist a girdle of gold, studded with emeralds, any one of which would have raised a regiment in her country, where they are sometimes required.

And at a fancy-dress ball in the Foreign Ministry on 20 February 1865: 'The Rimsky-Korsakov, in a Russian court-dress, splendid, her robe literally massive with precious stones'.[9] As already suggested, la Rimsky-Korsakov was one of Worth's more difficult clients, with far more money than taste. She was one of the most outrageously extravagant dressers of her period, and always strove for the maximum effect, being quite unable to leave well alone. Apart from ruining the costume copied from the same picture as that worn by the empress, she insisted that a feathered dress Worth made for her be smothered in plumes. Consequently she was a favourite topic for the reporters: 'The Rimsky-Korsakov had a bird of paradise in her hair, a dress trimmed with feathers of the same, and looked quite fit to fly away with that bird.'

28. Worth's peacock dress, made for the Princesse de Sagan in 1864.

On one occasion she went too far, turning up at the Palais des Tuileries as Flaubert's Carthaginian heroine, Salammbô, with a bodice so transparent that the empress took one look and had her quietly conducted straight back to her carriage. This incident made no difference at all to that princess's attitude. She considered herself a *femme du monde* who was above such narrow considerations as modest clothing, and thought those who made a fuss about such things were hypocrites. In 1866 she set Worth a real problem when she asked him to design an outfit that would leave her naked but chaste, dressed but not prudish. Not surprisingly, Worth found this a real puzzle, and suggested that perhaps she ought to go to her jeweller, for one could be dressed in but a single jewel, so let her cover her own treasures with others. In the end he allowed himself to be persuaded and did create a daring gown. *La Vie Parisienne* commented: '*Worth exigea d'énormes sommes pour l'habiller si galamment. Elle était en plaisir des hommes.*'

Another Worth customer who was even more interested in attracting the men was the Comtesse de Castiglione, one of Napoleon III's mistresses. The emperor might have a very beautiful wife but, like other men in positions of great importance, he was selfish and used his prestige to bring him pleasures which he might not have enjoyed otherwise. The countess herself was no better. An extremely vain woman, a proud cold beauty, she thought all men should fall at her feet. Among those who did were the Duc d'Aumale, Lord Hertford, and Comte de Nieuwerkerke, who was Princess Mathilde's treacherous lover. Needless to say, Empress Eugénie hated seeing the countess at court, and the latter in her arrogance tried to compete with the empress in appearance.

> Rivalry in hair-dressing nearly cost Madame de Castiglione her invitations to court. But, as might be expected, there were other points of discord on the subject of dress between the sovereign and her Florentine guest, the former being essentially conservative and the latter almost revolutionary.[10]

Masquerade parties gave the countess the opportunity to display herself in a variety of daring costumes, with which the empress could not lower herself to compete. One of the most shocking was a black velvet gown, slit up to the waist at one side so that a whole leg was revealed, which she dared to wear at the Tuileries. In 1856 she flaunted her reputation by appearing at a ball as the Queen of Hearts, discarding her corset to reveal the modelling of her breasts, which she considered works of art. The costume was decorated with hearts, which were placed on the strategic points of her person, symbolizing the men she had conquered. Empress Eugénie remarked with acid scorn that one of her hearts appeared to have slipped too low.

The Comtesse de Castiglione dressed with Worth because the empress did. She was particularly fond of *tableaux vivants*, so Worth was called upon for symbolic costumes. He dressed her as Sadness in drooping draperies, and as Amorous Conquest in a mixture of martial and voluptuous clothes. The empress had appeared as the Doge's wife, so la Castiglione wanted a similar outfit, only one that was more *risqué*. In 1867 she caused considerable offence by representing Pious Meditation wearing a nun's habit – this really shocked society. Fortunately, Worth was not responsible for that particular costume. Such was the countess's vanity, however, that she even had herself photographed in the habit and her other costumes, so that posterity might have the privilege of seeing her beauty preserved. Obviously she was unaware that concepts of beauty change, and that what was considered a fine figure in the 1860s would appear too short and plump a century later.

She was noted for her withering tongue, from which even the sovereigns were not spared. In 1860 Prince Jérôme gave a ball in honour of the empress at the Palais Royal, and when the imperial couple took their leave at 1 a.m. they met the countess on the staircase, who was just arriving.

'You are very late, Madame Countess,' said the Emperor to her, gallantly.

'It is you, sire, who are leaving too soon.' And she entered the fête with that disdainful and crushing air with which she seemed to look down on all humanity.[11]

The empress did her best to ensure that the countess did not receive invitations to court, and her visits became rarer as the decade advanced. The last costume Worth created for Castiglione to wear at the Tuileries was in 1869. How she succeeded in gaining admission no one knew, but she appeared, dressed all in black, representing the widowed Marie de' Medici. The costume was greatly admired but its occupant was not. The empress summoned a chamberlain, who offered the countess his arm and led her back to her carriage, for she was now firmly classified among the *personnes reconduites* – the inadmissible – for even the emperor had grown tired of her arrogant ways.

Fortunately such customers were in the minority, and Worth could create fantastic costumes for other ladies, secure in the knowledge that they did not have to be too outrageous. His loyal American client, Mrs Charles Moulton, enjoyed masquerades immensely, but her outfits were modest. For the Carnival of 1863 Worth dressed her as a Spanish dancer in a yellow satin skirt covered with black lace, a bolero embroidered all over with steel beads, a red rose in her hair and red boots. As a matter of fact she would have liked something more fanciful, and found the price too high. She was more satisfied, however, with Worth's next effort, when he turned her into a salamander for a masquerade ball at the Foreign Ministry in May 1863. She wrote home to the USA:

> I must tell you about my dress. It was really one of the prettiest there. Worth said he had really put his whole soul in it. I thought he had put a pretty good round price on his soul. A skirt of gold tissue, round the bottom of which was a band of silver, with all sorts of fantastic figures, such as dragons, owls, and so forth, embroidered in different colors, under a skirt of white tulle with gold and silver spangles. The waist was a mass of spangles and false stones on a gold stuff; gold-embroidered bands came from the waist and fell in points over the skirt. I had wings of spangled silvery material, with great, glass-colored beads sewed all over them. But the *chef d'oeuvre* was the head-dress, which was a sort of helmet with gauze wings and the jewels of the family (Mrs M.'s and mine) fastened on it. From the helmet flowed a mane of gold tinsel, which I curled in my hair. The effect was very original, for it looked as if my head was on fire; in fact, it looked as if I was all on fire. Before I left home all the servants came to see me.[12]

The amount of work involved in these costumes was clearly considerable, and very intricate shapes had to be heavily embroidered in metal thread and beads. Whereas day-wear was relatively simple, masquerade clothes called for elaborate detail. Maison Worth et Bobergh set itself the highest standards in dressmaking, and there was no let-up for masquerade costume. That had to be just as excellent in its finish as fashionable gowns. This increased the House's reputation abroad, and resulted in foreign orders for, as shown by Mrs Moulton's letters, Worth's customers were eager to let their relations back home know what wonders could be had from his hands. In Madrid the Duchess of Medina Celi heard the reports, and ordered a masquerade costume at eight days' notice, insisting that it had to be special. Worth obliged by creating a mermaid costume of watery green and blue tulle, set with silver scales, which was then dispatched by express train. The duchess was so delighted with it that she ordered another by an exchange of telegrams. This time Worth devised a gown of black velvet draped with pearl-grey velvet, the train lined with pink satin to give occasional flashes of brilliance, and accompanied it with four costumes for pages, all in white.

Sometimes masquerade balls had a theme. At one given by the empress's sister, the Duchess of Alba, the ladies performed a quadrille of the four elements; those representing earth were covered in emeralds and diamonds, those as fire were in rubies and diamonds, those as air were in turquoises and diamonds, and those as water were in pearls and diamonds. At one of Count Walewski's balls there was a cortège representing the different parts of the world, with the Marquise de Chasseloup-Laubat as India in a palanquin surmounted by peacock plumes, and Madame Bartholoni as Africa in a golden chariot. In the main, however, these balls had no central idea, and were a mixture of all the costumes imaginable. Another Walewski ball in 1865 had a Mary Queen of Scots and an English Cleopatra, while the men came as Julius Caesar, an Indian prince, a Hungarian chief, a Don Quixote, a knight in armour, and one genuine Gordon Highlander, with some sorry French imitations in unbelievable tartans. But it was the eighteenth century which set the pace for masquerades, and the number of such costumes which flowed from Maison Worth exceeded any other. There were innumerable Marie Antoinettes from 1860 until the day Worth died, and how it must have taxed his imagination to give each one a touch of originality: some could be straight copies from portraits of that queen, others could be entertaining sugar puffs of chiffon and tulle. What a relief it was to turn to costumes which did not try to represent anyone or anything in particular, so that Worth could sculpt and swathe sumptuous fabrics

29. Miss Van Wart as one of the innumerable Marie Antoinettes which Maison Worth had to churn out over the years.

as he willed, free of any preconception. He was able to conjure a costume from a mixture of materials at only a few hours' notice, whipping items together in a flurry of creation. Take a length of velvet, catch it up with a bejewelled brooch, add a bright satin for contrast, scatter some embroidery across the bodice, swirl some chiffon here and there, *et voilà*, a masterpiece for a masquerade. Given the hundreds of orders which his house received, speed of invention was an essential asset.

Whilst Worth et Bobergh was a ladies dressmaker's, there were occasions when it clothed men for masquerade balls. As Worth's reputation increased, he became regarded as an authority on all aspects of dress, so when men were faced with the problem of finding a suitable masquerade costume, Worth was the obvious person to turn to. With his wide knowledge of painting and historical dress, he could come up with an answer that would not make a chap look too ridiculous, for men were very sensitive about their dignity, which was why Napoleon III did not dress up. Among Worth's male customers

30. Mme de Benardaki in a fancy dress which Worth improvised in a few hours in 1890.

was an American in Rome, a Mr Marshall, who received an invitation to Duchess Fiano's fancy-dress ball in 1881. While not rich he decided to be reckless and ordered a costume from Worth which cost nearly as much as his annual income. It was of the period of Henri II: 'A light-blue satin jacket, and trunk-hose, slashed to exaggeration, with white satin puffs, a jaunty velvet cap with a long feather, and white satin shoes turned up at the ends.'[13] As he had skinny legs and wore glasses it is unlikely that Mr Marshall struck a very striking figure, but he was very proud of his masquerade outfit and, in view of the expense, decided to have himself photographed in it. He set off in a cab to go to the studio, but on the way the horse fell and could proceed no further, so Marshall had to get out and walk. Unfortunately it then poured with rain and all the blue dye in his costume ran. *Sic transit gloria.* . . .

Dressing men was never a major part of Worth's business, but it was a regular feature, and a very lucrative one, for the same philosophy of nothing but the best was applied to men as much as to women. Brocade, satin, silk, and lace were all employed, and all the jewels were real. Renaissance princes, Van Dyck cavaliers, eighteenth-century fops and Regency bucks were the principal kinds of costume created for these customers. Even after the collapse of the Second Empire, masquerade dress continued to be in demand. The Paris exhibitions of 1878 and 1889, and Queen Victoria's Golden Jubilee in 1887, were all excuses for lavish celebrations, and the Paris season never lost its appeal to foreign rich and royalty. The Prince of Wales loved the place, and he had no objection to dressing up. Indeed as a prince he had been required to wear all sorts of fanciful uniforms, so a masquerade costume was not an embarrassing proposition as far as he was concerned. The same could be said of the Russian Grand Dukes and Austrian Archdukes who made Paris their playground. All were willing to oblige a comtesse or duchesse by wearing masquerade costumes to their parties; after all their dignity was guaranteed. Napoleon III's doubts on the subject only served to show that he was not really royal.

Apart from costume balls, Worth's clients also went in for charades and elaborate japes, for they lacked sufficient education for more serious pursuits. One of the court beauties whom Worth dressed regularly was Melanie, Comtesse de Pourtalès, who was a member of a club called the Imps, which specialized in playing pranks. On one such occasion a Worth creation came in for the sort of treatment which would have made him fume. Mme de Pourtalès's parties were usually very well organized and she always spent a small fortune on flowers alone, but one dinner party proved an exception. When the guests arrived they found her house staffed with a new set of servants, who were all very clumsy and confused everyone's names.

Just then, impetuous and quick-tempered, Madame de Metternich entered the room, announced as 'Madame de Materna', considerably ruffled because her superb cloak, fresh from the hands of Worth, had been rolled up by a clumsy lackey like the commonest mantle. 'Really, my dear Melanie,' she exclaimed, 'what has happened to your servants? What sort of people have you engaged?'[14]

Worse was to follow. When the guests entered the dining-room they found the table occupied by these self-same dreadful servants. There was uproar until the truth dawned. The servants were all the noble members of the Imps.

The treatment of Princess von Metternich's cloak was not that far removed from reality, for a clumsy servant in the wardrobe was a disaster. Lady Paget wrote furiously from Longleat in October 1877: 'I've had to tell Mrs. Hurley she must depart . . . I found one of my best Worth dresses shoved into a window on the servants' staircase at Heron Court, with my shoes thrown on top.'[15] That was no way to treat the most expensive clothes in the world. Anything from Maison Worth et Bobergh was expensive, because it was the leading couture house, the first one of its kind. What is more, masquerade costumes could cost more than ball gowns, for they were much more elaborate. Although intended for only one night's frivolity, the masquerade costumes from Worth were just as well made as anything else emanating from that establishment, for his policy that everything must be the best of its kind was applied with equal force in this department.

Masquerade parties could fall into two main types: the *bals masqués* at which masks were all-important, and the *bals costumés* at which fancy-dress dominated. These terms were used by London high society as much as by Parisian society, French terminology being part of the snobbism of the period. In the 1870s the Duke of Marlborough was considered a leading presenter of *bals costumés*, and in the 1890s, the Duke of Devonshire.

Nowadays when fashionable clothes are not very ornate, masquerade dress can seem too extreme and elaborate. The view was different in the nineteenth century, when fashionable wear owed a great deal to historical costume. The past was repeatedly plundered for inspiration, and such items as lace collars, capes, bustles, sleeves, and hats were often copies of previous modes. Thus the gap between normal day-dress and historical costume was much narrower than it is today, so that the masquerade was not looked upon as alien. A modern girl, accustomed to short skirts, would have to change her whole manner of walking if put into a crinoline and full court train, but the nineteenth-century girl was used to wearing such clothes in the day-time, and found no difficulty in managing a similarly ornate masquerade costume in the evening. Flamboyantly impractical clothes were part of her life-style, and showed that she was most definitely not one of the workers. Masquerades were simply another aspect of that social display which poured money into Worth's coffers. He was catering for those who liked to be conspicuous.

Notes

1. F. Whitehurst, *Court and Social Life in France under Napoleon III* (1873), vol. II, pp. 14–15.
2. *Souvenirs de la Princesse Pauline de Metternich 1859–71*, notes by M. Dunan (1922), Librairie Plon, p. 67.
3. Frédéric Loliée, *Women of the Second Empire*, trans. Alice M. Ivimy (1907), p. 232.
4. These volumes are now in the possession of the Victoria and Albert Museum, London.
5. Mme Valerie Feuillet, *Quelques Années de ma Vie* (1894), pp. 207–8.
6. F. Whitehurst, op. cit., p. 168.
7. Loliée, op. cit., p. 101.
8. In the collection of the Museum of London, Dept. of Textiles, cat. no. 32.155.
9. Whitehurst, op. cit., vol. I, p. 46.
10. Loliée, op. cit., p. 13.
11. Mme Carette, *My Mistress, the Empress Eugénie; or Court Life at the Tuileries* (1889), p. 245.
12. Lillie de Hegermann-Lindencrone, *In The Courts of Memory* (1912), p. 48.
13. L. de Hegermann-Lindencrone, *The Sunny Side of Diplomatic Life 1875–1912* (1914), p. 110.
14. Loliée, op. cit., p. 325.
15. Walburga, Lady Paget, *Embassies of Other Days and Further Recollections* (1923), vol. II, p. 320.

Chapter 7

Worth and Fashion
during the Second Empire

Once Worth became established as the dominant figure in the world
of French fashion, it was inevitable that later periods would come to
look on him as the fountain head of all styles which emanated from
Paris in the second half of the nineteenth century. Not only
mainstream high fashion, but the multitude of temporary sub-
fashions were all thought to be his creations, as if he was some sort of
cornucopia capable of an infinite number of luxuries. The true
picture is far more complicated. Every fashionable dressmaker liked
to have some new features for each season, and a lot of the sub-
fashions had nothing to do with Worth, although his name was
sometimes used to suggest that an innovation had his blessing behind
it – a common practice of the period. Foremost among the
fashionable myths is the one which states that Worth both invented
the crinoline and introduced it to the Empress Eugénie, but like many
a myth this does not stand up well to examination. The empress first
started wearing a *cage*-crinoline in 1856, when she was expecting the
Prince Imperial, which was four years before she invited Worth to
become one of her dressmakers.[1] Furthermore, the question must be
asked, for which kind of crinoline was Worth responsible? for there
were a great many varieties.

Crin is French for animal hair, and crinoline in the 1840s meant a
horsehair petticoat. Being relatively stiff, such petticoats gave the bulk
which fashion demanded for skirts. As it is in the nature of styles to
develop to their utmost extent, the insistence on width became even
more marked in the 1850s, and by 1854 petticoats stiffened with
whalebone and petticoats of horsehair were both being worn. By
1856 petticoats held out by steel bands were being introduced, and
they were known as *cage*-crinolines. These wire crinolines were
considered far superior to cheaper methods of holding out the skirt,
such as buckram petticoats or split sugar cane, which were unwieldly
and lacked flexibility.

There was some confusion even at the time as to whether France or

England was responsible for the invention of this steel frame. Henry Mayhew was of the opinion that crinolines orginated in France,[2] and *Punch* shared his view:

> That Crinolinomania is of foreign origin Dr Punch considers there is little room to doubt; indeed he would say without hesitation that the malady broke out in Paris. Dr Punch has ample grounds for his belief that the persons first affected were the ladies attached to the Imperial Court; and that the symptoms of the mania were primarily betrayed by the young and lovely Empress.[3]

This opinion was shared by one Frenchman, Comte Fleury, who reported that the inventor of the crinoline was an individual with the highly unlikely name of Auguste Person from Champagne, who sold the patent for a mere 4,000 francs, although others gained millions from it.[4] He added that the crinoline was first known in France as a *cage*, so that women wearing it were said to be caged, which caused a lot of humorous comment. All this talk about it only caused the *cage* to sell. Another French writer, Bertall, however, considered that responsibility for such enormous frames could only lie with the English:

> If we are well informed, the crinoline and its iron carcass are an evil of English origin, a fatal virus which propagated itself across the surface of the globe with the rapidity and inflexibility of lightning. It is highly appropriate that it is the English, a gauche, mercantile, ungainly race, who are responsible for the creation of these rigid bells, the grave of grace and style.[5]

The truth probably lies somewhere between the two attitudes, with developments in the structure of the crinoline taking place on both sides of the Channel at the same time. It was after all a straightforward engineering problem – how to achieve the maximum width with the minimum of support. Both the construction of the Crystal Palace in 1851, and the new railway termini, with their broad spans of iron ribs, could suggest to more than one mind a method for achieving greater expanse in skirts. Mayhew drew attention to the technique that enabled iron to be turned into steel, which could then be drawn out into fine wires. Indeed this process was vital to the invention of the flexible *cage* frame. This form of crinoline was a true child of the Industrial Revolution, for it could not have taken place without it. By 1858 there were factories which made nothing but crinoline steel, and shops which sold nothing but crinolines. The *cage* was without doubt the first industrial fashion, a true representative of its age.

The new petticoat exploded across France, England and over to the United States within months of each other. The number of crinoline makers became legion, and almost every issue of any fashion magazine carried advertisements proclaiming the advantage of this or that variation on the *cage*. Some claimed that their product never got caught in the feet, others that their springs never sprang out of order, and others that their crinolines could not flare up in a high wind. With so many competitors in being, one can only point to scores of adaptors and developers, rather than to any one inventor.

The enormous popularity of the *cage*-crinoline was due to the new freedom it brought to fashion. An English lady was reported as saying: 'In walking it permits a degree of comfort and freedom in movement, to which, before its use, I had been an utter stranger.'[6]

For the first time in decades women's legs did not have to fight against quantities of petticoats piled on top of each other to achieve width. The *cage* gave width without bulk. In the opinion of Dr Barthez, physician to the infant Prince Imperial, Napoleon III's heir, this explained why Empress Eugénie was so fond of this new fashion. In a letter of 22–26 September 1856, written at the empress's villa at Biarritz, he said:

> The amplitude of these dresses is something fabulous. It is beyond any idea that you can form from what you have seen in Paris. All this stuff is supported by a sort of skeleton of extremely flexible iron. The Empress is greatly attached to this cage, which to us seems very ungraceful and inconvenient. She sticks to it in spite of the quips of the Emperor, to whom she simply replies that she does not know how she lived so many years without a cage. I can find only two excuses for this fashion. One is that women who wear it have their legs free in walking, and are not hampered by skirts and petticoats hanging on their calves and thighs and impeding their movements; the other, in her case, is that there is a sort of harmony between the amplitude of the woman and the size of the apartments in which she lives.[7]

His first excuse is the correct one, his second is ingenious but hardly applicable. If the size of imperial apartments had ever determined the width of skirts, empresses would have been wearing crinolines since antiquity! The reason why that champion of women's rights and dress reform, Mrs Amelia Bloomer, advocated Turkish trousers for women in 1851 was because such garments liberated the legs from petticoats.[8] In a way *cages* answered her complaint by abolishing the need for layers of petticoats, although they did not solve her other objection: that long skirts were unhygienic because they dragged in all the mud and filth of the streets. There was a price to be paid for this new freedom, however – extremely wide skirts caused many young ladies to be burned to death through standing near an unguarded fire or stove and not knowing that the far edge of the dress had caught alight. In addition, mortalities were caused by girls being blown under the feet of horses, tumbling downstairs, falling over their own hems, and even over cliffs. The crinoline was not the first fashion to demand some human sacrifices among its devotees.

When did Worth enter this complicated scene? As can be seen in Chapter 3, he was definitely an early advocate of wider skirts, with his 'great novelty' advertised in *Le Moniteur de la Mode* in 1852–3 (fig. 12). However, all the emphasis in that design was on width, recalling the panniers of the mid-eighteenth century, rather than the round bell shape which was to be characteristic of the *cage*-crinoline. He can certainly be seen as an early experimenter in the field, but his novelty was not the one which excited the fashion world three years later. Moreover, it is most unlikely that Worth was *au fait* with the development of processes in the steel industry. It probably took minds which had some access to factories to appreciate the possibilities of sprung steel for skirts, rather than a dress designer who never went near steel mills. The first promoters of *cages* evidently took their inventions straight to court if Empress Eugénie was wearing them in 1856, and not to a dressmaker who had still to make his name in the world. Of course once Worth had won his imperial appointment in 1860, inventors came to him before anyone else, but this was five years after the sensation of the *cage*. In 1856 Worth was still at Gagelin and not his own master. His employers might have allowed him to start a dressmaking department, but it is most unlikely that they would have permitted him to fill their august emporium with *cage*-crinolines, which were undergarments, not gowns.

Jean-Philippe remembered an English inventor called Thomson coming to his father in about 1860 with a cashmere petticoat mounted on three steel or whalebone hoops, which Worth agreed to promote.[9] 1860 was the date when inventors would turn to Worth, with their latest variation on the *cage*, but they would hardly have been aware of his existence before then. The Mr Thomson concerned may have been William Thomson of Thomson, Sparks & Co. at 97 Cheapside, London, manufacturers and patentees of prize medal crinolines, who won awards for their product at the London exhibition of 1862 and the Paris one of 1867.[10] There are no other Thomsons, crinoline makers, in the Post Office Directory for London around that date.

Crinolines fell into two types. There was the skeleton frame of steel, which was the *cage*, and crinoline petticoats in which the ribs were built into the wool or cotton of the petticoat proper. According to an official report of 1867, crinolines were made in all the towns in

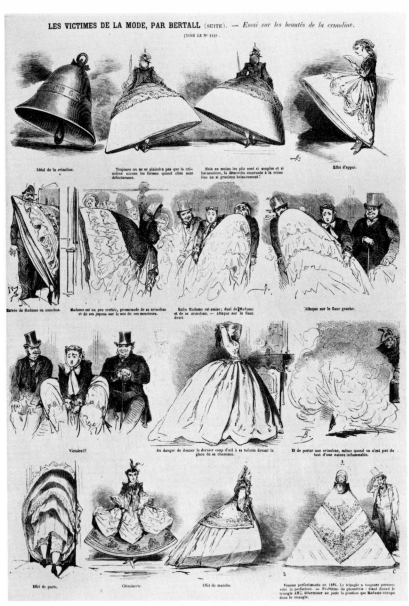

31. Bertall cartoon on the problems of the crinoline – difficult to manage, impossible on an omnibus, liable to conflagration, and turning madame into a triangle. 1864.

France. The rolled steel came from British and French mills, and the cotton and wool from Roubaix, Amiens, Tarare and St Quentin, with cambric muslin and other fancy tissues coming from Mulhouse, Rouen and St Marie-aux-Mines. The value of the trade was put at 20,000,000 francs, with half the output exported. In other words it was an industry.[11]

Once the principle of expanding skirts over *cages* had been discovered, it was exploited to the full, resulting in the early 1860s in enormous skirts, which were increasingly difficult to manage, as Mme Carette remembered:

> To walk with so immense a paraphernalia around one was not very easy; and the narrow bust placed in the centre of this volume of material, appeared to be detached from the rest of the body altogether. To be able to sit so as not to cause the rebellious springs to fly open, required a miracle of precision. To ascend a carriage without rumpling such light texture, at a time when evening toilettes were made of tulle and lace, required a great deal of time, much quietness on the part of the horses, and much patience on the part of fathers and husbands, whose complaisance was put to an enormous test, compelled as they were to remain motionless in the midst of these *nuages fragiles*.[12]

The problems were how to travel, how to rock a baby in the cradle, how to take hold of a child's hand, for a woman was now surrounded by a barrier two metres in diameter. The courtesy of a man offering his arm to a lady now went out of fashion, for the simple reason that it was impossible physically. The *cage*-crinoline emphasized a woman's natural shape below the waist, but at the same time made her unapproachable, which illustrates the dichotomy in the nineteenth-century's attitude to women. By 1865 the size of such skirts was being criticized with increasing intensity. When a Dr Jules Meugy petitioned the French Senate that year asking that the enormous amount of prostitution in Paris be made illegal, he was supported by the Procurator-General Dupin, who said it was fashion which drove women into prostitution. Poor females were trying to ape the rich with huge dresses and *cages*, and had to sell themselves in order to find the money. Certainly poverty did drive women into whoredom but it was the need for bread rather than a need for a dress which made them do it, although of course there were some women who saw it as an easy way to make money out of men. Dupin picked out the *cage*-crinoline for particular criticism, in a speech to the Senate:

> La Fontaine, in one of his fables, mocks the frog who wished to be as big as an ox; but, with today's fashions, he would be able to

do it! (General hilarity. Very good! Very good!) It would suffice for this idiot to tie these elastic dimensions around his waist, which would make him as enormous as the model he desires to imitate.[13]

No one was more aware of the increasing absurdity of the *cage-crinoline* than Worth himself, for he was surrounded by them night and day. As his salon was increasingly filled with ladies of enormous width, who could not help but collide with each other or knock chairs over, and as his own wife could not handle their children, he could see for himself that something would have to be done.

In 1864, a year ahead of Dupin, he embarked on a campaign of reform. The main problem was that the *cage* was round, with as much material in front as in the back. To abolish *cages* overnight was out of the question. Everyone was used to women being extremely wide, and the sudden introduction of a narrow line would have been too sudden a shock. Worth decided on a slower approach – on reform rather than

32. The crinoline at its widest. Worth's design for a jacket and skirt showing strong eighteenth-century influence.

revolution. The most sensible thing to do was to flatten the *cage* in front, and push all the fullness out of the way round to the back, thereby enabling the wearer to be able to make some human contact with her hands. This idea was ridiculed by the press at first, claiming that the backs of dresses would now need relays of lackeys to carry them, but it was such a practical innovation that women took to it. Madame Carette said that Worth was a deliverer of women from the tyranny of *cages* when he introduced his flat-fronted crinoline, and the court at once adopted it in 1864. This was the form of crinoline which Worth definitely invented.

It took a couple of years for the change to percolate down the social ladder. In 1865 Whitehurst could still report:

> I confess that I have seen no signs of that salutary reform which we are taught to expect from the startling revelations and bitter diatribes of M. Dupin. I certainly think that at the theatre . . . at least in the boxes, the ladies have left off their crinolines. How

33. Worth design for a swept-back dress, *c.* 1864.

indeed to get into a box without? But then, judging from what meets the eye above, they have left off their dresses too, and that, I suppose, is hardly the kind of economy advocated by the Reformer of Robes.[14]

The theatre was one place where huge skirts were never welcome among the audience. A hundred years before, when panniers were all the rage, playhouses used to request that ladies leave their hoops at home. In February 1866 the observant reporter could still see *cages* at a ball given by Baron Haussmann, and could only wonder at their sheer impracticability: 'How those feet get round without tripping themselves up in their own steel hoops, or the voluminous petticoats worn under their very luminous robes, is to me a miracle.' But by the following month he could see that some women had abandoned *cages*.

Thanks to Worth the fashionable emphasis was now on the back of the dress, and no one produced such magnificent versions of the new

34. The swept-back look in a lace skirt.

35. One of Worth's experiments with dress construction: Marie Worth in a
prototype princess dress without a seam at the waist.

style as he did, with great sweeping skirts which conveyed an air of grandeur upon the wearer. Nevertheless he always kept them simple, with just ribbon, bows or lace as the decoration, for extremes of ornamentation were never characteristic of Worth. His reputation for taste was based upon this avoidance of excess, and many of his designs in the 1860s were the essence of simplicity in an age when an over-abundance of decorative detail was only too common.

During that decade Worth concentrated a lot of attention on the construction of skirts. As early as 1863 he was experimenting with a dress in which the waistline was dropped to the top of the hip – the fit at the waist proper was achieved by darts. He was trying to see if it were possible to create a gown without a waistline seam: the skirt and bodice as one. Marie Worth was the only person to wear this experimental gown at the time, and while Worth did not proceed with this idea in the 1860s, he was to return to it in the 1870s, as we shall see later. Matching separates were another of his developments at this time, as in the green silk dress with a striped hem, teamed with a cape with a similar hem, which was bought by Princess von Metternich.

36. The Duchesse de Morny in 1863 wearing one of Worth's simple gowns with a moiré sash.

Once again it is the simplicity of the design which is most striking. Such plainness had the added advantage of displaying the perfection of Worth's fit to the full, for there was no clumsiness which needed to be hidden under trimmings.

It was at the request of Empress Eugénie in 1863 that Worth turned his attention to the length of skirts. As she was fond of long walks in the country or at the seaside, she liked to go on excursions but found ground-length hemlines a considerable nuisance because they got so

37. Worth's design for a dress and cape with striped hems, 1865.

dirty, picking up mud or sand at every step. Peasant women and fisherwomen coped with the problem by hitching their skirts up, and had been doing so for generations, but it did not become the Empress of the French to hitch up her skirts. She asked Worth to invent a solution which would be practical while remaining respectable.

Fashionable hemlines had been ground-length for nearly thirty years. Not since 1830 had ankle-length skirts been in fashion, but Worth decided to take the bold step of raising the hemline, as the easiest solution to the problem. Ten centimetres cut off the bottom was enough to clear the ground, while leaving the ankles demurely concealed. The empress, of course, was not the first to wear the new walking skirt. It was Marie Worth who had to brave the Parisian promenades, the raised eyebrows, the shocked glances, and the muttered comment. The innovation was, however, so manifestly practical that only a literal stick-in-the-mud could see any real objection. The empress's ladies appeared in it, and then the empress

38. Princess von Metternich wearing the dress shown in fig. 37.

herself, wearing the walking skirt at Trouville. By April 1864 the skirt was common enough in town for *Le Charivari* to publish a cartoon in which two old street cleaners complained that these new short skirts did not sweep the streets for them.

Worth's other bold innovation in 1863 was the rakish hat, again first worn by Marie. Ever since the 1790s bonnets had become the dominant headgear for women, to such an extent that hats with brims were considered extremely masculine. The more demure the

87

39. E. Boudin – Empress Eugénie and her ladies wearing the shorter skirt on the beach at Trouville in 1863.

40. Marie Worth, the first person to wear the short walking skirt in 1863 – and with a hat instead of a bonnet. With her are her sons, Gaston, then aged ten wearing a cap, and Jean-Philippe aged seven.

nineteenth-century woman had to be, the more she retreated into her bonnet. A frill at the back, the *bavolet*, concealed her neck, the depth of the brim blinkered her vision and made her face more remote, the tie bow in front hid her throat and chin. There was a vogue for sun hats in 1855 for the seaside, but in town, bonnets were almost compulsory. According to Charles Dickens, Worth allowed a bonnet-maker to operate on the ground-floor of his establishment to whom he would refer customers for bonnets to match his creations.[15] As Worth loathed clutter in any form, he probably consulted this lady about his ideas and got her to try out alterations.

His first step was to discard the *bavolet*, and once again it was Marie Worth who exhibited the innovation in fashionable society. Princess von Metternich approved and adopted the reformed bonnet herself; bare necks became acceptable for day time outdoors. But if one could now show the neck, why stop there? What was wrong with showing the hair as well? Hats, said Worth, and out went Marie wearing a hat with a brim, which to some people was akin to a woman wearing trousers it smacked so much of dashing masculinity. No lady should ever make herself conspicuous. Even Marie Worth must have had a few doubts about the propriety of some of her husband's ideas – there was sometimes a tearful scene if she felt that he was asking her to do something too outrageous for genteel taste.

Hats were too bold for her initially, but Princess von Metternich had no qualms and, with the princess for support, Marie Worth rode round Paris in a hat with a jaunty brim. Interestingly, Worth had first looked at hats in 1860 when he made the princess a tiny round hat to perch on top of her head, but that did not compare in audacity with Marie's hat with its mannish brim.

Worth's principal launching ground for new fashions was the racecourse at Longchamp. Opened in 1859, it was, along with the French Jockey Club, closely modelled on English examples, and rapidly became established as one of the smartest rendezvous for Parisian high society, which made it an ideal location for a dressmaker to try out new effects. One visitor recorded:

> The prettiest women, the prettiest carriages, the prettiest toilettes, came together at Longchamp. It is there that Worth – who was then ruling without rival – launched his models. I think that Laferrière was beginning to hardly exist.[16]

It will be remembered that Laferrière made the empress's ordinary frocks. During the racing season, the aristocracy paraded up and down at Longchamp, but once the races started, the ladies retired to the grandstands and the men stood on the ground near the rails. This form of segregation was also practised in the theatres, with ladies in the balconies and men in the pit.

As Worth hated fussy effects, one of his targets for improvement was the shawls and cloaks with which women draped themselves before going out. It was considered indelicate for a lady to reveal the shape of her bust and shoulders to vulgar gaze, so no lady ventured out of the house without concealing such features in metres of drapery. What with bonnets with *bavolets*, Paisley shawls and crinolines, a woman outdoors looked like a triangle swamped in material from head to foot. As Worth took so much trouble to see that the fit of his gowns was perfect, it was annoying that all that elegance should then be buried under shawls and mantles as soon as it left the salon. But Marie Worth would not walk outdoors without a mantle, no matter what he said, and so it was necessary to recruit Princess von Metternich as well and send them to Longchamp together. He dressed the princess in a gown of vivid green which he had christened Metternich green, and his wife in purple and blue taffeta. As both ladies felt naked without something round their shoulders, Worth allowed them wisps of material instead of wraps, a mantilla for the princess, and a confection of taffeta and Chantilly lace for his wife. The arrival of these 'undressed' women at Longchamp caused a sensation, but as Worth was the arbiter of dress no one dared to ignore his edict. Two weeks later shawls and mantles had vanished from the grandstands at Longchamp.

Other gowns which Princess von Metternich wore at the races were one of yellow taffeta decorated only with black velvet bows, and a plain black dress accompanied by a bright red parasol; both being good examples of Worth's ability to make striking effects very simply. When Comtesse Sibylle de Martel de Janville, who wrote under the name Gyp, was in her teens, she saw the princess in the yellow taffeta and was astonished at her big mouth with violently red lipstick and short nose but, as the princess said herself, she was no beauty. On the same occasion Gyp noticed that some ladies were standing on chairs to watch the races, and the pressure of the crinolines against the backs of the chairs forced the backs of the crinolines to stick up, revealing a variety of legs and underwear. One undergarment in particular attracted the girl's attention and she asked her uncle very loudly what it was. Open pantaloons, he replied with patent embarrassment, at which the ladies in horror struggled to descend.[17] This form of pantaloon enabled a lady to use a *pot de chambre* without removing her crinoline, because 'the smallest room' was often too small to get into.[18]

Simplicity was a fundamental principle for Worth's approach to design, as Dickens realized. Writing in 1867 of the sleeveless fitted jacket Worth had just introduced, rich in gold and coloured embroidery, he remarked on the absence of sleeves: 'Mark that touch of genius, for there is as much talent in knowing what to abate as in knowing what to add.'[19] Simplicity was also the key to Worth's tunic dress, which Whitehurst first saw at the first imperial ball of 1866. It was nothing more than a short bodice and skirt, worn over a long skirt, but the number of variations that could be obtained by using contrasting fabrics was considerable. Empress Eugénie wore a tunic dress when entertaining the Czar Alexander II and the King of Prussia in 1867. It was simply a lace tunic worn over a silk skirt, but therein lay the essence of elegance. The tunic style lasted until 1874, when Worth himself began to abolish it, and there were many variations on the theme, such as apron overskirts where only the overskirt was in a different fabric from the gown proper. The permutations he employed were such contrasts as brocade tunics over velvet skirts, velvet tunics over brocade skirts, lace tunics over silk, silk over lace, tulle over chiffon, chiffon over tulle. Only the number of textiles in existence limited the possibilities.

In 1868 Worth was again busy with skirts, as the *Daily Telegraph* reported:

> I am informed that the last new thing in dress is a 'puff petticoat', which sticks out in a bunch, and causes the female form divine to look rather like the Gnathodon or the Dodo. It is said to have routed sleep from the couch of the oft-recorded Worth, who laboured day and night at its invention.[20]

But the impact of this puff skirt was overshadowed by Worth's other innovation of that year: he dared to abolish crinolines altogether. It was four years since he had tamed them with his flat-fronted form, and now he felt that the time was ready to discard the *cage* in any shape. It was a dangerous step, for crinolines had been in fashion for thirteen years, and fullness had been normal in skirts since the late 1820s. To the eyes of 1868, conditioned all their lives to full skirts, a return to natural shape and slimness could only seem like indecent exposure – a revelation of fundamental feminine shape which had been concealed for generations. It took a very brave woman to be the first to wear a skirt without a crinoline, but Pauline von Metternich would dare what other women would not. Indeed, without her bravado, Worth would have found it difficult to introduce some of his fashions.

He created a skirt of heavy satin which fell straight down to the ground without any form of under structure whatsoever. With it went a Spanish type bolero with very long sleeves – a salute to the empress's Spanish ancestry. The ensemble had a classic simplicty, without pleats

41. T. van Elven – Empress Eugénie in a Worth tunic dress, accompanied by Czar Alexander II, followed by Napoleon III and the King of Prussia, during a reception at the Palais des Tuileries in 1867.

or trimmings, and thus achieved great purity of line. It was subsequently hailed as the pinnacle and zenith of design. Nevertheless it created a problem: if one removed the crinoline the dress above it was now too long. For a while it became fashionable to wear dresses which trailed on the floor and ended in very long trains, but this could only result in 'that perpetual rending of garments' which Whitehurst so often saw in ballrooms. Indeed after any ball of the Second Empire there would be some wisps of finery left on the floor. Obviously, something had to be done; so Worth looked to history for inspiration.

42. The sensation of 1868 – Princess von Metternich in Worth's flat-fronted dress with no form of crinoline whatsoever.

As a great admirer of late Baroque styles, he knew that large quantities of material had been caught up at the back of a gown and supported over a small frame, then called a *cul de crin*, or horsehair bottom, and he decided to do the same with the surplus stuff of 1869. For one of the empress's ladies he created a dress that was so like a gown of 1696 that he must have copied the original engraving. The

93

Comtesse de Pourtalès wore a skirt looped back and edged with lace, and a petticoat of tiers of frills, much the same as that worn by the Queen of Denmark 173 years before. The principal difference was that Worth raised the waistline, calling it the Josephine in an obvious echo of the First Napoleonic Empire, whereas the Baroque waist had been lower. His general effect was rounded, whereas the late seventeenth-century emphasis was upon stateliness and height. A fashionable revival is always a reinterpretation and never an exact copy.

43. The bustle in 1696. A. Trouvain – Charlotte Landgravine of Hesse Cassel, Queen of Denmark.

Ideas for fashions came from everywhere: it was seeing acrobats in sleeveless jackets which inspired Worth to create his own jacket; it was Empress Eugénie's interest in the Scottish side of her family, together with Queen Victoria's fondness for Balmoral, which led to Worth using tartan sashes and trimmings on dresses; it was the French conquest of Algeria which led to Worth using the burnous as a wrap. In addition, ideas could come up from below which the couturier then had to accommodate and improve: the success of Garibaldi's landing in Italy led to red shirts and pill-box hats becoming all the rage. As a result the shirt and skirt combination entered the female wardrobe on a permanent basis, instead of the invariable gown. In 1869 Worth designed a blue walking suit which had a white linen shirt cut exactly like a man's.

44. The bustle as revived by Worth in 1869, and worn by the Comtesse de Pourtalès.

Although Worth was the dominant figure in French fashion, he still did not publish his designs in the fashion magazines because of the enormous amount of piracy and unlicensed copying which went on. Once a design was illustrated it could be copied from St Petersburg to Chicago, without the designer getting a penny. When *Harper's Bazar* [*sic*] was first published in New York in 1867, it had an arrangement with European magazines, particularly the German, *Der Bazar*, to receive fashion plates at the same time as the European magazines were publishing them themselves; so American pirates could reproduce French models as soon as anybody else.

The blue walking suit mentioned above was one design stolen from Maison Worth in 1869, when a series of designs was published in

London as *La Mode Artistique* by Gustave Jannes, some of which are identical to original drawings in the Worth sketchbooks. *Harper's Bazar* then reproduced some of these designs in May 1869, without attributing them to Worth or to Jannes. Furthermore, the designer's very name could be stolen. In 1882 there was a *corsetière* in Hanover Street, London, calling itself Worth et Cie. It published designs for corsets and layettes, and only in the tiniest print does it admit that the Madame Worth running the business had no connection with Worth et Cie of Paris. There was very little Worth could do about this, short of employing a huge army of spies across Europe and the United States to keep track of unlicensed copying. Far better to keep out of the fashion magazines altogether, for he did not need to advertise; the society press and the aristocracy did that for him.

Nevertheless, Worth himself did take some fashion magazines just to see what the lesser fry were up to. Gagelin had retained the dressmaking department he started, so it was amusing to keep an eye on its activities. His success had caused other Englishmen to try to set up in Paris as couturiers; Poole and Smallpage were both active in Paris in 1869, having started with premises in London, but neither could topple Worth from his throne. The magazines Worth took to watch such competition were *Le Follet*, 1846–73; *Le Journal des Demoiselles*, 1845–73; *La Mode Illustrée*, 1864–86; *Les Modes de la Saison*, 1873–8; and *The Monthly Belle Assemblée*, 1841–70. There was, however, one line of defence he could take: if he sold a dress or a pattern to a dressmaker only to find that design being published later, he could blacklist that dressmaker thereafter; so fashion magazines could be quite helpful here.

There were a few who sighed at Worth's establishment in the fashion world. Why did all the world have to rush to his door?

> I presume it is absolutely necessary to come here to learn how the French dress or do not dress themselves, in order that London may be covered up or exposed *à la mode de Paris*; but when I see my respected friends the Boodles of Bangor clothing themselves at Worth's . . . I can only sigh for poor B.'s banker's book, and feel that the ladies would have been as well dressed, and half as cheaply at home. . . .'[21]

wrote Whitehurst to his British readers, but this did not stop them coming. It was a status symbol to shop at Worth's. As Gyp noticed when she first arrived in Paris in the late 1860s, '*On ne parlait encore que de Worth.*'

Notes

1. A. Adburgham, *A Punch History of Manners and Modes* (1961), Hutchinson, p. 55.
2. H. Mayhew, *Shops and Companies of London* (1865), vol. I, p. 59.
3. Adburgham, loc. cit.
4. Comte Fleury, *Memoirs of the Empress Eugénie* (1920), vol. I, pp. 383–4.
5. Bertall, *L'Illustration*, July–December 1864, vol. XXXXIV, p. 339.
6. Mayhew, loc. cit.
7. Dr A. Barthez, *The Empress Eugénie and her Circle* (1912).
8. For a consideration of Bloomerism *see* Stella Mary Newton, *Health, Art, and Reason* (1974), John Murray, ch. 1, and Diana de Marly, *The History of Haute Couture 1850–1950* (1980), Batsford, ch. 4.
9. J.-P. Worth, *A Century of Fashion* (1928), p. 50.
10. Post Office Directory, London (1870).
11. *Complete Official Catalogue* (1867), Paris Universal Exhibition, p. 399.
12. Mme Carette, *My Mistress, the Empress Eugénie; or Court Life at the Tuileries* (1889), pp. 173–5.
13. Dupin, *Le Luxe effréné des Femmes* (1865).
14. F. Whitehurst, *Court and Social Life in France under Napoleon III* (1873), vol. I, p. 128.
15. C. Dickens, *All The Year Round*, June–December 1867, vol. XVIII, p. 564.
16. Gyp, *Souvenirs d'une petite fille* (1928), vol. II, p. 265.
17. Gyp, op. cit., pp. 269–72.
18. Betty Askwith, *A Victorian Young Lady* (1978), Michael Russell, p. 146, wonders if a lady would relieve herself upon the lawns at Hurlingham, while conversing with a gentleman, the long skirt and open pantaloons both concealing and making the operation possible. Possible but not to be confessed.
19. Dickens, loc. cit.
20. Whitehurst, op. cit., vol. II, p. 85.
21. ibid., vol. I, p. 122.

Chapter 8

Maison Worth and
Worth's Attitude to Dress

Every day between ten and twelve in the morning, and three and five in the afternoon, the carriages of the great and wealthy loitered up and down the rue de la Paix, while their owners were closeted inside No. 7 with Worth. No lady was too proud to condescend to visit Maison Worth et Bobergh. When one princess had the audacity to command his attendance at her town residence, she received the reply that Worth was too busy with the princesses who had come to him. The imperial couturier did not rush all round Paris to measure

45. The imperial couturier at forty; not a man to be trifled with. At this date the shoulders of men's jackets were not padded, and the sleeves were made curved not straight.

clients; they all had to drive to his salon, with the exception of the empress herself and her ladies. Even Russian Grand Duchesses went to Worth, not he to them. Their increasing respect for Worth's taste and judgement, and his approach to dress, were helping to build him a towering reputation. The sight of royalty paying court to a dressmaker made some people furious. What was society coming to when a maker of fashions could order the aristocracy to obey his whim? Hippolyte Taine published a libellous description of Worth in his chapter on the world today in *Notes sur Paris* of 1867. Ostensibly writing about an old photographer whose wife ran a dress shop, he complained:

> . . . it is necessary to have an introduction in order to be served by him. Mme Francisque B . . . , a person of true society and elegance, came last month to order a dress. 'Madame, by whom are you presented to me?' 'What do you mean?' – 'That it is necessary to be presented to me in order to be dressed by me.' She went away, suffocated with rage.[1]

This was untrue, as Dickens says, 'The man-milliner professes to know no distinction nor degree. He is open to all, like the law.' No one was refused admission to Worth, provided they could afford to dress there, but the difference was that he had an appointments system. So many women wished to avail themselves of Monsieur Worth's good taste, that a system like this was the only way to cope with the demand; but this was unheard of in the world of dressmaking, and made critics like Taine feel that Worth was giving himself airs and behaving as if he were a member of the professional classes! To begin with, Worth did put the emphasis on being a gentleman dressmaker, and not a tradesman. Dickens described him as a perfect gentleman, always freshly shaved and with his hair perfectly dressed, attired as a gentleman should be:

> Black coat, white cravat, and batiste shirt-cuffs fastened at the wrists with gold buttons, he officiates with all the gravity of a diplomatist who holds the fate of the world locked up in the drawers of his brain.[2]

In his own time he was described as a sort of Minister of the Robes without portfolio, and his establishment certainly radiated this atmosphere. While every fashionable dressmaker would have had a number of duchesses calling at her premises, the sight of almost every leading lady in society going to Worth gave his House a prestige and eminence which dressmakers could not rival. He was acquiring a positive monopoly of important custom, which gave the firm an air of grandeur that was reinforced by the very imposing way in which that House conducted itself. It was not a dress shop but a palace of costume.

When Joseph Primoli, Princess Mathilde's nephew, went to Worth's with his mother in 1868 he said that it was like an embassy, where 'all the young men look like embassy attachés with their English accents, curled hair, pearl tie-pins and turquoise rings' while the apartment 'exhales some atmosphere of degraded aristocracy, some heady fragrance of elegance, wealth, and forbidden fruit'.[3] Perhaps Primoli was rather overcome by the sight of beautiful models parading up and down, and remembered the claim that Maison Worth was a de luxe brothel. He was certainly amazed at the range of customers who could be found there, from the elegant *grandes dames* of the faubourg Saint-Germain, to the wives of officials, and even the mistresses and courtesans patronized by the aristocracy. No woman's reputation banned her from this couture house; the only requirement for would-be clients was an ability to pay the bills.

And what bills they were! As Princess von Metternich had lamented, once Worth had obtained imperial custom, dresses at 300 francs no longer saw the light of day. Worth became '*cher, horriblement cher, monstrueusement cher*', she cried, but acknowledged that he recognized the fact more than anyone else in his position would have done.[4] In 1857 the most expensive dresses Professor William Senior had encountered in Paris were at a British embassy ball, where the ambassadress, Lady Cowley, informed him that the average cost of the gowns was between 1,000 and 1,200 francs, which took his breath away (£40 to £48 each). A professor's wife might have a dress allowance of 10,000 francs a year, which did not allow for ballgowns at over £40.[5] The simplest day costume at Worth's cost 1,600 francs – over £60, more than the most luxurious ballgown elsewhere. An evening gown at £100 was the sort of price one had to pay *chez* Worth, which made people reel with shock.

He himself admitted in 1871 that respectable women in Paris could dress on £60 a year, but stressed that his clients were a different class altogether. He provided the best clothes for the best people, and his prices were rated accordingly. In 1869 a man was considered wealthy if he had £5,000 a year, and the professional man might earn £500 a year.[6] Worth said that his customers spent between £400 and £4,000 a year on his creations, and that the most expensive gown he had ever made was of lace at 120,000 francs and a fur cloak at 45,000 francs (*c.* £5,000 and £2,000). In other words it did not suffice to be merely wealthy to go to Worth, a client had to be in the millionaire or rich aristocratic class.

There were probably two reasons why Worth charged such unheard of prices. Firstly there was no guarantee that Empress

Eugénie's patronage would last for ever, for she had changed her dressmakers quickly enough in the past. Having seen his own father lose all his money, Worth would want to make as much as he could while his good fortune lasted to ensure himself against bankruptcy. Secondly he was designing and making the most superb clothes in the world. Perfection was his object, and no garment was ever allowed to emerge from his House which was not as excellent as human ability could make it. Not only did he use the most expensive materials and trimmings, but the workmanship was impeccable also. Ladies went into ecstasies when they saw the finished product, for its like could not be found elsewhere. He was selling an exclusive article, so he could charge as much as he liked for it. Significantly, when Worth adopted a coat-of-arms he took as his motto the phrase *'obtenir et tenir'* – to obtain and retain, in other words, to do the very opposite to his father.

He succeeded in doing so, and made a clear profit of over £40,000 a year. This set him on the same financial level as his royal and imperial customers, so he could afford to live like a prince. By 1868 he had built himself a luxurious country house to the west of the Bois de Boulogne, overlooking the Seine at Suresnes. It was reputed to be so splendid that the nobility vied for invitations to it, in much the same way that they craved invitations to the imperial châteaux at Compiègne and Fontainebleau. Here was wealth on a scale that other dressmakers had not dreamed of.

The size of Maison Worth was also astonishing. The average Parisian dressmaker employed up to forty seamstresses; Worth began with 20 in 1858, but had 1,200 by 1870, and still employed that number at the time of his death. After all, he was turning out hundreds of new gowns every week, so he had to operate on an unprecedented scale. As Bobergh is never mentioned as a designer, it is likely that he managed this enormous enterprise, leaving Worth free to concentrate on creation. It was normal practice for seamstresses to live on the premises, but this was clearly impossible at Worth. Some girls did sleep there, for staff were kept on call at all hours, ready to make a gown at a moment's notice should any client have a clothing crisis; but the building in the rue de la Paix could not accommodate them all. Obviously Maison Worth had other workrooms and dormitories scattered round the area. The comfort of staff was one of the last things which employers bothered about in the 1860s, and accommodation was rarely purpose built. When Worth's former employers Lewis & Allenby erected a new building at 61–65 Conduit Street, London, in 1866, it was one of the first shops to have proper dormitories for the staff, instead of expecting them to sleep under the attics or beneath the counter. Worth did add extra floors to

No. 7 for workrooms, but he was never in the forefront of reform for staff. Seamstresses as a whole were very badly paid, and Maison Worth simply followed the existing pattern. Seamstresses were apprenticed at thirteen or fourteen, and they worked the usual twelve-hour day immediately. Once qualified they became a second hand, assisting the first-hand seamstress. Men in dressmaking could expect five francs a day, women a mere two francs, twenty-five centimes. The wage of English seamstresses at this time was 1s. 6d. or 2s. (7½p or 10p) a day, plus their keep. The art historian, Mary Merrifield, was one contemporary who did consider these wages scandalous. The work done by men house painters or carpenters was no more arduous or difficult than that done by seamstresses, yet they received 4s. 6d. a day (22½p), so she demanded:

> What reason can be assigned why a woman's work, if equally well done, should not be as well paid as that of a man? A satisfactory reason has yet to be given; the fact, however, is indisputable that women are not in general so well paid for their labour as men.[7]

Worth and Bobergh, however, were far too busy building up their business to stop and think about justice.

In addition to hundreds of seamstresses, Worth depended on another component that was equally essential in dressmaking: the sewing machine. These inventions were not new, but had seen some thirty years of experiment and improvement. Thanks to the unscrupulous Isaac Singer, considerable advances had been made,[8] and by 1867 the French government could note 'the growing use of the sewing machine' in the dressmaking business. Worth could not have operated on such a huge scale without it, with all the courts of Europe demanding his gowns. He had to mass-produce, and he used the techniques of the industrial age, evolving a series of standardized patterns with interchangeable parts. Thus it was possible for a gown to consist of standard bodice type A, with sleeves pattern B, and skirt pattern C. These would then be put together on the sewing machine, which made the long seams and the trimmings. The finishing, the embroidery, the perfect cut, were done by hand.

A large and efficient filing system was also necessary at Maison Worth. As the House had customers all round the civilized world, some of whom never came to Paris, it was imperative to build up a highly detailed catalogue of the individual lady's size, height, colouring, peculiarities and preferences, to which adjustments could be added as the years advanced. From these details dummies could be constructed, if the lady was a regular customer, and dresses be fitted upon it, as if upon the wearer herself. Furthermore a careful check had to be kept of where individual designs went.

If a Russian princess ordered a gown in blue for a state ball in St Petersburg, it was imperative to ensure that any other Russian princess who bought that design, and who might go to the same ball, did not get the dress in the same blue. When a model gown was sold to a member of a royal family, that model was then withdrawn so that it could not be copied. Worth's reputation depended on not making any slips in this area. A lady who bought an exclusive design had to be certain that it was exclusive. Models for reproduction were also sold to foreign dressmakers, as Dickens observed: 'Milliners from every decent capital come to wait on Worth. They go away bearing a dress or a pattern, for which they pay fabulous prices.' Keeping the price high was another way of limiting the amount of reproduction which would take place, for the foreign dressmaker would have to charge a high price to recover her expenses, which helped to maintain the exclusive connotation, even in a copy.

During the first seven years of Maison Worth et Bobergh's existence, Marie Worth was of considerable importance as the chief mannequin and *vendeuse* rolled into one. She could either model a gown herself, or sell a dress worn by one of the mannequins whom she had trained. A great deal more style was required to model a gown at Worth's than had been necessary in a mercer's shop. However, while Marie Worth is often singled out as the world's first professional model, she was really nothing of the sort. Any leading dressmaker had a few model girls on call, but at Maison Worth, as with everything else he did, the numbers were greater. During the season he was continually besieged by customers, so a large number of mannequins was a necessity in order to satisfy the hungry crowds of clients. What made Marie Worth unusual was that her husband sent her out of the salon to model his creations among high society. The ordinary model girl was not allowed to wear her employer's gowns outside the premises, but Marie Worth wore them at the races, at the opera, and at imperial balls. Hitherto, once a dress had been sold, how well it appeared in society depended entirely upon the customer's ability, or lack of it, to wear a dress with style. Marie Worth had been trained to move with grace and elegance, to turn in such a way that it showed a gown to best advantage, and to pause for effect. Accordingly, when she wore a gown among the rich and the titled, she could do so better than they could. Moreover, she had to conduct herself like a great lady, with Princess von Metternich taking her to the same receptions as herself, and Empress Eugénie inviting her to the palace dances. It was the range of Marie Worth's work which was so different.

She was so important as a fashion setter in those early days, that a change in her attire could produce a change overnight in the whole court. One evening when every lady going to the Tuileries ball had the same low set headdress, Worth for the sake of variety sent Marie with a tall aigrette. At the next ball aigrettes were *de rigueur*. Marie gave up modelling in 1865 after an attack of bronchitis. Worth sent her to the South of France to recuperate, and would not allow her to work thereafter. Nevertheless whenever she went out she was still a travelling exhibition of her husband's style, and she never lost her reputation as one of the most elegant women in Paris. Couturiers since have used their wives to promote their creations in the world outside the salon, repeating, as they do in so many ways, the pattern established by Worth.

As will have been observed at the start of this chapter, the House employed a number of young men – unlike later couture houses where all the staff on view, the *vendeuses*, the fitters, the models, were all women. They were there to sell fabrics, for Maison Worth never forgot that it had begun in a textile shop. The leading salesman was a Swede, Carlsson, probably recruited by Bobergh, whom Princess von Metternich considered a very good type. Most of the display was devoted to fabrics, with very few dresses on view. Black and white silks occupied the first salon, coloured silks the second, velvets the third, brocades and similar heavy materials the fourth, together with a few examples of the latest gowns arranged against mirrors. The fifth salon was the Salon de Lumière lit entirely by gas, with all daylight

46. Lyon silk with feather pattern used by Worth for Empress Eugénie.

excluded, so that customers could try on ballgowns in the same lighting conditions that they would find at receptions – a very sensitive consideration.

The fabrics Worth favoured most were tulle, silk, satin and brocade, instead of the moirés, grosgrains and velvets that had been in vogue. It was textiles which dominated his whole approach to design, for with no drawing talent or training to rely on, he had to start with what he knew best. To record ideas, he had a series of lithographed heads and busts stuck in drawing books to save him the trouble of trying to sketch them, and designs for dresses would be painted on underneath. More than one hand was responsible for the designs in the Worth albums, so some assistant designers may have been engaged as well. Indeed, given the size of his business, additional help in this area was essential and so Worth probably ran his design studio in much the same way as a fashionable portraitist ran his: with assistants contributing ideas and undertaking parts of the design, but with the artist controlling the style of the final product. Unfortunately no staff records survive to say who these assistant designers might have been.

The modelling of a silk or satin upon a client or model, was Worth's particular prerogative, and of course it was this idea of a man fitting a woman which had caused all the scandal. How he approached this problem was described by Dickens in his first report on Worth in 1863:

> When he tries a dress on one of the living dolls of the Chaussé d'Antin, it is with profound attention that he touches, pricks, and sounds it, marking with chalk the difficult fold. From time to time he draws back in order to judge better of his work from a distance: he looks through his hand, closed into the shape of an eyeglass, and resumes with inspired fingers, the modelling of the drapery on the person of the patient.[9]

Worth would apply the trimmings, the flowers or bows, then retire to a sofa and ask the lady to parade round the room:

> 'To the right, madame.' The client performs a quarter of a revolution.
> 'To the left.' The patient turns in the opposite direction.
> 'In front.' Madame faces the artist.
> 'Behind.' She turns her back.
> When all is over, he dismisses her with a lordly gesture: 'That will do, madame.'

It was Worth's dictatorial attitude which infuriated critics. Not only did he tell women to parade up and down before him, as if he were a

47. Black satin with design of tulips in pinks, yellows and greens, made for Worth at Lyon by Gourd, Payen et Cie in 1889. The design repeat is over one metre.

sultan in a harem, but he would not even allow them to express their own ideas. No lady could tell Worth what she thought she ought to have; she went to receive his opinion, as to an oracle or sage. This sight of a dressmaker behaving in such a lordly manner made Taine absolutely furious:

> This dry little being, dark, nervous, who looks like a dwarf scorched by the fire, receives them wearing a velvet jacket, proudly reclining on a divan, a cigar between his lips. He says to them 'Walk, turn; good; come back in eight days and I shall compose a toilette that will suit you.' It is not they who choose, it is he; and they are only too happy to let him.[10]

48. Worth supervising a fitting in 1880, and laying down the law.

No wonder Taine does not mention Worth by name; this could have landed him in court. Worth was not a swarthy dwarf, for the family has always been quite tall.

Worth reinforced his control over what clients wore by leaving the final touches until the last minute. Thus before balls at the Palais des Tuileries or the Hôtel de Ville ladies would drive to Maison Worth at 10 p.m., where they were ushered into a waiting-room, and served with Malmsey Madeira and pâté de foie. Each lady was given a ticket with a number on it, and had to await her turn. Taine considered such goings-on truly astonishing and unprecedented, but the proudest women in the land submitted to Worth's system. Princess von Meternich thought Worth's last word essential:

> Worth composed dazzling dresses and used to make certain adjustments at the last minute, changing this, changing that, in short the last look from the master and creator was indispensable.[11]

It was because women regarded Worth as '*le maître et le créateur*' that they willingly yielded to his authority. No one could match him where the judgement of taste and style was concerned. Was he not an expert in abolishing clutter, in making crinolines more practical, in creating clothes which fitted like a second skin? Did not the empress listen to what he said? Of course one should heed Monsieur Worth. So ladies waited their turn, no matter who they were, and modestly received the great man's directives. 'He looks, he inspects, gives a finishing touch, arranges a flower, and madame has realized the epitome of elegance.'[12] The woman who emerged was confident in her heart that in no way could her appearance be better than it was now. Worth himself explained his policy in an interview given later in his life, and it was all part of his philosophy of absolute excellence.

> Those ladies are wisest who leave the choice to us. By so doing they are always better pleased in the end, and the reputation of the house is sustained. Curiously enough, the persons who realize this fact most clearly are precisely those whom you might fancy the most difficult to please. For example, a telegram comes from the Empress of Russia, 'Send me a dinner dress!' Nothing more. We are left absolute freedom as to style and material. Not that the Empress is indifferent in the matter of dress. Quite the contrary. She will sometimes require that all the ladies' costumes at a certain ball be pink, or red, or blue. And her own dresses are always masterpieces of elegance. The point is that she trusts our judgement rather than her own. In the same way recently we have received over twenty telegrams from Madrid for ball dresses, and we shall make them up as we think fit.[13]

A man to whom empresses bowed was entitled to feel rather special. The term 'genius' was used of Worth with increasing frequency, but he did not let it go to his head. Whitehurst remarked that this genius was very modest and thought 'the very weakest tea' of himself. Nevertheless anyone who was anybody ought to know about Worth, as Frances Hodgson Burnett made clear in her novel *Louisiana*. Miss Ferrol from sophisticated New York encounters an innocent creature called Louisiana in the country, and thinks that she has certain possibilities as a fashionable *ingénue*, but determines first to check the girl's education:

'Do you know who John Stuart Mill is?' she said.

'No,' she replied from the dust of humiliation.

'Have you never heard – just *heard* of Ruskin?'

'No.'

'Nor of Michael Angelo?'

'N-no – ye-es, I think so, but I don't know what he did.'

'Do you,' she continued very slowly, 'do-you-know-anything-about-Worth?'

'No nothing.'

Her questioner clasped her hands with repressed emotion.

'Oh,' she cried, 'how – how you have been neglected.'[14]

Appalled at her own ignorance Louisiana asks if Worth might be a poet, and thought her hostess was more astonished at her stupidity concerning this artist than all the others. Great was her surprise to be told that Worth both made dresses and was a man dressmaker at that.

'Does' – guilelessly she inquired – 'he make nice ones?'

'Nice!' echoed Miss Ferrol. 'They are works of art. I have got three in my trunk.'

'O-o-h!' sighed Louisiana. 'Oh, dear!'

A cream-coloured silk evening dress was produced, with a golden fringe and golden flowers embroidered upon it. When Miss Ferrol suggested that Louisiana try it on, the girl was horrified. It was too beautiful for her to dare, but on it went, and it fitted well:

There was not the shadow of a wrinkle from shoulder to hem: the lovely young figure was revealed in all its beauty of outline. There were no sleeves at all, there was not very much bodice, but there was a great deal of effect. . . .

The man responsible for such creations did not make dresses; he composed toilettes. Worth used this term very much in the 1860s and it became accepted language to describe his superior approach to dress design. After all, the imperial couturier should show a certain flair:

When this truly great man is composing, he reclines on a sofa, and one of the young ladies of the establishment plays 'Verdi' to him; he composes chiefly in the evenings, and says that the rays of the setting sun gild his conceptions.[15]

The adoption of a pose to impress the newspapers might seem rather ridiculous, but it was good publicity and Worth really did believe that he was above all other dress designers. Certainly, success and the good opinion of high society told him that he was. What is

"Walk across the floor," commanded Miss Ferrol.   P. 16.

49. G. C. Hellawell – Overcome by her first Worth dress. An incident in
Frances Hodgson Burnett's novel *Louisiana*, 1880.

more, the man whose gowns were called works of art need not think
of himself as a dressmaker, but as an artist. He was applying the
standards and principles of fine art to dress design, and elevating the
subject to a higher plane. It was not simply a craft; it was part of
aesthetics. This was recognized by a lady-in-waiting, Carette: 'We owe
to the artistic taste of this great milliner, and to his intuition for
aesthetic elegance, the revival of grace in dress.'[16]

Worth began to stop dressing like a gentleman, and transformed
himself into an artist proper, modelled after Rembrandt, with a velvet
beret which he wore all the time, a flowing coat edged with fur at the
neck, and with a floppy silk scarf knotted at his throat instead of a
cravat. This was accepted artistic dress of the period; Wagner wore a
velvet beret, and Tennyson favoured flowing cloaks, while the floppy
bow was an immediate signal that the wearer was above the
pretension of being a gentleman.

Worth's importance in bringing art into dress design was fully
recognized by *L'Illustration*, which stated that the bourgeoises of the
time of Louis-Philippe and the early days of Napoleon III had only
the vaguest idea about great artists from Titian and Velasquez down
to Watteau and Mme Vigée Le Brun, and still less idea of the costume
of the Renaissance and eighteenth century. It was Worth who went to

50. Méaulle after Nadar – Worth the artist in 1892.

all the museums, studied the paintings, leafed through albums of drawings, and hunted through collections. From all this he arrived at an aesthetic whereby *'la modernité s'inspirait de l'Histoire'*.[17] The history of art and the history of costume were the twin foundations upon which modern dress design should rise, and from which it should draw its strength. Worth had taught himself much, gathered the artists and the styles to his fingertips, and could now lay down the law on all that concerned taste in dress. Moreover, painters themselves recognized his importance in this field, and came to draw on his knowledge when portraits were to be painted. Together with Mme Virot, Empress Eugénie's hatmaker, he would be invited to a studio.

> It may not be known to all that Worth and Madame Virot often collaborated with great artists, and in the beautiful portraits and busts of the period one recognizes their taste intermingled with the inspiration of the masters'[18] –

wrote Carette, who herself would have been on duty at sittings. This can be seen very clearly in the *œuvre* of Winterhalter. Worth used clouds of tulle by the scores of metres. Whereas Winterhalter did not envelop his portraits of Queen Victoria with this material in the 1840s, during his time in Paris in the 1850s and 60s the amount of tulle in his pictures was considerable, and played an important part in creating the misty romance so typical of his work at that period. Moreover, many of Winterhalter's sitters around this date were Worth customers, so naturally they would choose to be painted in the most expensive and glamorous gowns they possessed. For Princess von Metternich to be so depicted, was a way of commemorating her role in Worth's establishment as the commanding figure in the world of fashion, as well as just being a portrait of the princess herself. The painting was done in 1861, so it was very close to the actual day in 1860 when the princess wore her first Worth (fig. 16). A tulle ballgown, softened at the neckline and sleeves with gathered tulle, and with a veil of tulle billowing from her hair, reveal the princess in Worth's best. She does not say in her memoirs whether this was the actual gown (fig. 51) which she wore to that important meeting with the Empress Eugénie, but the possiblity certainly exists, for it has the matchless simplicity which was so admired on that occasion.

When Winterhalter came to paint the lovely Duchesse de Morny he used the same formula – that of a gown amidst wisps of tulle (fig. 26), and the portrait can be compared with a photograph of the duchess in one of Worth's day dresses (fig. 36) to show that the elegant simplicity was real, and not an illusion, existing only in the artist's imagination. Of course when la Rimsky-Korsakov came to be painted by Winterhalter she did not want the restrained formality of a ballgown and pearls. For her, the daring undress of a *robe de chambre* almost falling off her shoulders was the image she wished to present at a time when no lady would have dared to be so informal in a public portrait. With la Rimsky-Korsakov such considerations did not apply, for she thought herself above conventional morality. She was proud of the length of her hair and the slope of her shoulders, so let the world admire. There was no end to the woman's fondness for immoderate display, as Whitehurst never failed to mention; thus at a ball at the Hôtel de Ville in January 1867, 'The great event of the evening was the dress of Madame Rimsky-Korsakov, the train of which took up standing room for about ten men.'[19] Marie Worth had a *robe de chambre* of foaming lace bedecked with bows, but she never dreamed of being painted *en déshabillé*.

Spangled tulle was another of Worth's characteristics in the 1860s. He had used it spangled with silver for Princess von Metternich, and he subsequently used it spangled with gold for Empress Elizabeth of Austria in the famous Winterhalter portrait, which presides over the conference room in the Imperial Palace in Vienna. Either form of tulle allowed Worth to create dresses which were very simple – the essence of his style – but which were given a sparkling air of richness by the gold and silver thread. Thanks to his co-operation with Winterhalter, the beauty of such gowns can still be seen today, whereas the original tulle was not robust enough to survive the century. The impact of these plain but very bright gowns among the over-decorated and fussy products of other dressmakers can be imagined. They took the breath away by their very understatement, yet by some rare magic were also alight with stars. To emphasize the point, Empress Elizabeth put stars in her hair. The spangled tulle was a new development in textiles and Worth exploited its possibilities to the full.

One more of Worth's variations on the use of tulle can be seen in another Winterhalter portrait, now in Leningrad, where the filmy material is controlled by bands of ribbon spreading out from the waist (fig. 51). This technique can also be seen on one of the original Worth designs which has the same arrangement on the skirt, where puffs of tulle are caught up by the ribbon (fig. 52). Shirred tulle, pleated tulle, draped tulle, puffed tulle, and layers of silk tulle upon silk tulle, were all employed as Worth conjured up these *nuages fragiles*. And what a gift to the portrait painter such gowns were. No need to labour for days on end painstakingly recording every leaf in a patterned brocade, or the minutiae of embroidery, but let the brush swoop across the canvas in great sweeps of translucent cloud, for they allowed for a much freer style.

Many artists, such as van Elven, Baron, Carpaux and Gérôme,

113

depicted court events where Worth gowns were prominent, but none of these are as important as the portrait for revealing the detail of Worth's collaboration. Looking at his later career, the portraitists, Carolus-Duran, that influential teacher of future artists; Dagnan-Boureret, and John Singer Sargent together with Giovanni Boldini all portrayed the society ladies who queued up to be dressed by Worth. To take one example, Sargent's portrait of Worth's American customer, Mrs Henry White (now in the Corcoran Gallery, Washington), shows all the historical features which Worth was putting into

51. Winterhalter – T. A. Iocynosou, 1858.

contemporary fashion. The dress has a fichu and elbow frills, and a skirt looped back over a petticoat, showing a strong debt to the 1780s, and making a diplomatic salute to what Americans called the Martha Washington Look, not that there was anything specifically American about that form of costume. Sargent in particular was an artist who liked women sitters to wear evening dress or some other form of ornate attire in order to produce the sumptuous effect so characteristic of his bravura style. Consequently Worth gowns suited him completely.

Worth's co-operation with art can be seen most clearly in his adoption of aesthetic dress. This was a form of clothing which began in England, and which grew out of the rejection of contemporary fashion by artists of the Pre-Raphaelite Brotherhood, who were interested in evolving a form of dress which did not change every season. Rossetti experimented with looser gowns without corsets, in order to study the effects of folds over the limbs. This could not be studied in fashionable dress in the 1850s when *cage*-crinolines

52. Worth evening dress design with the same skirt as fig. 51.

concealed the body and had no gentle falls of fabric in fold and pleats. The Brotherhood undertook such research for their own purposes to use the results in their paintings which specialized mainly in medieval subjects where clinging garments had been worn. They were not dress reformers with a campaign to remedy contemporary fashion; rather they ignored it, but over the years women who admired Pre-Raphaelite painting came to adopt Pre-Raphaelite principles in their clothing. Increasingly from the late 1850s, women with artistic tastes were wearing aesthetic dress instead of the products of Parisian high fashion, and by the 1870s the style was all the rage among the more sophisticated and cultivated members of the middle class. The main principle was that the costume should fit loosely and never impede the body in the way that many fashions did. Mary Merrifield in 1855 had objected to the fact that many Parisian dress designs disregarded the fundamental nature of the female shape, and imposed all sorts of impossible forms on the body, which damaged the woman who was so unwise as to follow fashion blindly.[20] There was concern in medical circles about the distortion of the body, which was caused by tight lacing, and aesthetic dress was one method of avoiding such extremes.

To Worth the vogue for aesthetic dress was a godsend, for it allowed full expression of his artistic principles. While the style began in England, spreading from Oxford to London, its theories found favour in sophisticated society in the United States, France, Germany and Scandinavia, and once Worth gave the innovation his blessing, this was a directive that it was safe for other women to wear it, even if they did not claim to be in the forefront of artistic appreciation. Worth used many historical styles in his aesthetic gowns, from the Renaissance to the Neo-Classical and First Empire. Sleeves were inspired by examples in the works of Moroni, Rubens, Van Dyck, and Gainsborough, as were collars, cuffs, and hats. He even designed some with empire waistlines in the low-waisted 1880s and 90s for those ladies who dared to be entirely independent of fashion. Dagnan-Boureret and de Beers were two of the society painters who came to consult Worth over the suitability of aesthetic dress for portraiture, for it was felt that such costume would prevent the picture from dating as quickly as one with fashionable clothes, although this overlooked the point of view that the artist himself might go out of date just as swiftly. Nevertheless aesthetic dress was about as close to timelessness as a costume could get. Worth also applied these concepts to tea gowns, those loose gowns for informal at-homes, which could either be worn over the underwear like a négligée or on top of a dress. One of his tea gowns of 1891 was considered a masterly creation in beige-coloured cloth with wide revers of white plush, falling in Watteau pleats at the back, over a dress of stamped velvet in tones of maroon, in a sweetness and elegance that defy the date.

Worth's collaboration with artists and his own artistic attitudes were outrageous as far as Taine was concerned, and he satirized the couturier bitterly, putting the following arrogant declaration into his mouth:

'I am a great artist. I have Delacroix's sense of colour and I *compose*.

A toilette is worth as much as a painting.' If one is irritated at his unreasonable attitude, he says:

'Monsieur, in every artist there is a bit of Napoleon. When M. Ingres was painting the duchess of A . . . he wrote to her one morning: "Madame, I need you this evening at the theatre, in a white dress, with a rose in the middle of your coiffure." The

53. An artistic creation: a Worth tea gown in 1891.

duchess cancelled her invitations, put on the dress, sent out for the coiffure, and went to the theatre. Art is God, and the bourgeoisie was made to take our orders!'[21]

To Taine, fashion was a frivolity, a froth of nonsensical fancy, and so were the people in it, so he savaged the idea of a dressmaker being a serious artist, declaring that such a claim was nothing but vanity, an absurdity too preposterous to merit consideration. This suggests that Taine never put his head inside a studio or a workroom, for fashion is

54. Without this, Worth's dominion could not have reached overseas so speedily – the steamship *Europe* in 1871.

55. Without this, overland orders could not have been dispatched at a few hours' notice – the 4–4–0 locomotive 1814, in 1888.

not a form of activity where serious application can be dispensed with. On the contrary, to produce endless new ideas does require ability, to turn those ideas into wearable gowns takes talent, and to be able to spot the potentiality of a variation on a mode from which a new style could emerge needs both insight and imagination. How much more so when both art and costume history were to be applied to design, necessitating a wide knowledge of both disciplines? Taine might scoff but sophisticated society conceded that Worth was '*nôtre maître*', and anyone of taste should be able to speak of him as much as of Ruskin or Michelangelo. He had stated that dress was art and his pronouncements were to be taken seriously, for no one could deny that his dresses really were works of art. In fact, they could actually cost as much as a painting. Accordingly one both cherished the gown and the artist who had created it. Worth was positively revered.

Yet all that artistic taste, all that glamour and glory could only exist because of industry; it was improvements in looms and sewing machines which made Worth gowns possible. It was the construction of an international telegraph system which enabled customers to call him from afar. It was long-distance locomotives and trans-Atlantic steamers which conveyed his goods at unprecedented speed. Without them Worth would have gained a European kingdom similar to that enjoyed by Marie Antoinette's *modiste* Rose Bertin. With them he won a world-wide empire such as no previous dressmaker had ever achieved, or could have done. He was an artist, but on an industrial scale.

Notes

1. H. Taine, *Notes sur Paris* (1867), pp. 174–5.
2. C. Dickens, *All the Year Round*, June–December 1867, vol. IX, p. 9.
3. Primoli Diary, trs. Joanna Richardson, *La Vie Parisienne 1852–1870* (1971), pp. 240–41.
4. *Souvenirs de la Princesse Pauline de Metternich 1859–71*, notes by M. Dunan (1922), Librairie Plon, p. 138.
5. N. W. Senior, *Conversations with M. Thiers, M. Guizot, and other distinguished persons during the Second Empire*, ed. M. C. M. Simpson (1878), Vol. II, p. 130.
6. R. Dudley Baxter, *The Taxation of the United Kingdom* (1869), p. 14.
7. Mary Merrifield, *Dress as a Fine Art* (1855), pp. 101–2.
8. Ruth Brandon, *Singer and the Sewing Machine* (1977), *passim*.
9. Dickens, loc. cit.
10. Taine, loc. cit.
11. Metternich, op. cit., p. 140.
12. Dickens, loc. cit.

13. W. F. Lonergan, *Forty Years of Paris* (1907), Fisher Unwin, pp. 199–200.
14. Frances Hodgson Burnett, *Louisiana* (1880), pp. 13–16.
15. F. Whitehurst, *Court and Social Life in France under Napoleon III* (1873), vol. II, p. 85.
16. Mme Carette, *My Mistress, the Empress Eugénie; or, Court Life at the Tuileries* (1889), pp. 173–5.
17. Bertall, *L'Illustration*, 16 March 1895, pp. 217–18.
18. Carette, op. cit., p. 176.
19. Whitehurst, op. cit., vol. I, 27 January 1867.
20. Merrifield, op. cit., pp. 96–106.
21. Taine, loc. cit.

Chapter 9

Disaster and Survival

The Second Empire had grown wealthy and waltzed its way on clouds of almost untarnished glory, becoming a legend in its own lifetime. Through it Worth and Bobergh made their fortunes; they could not have had such enormous success at an earlier time, for it was the myth of Paris as *the* city worth visiting, *the* capital of receptions, parades and exhibitions, *the* centre of unending entertainment, of Offenbach operettas, of dances by Waldteufel and Strauss, of banquets and carnivals, of *la gaieté parisienne*, reported round the world by newspapers, illustrated journals and guide books, which caused the customers to come. Charles Frederick Worth had become part of that luxurious legend, he had helped to create that glittering image, and a visit to the rue de la Paix to see the most famous fashion House in the world was now on every tourist's list. There were some middle-class ladies who were tempted to spend a whole year's dress allowance on just one model gown from Worth. Everyone was eager to inspect the new Paris which the emperor had built.

Nevertheless there were danger signs in the air which Napoleon III chose to ignore. The ambitions of Prussia, her defeat of the Austrian Empire in order to win hegemony over the German-speaking world in 1866, and the build-up of armaments under Bismarck, should have made the emperor more suspicious of that Iron Chancellor's assurances of peaceful intentions. Even one of the court beauties could see the dangers, for Mélanie, Comtesse de Pourtalès, a native of Alsace, a border province, was so alarmed by Prussian military preparations that she warned the emperor herself, only to be told that she was imagining threats.[1] When Napoleon III did decide to challenge Prussia it was too late. The very latest guns, which Krupps had exhibited in Paris in 1867, pounded the French artillery to pieces. Despite heroic cavalry charges the French were routed on every front, and on 2 September 1870 the emperor was captured by the Prussians at Sedan. The glorious Second Empire was over. Ironically, one of the battles was at a place named Wörth. France was to suffer three bitter humiliations: the loss of Alsace-Lorraine, the German occupation of

Paris, and the sight of the King of Prussia being proclaimed Emperor of Germany inside the château of Versailles.

In Paris, the capture of Napoleon III was greeted by increasing demands for the establishment of a republic, by riots in the streets and by the tearing down of imperial insignia from public buildings. All those associated with the disgraced Second Empire were suddenly in grave danger, and the Prussians were approaching. The empress had been appointed regent in the emperor's absence, and now busied herself with organizing the defence of the capital, only too pleased to have an active role at last instead of always being the powerless imperial consort. In preparation for a siege, large naval guns were brought in, and huge flocks of cattle and sheep were pastured in the Bois de Boulogne and the Jardins du Luxembourg. But one evening, as she walked in the Tuileries garden, wearing a white lace scarf from Worth over her head, with Mme Carette for company, the brilliance of the setting sun made the empress exclaim with anguish that it looked as if the whole of the Tuileries were on fire.

On 4 September, now wearing one of her plain black silk dresses with a Worth shawl of violet braided with gold, she received a deputation from the Corps Législatif which asked her to hand over her executive powers to that assembly, so that there could be a legal transfer of authority to a republic, without undue violence. The

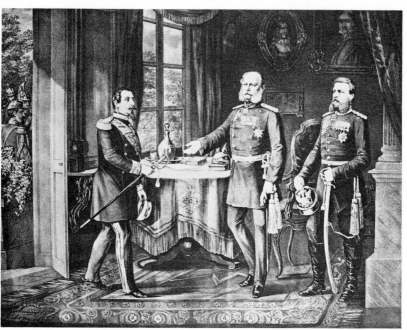

56. The end of an empire, Napoleon III surrenders to Bismarck.

empress replied that she would never desert the post with which she had been entrusted, and that they would have to depose her. At the Hôtel de Ville, however, moderate republicans had proclaimed the Third Republic, and the mobs were converging on the palace. Prince von Metternich urged the empress to leave. She refused at first, but as the armed mob burst into the Louvre courtyard, she agreed and was hurried through the echoing galleries by Prince von Metternich and the Italian ambassador, Count Nigra, to the door on the Place Saint Germain l'Auxerrois. Metternich went off to look for his own carriage, but Nigra spotted an empty cab and put the empress into it. In this humble vehicle the Empress of the French left her palace. Her reader Mme Lebreton was with her, and as the cab pushed through the excited crowds the empress saw that the insignia 'By appointment to Her Imperial Majesty the Empress' were being torn from shop fronts. 'Already,' she shrugged. One of the first establishments to suffer this assault must have been Worth et Bobergh.

The empress tried two addresses for refuge but the owners were out, and in desperation she turned to her dentist, the American, Dr Evans. He and a colleague Dr Crane agreed to convey the empress to the coast. As trains would have been too risky, they organized a relay of carriages. At five o'clock next morning, 5 September 1870, Empress Eugénie left Paris with the doctors and Mme Lebreton. The centre of Worth's world was going into exile, wearing that black dress, a travelling cloak, a Derby hat with a veil, and with no wardrobe beyond a pair of handkerchiefs. At dawn on the 7th an Englishman Sir John Burgoyne conveyed the empress aboard his yacht, through violent seas, to Ryde. Never again would she summon Monsieur Worth to the Tuileries.

In the midst of all the chaos and confusion there was someone who could do far more to provide the empress with clothes than Worth himself could in the present situation. Count Maurice d'Hérrison was ordinance officer to General Louis Trochu, whom Napoleon III had appointed Governor of Paris. Because of a row with another general, Trochu did nothing to save the Empire. He switched sides, and was elected President of the republican Government of National Defence. D'Hérrison was thus well placed to do something for the empress, when Worth would not have dared to be seen in the streets. The count went to the Palais des Tuileries and entered the realm where only one man, Worth, had entrée – the wardrobe. First he found fifty umbrellas; one of mauve silk covered with black lace, one of white silk garnished with valenciennes, and one of white silk, all designed to match Worth gowns. Next he came upon enormous cupboards in great rows, full of clothes: gala gowns, simpler dresses, cloaks, linen, lace, the proudest creations of the *grand couturier*. There was a special room for hats, another room for footwear, and a room for furs, while standing ready on duty were the four dummies, dressed in what the Empress Eugénie should have worn that day. With a *femme de chambre* to help, d'Hérrison filled fifteen trunks with clothes, and still all the cupboards seemed full. He had these trunks taken to the Gare du Nord, and despite the scene of panic and disorder managed to get them on a train to the coast. The empress, then at Hastings, subsequently acknowledged their safe arrival, so some of her Worths were saved. The count also filled a further twenty-three trunks with the empress's personal effects, which he lodged at the Austrian Embassy. The empress's furs, the count returned to the imperial furrier, Valenciennes, at 21 rue Vivienne. There were over seventy categories, from swansdown cloaks, to coats, muffs and tippets of chinchilla, silver fox and sables, which d'Hérrison valued at 600,000 francs. Princess Pauline von Metternich sent the empress's jewels to the safety of the Bank of England.[2]

Faced with the loss of its most important customer, what could Maison Worth et Bobergh do but close? There was not much hope for an imperial couturier in a republic. The princesses and the duchesses fled to their estates, and anyone with Bonapartiste connections was well advised to lie low. The Metternichs moved to Calais and Boulogne, then crossed the Channel to visit the exiled empress. Everyone was leaving. Worth never forgot what he owed to Empress Eugénie, and never failed to say so, as Pauline von Metternich acknowledged:

> Very attached to the Empress, he has not hidden his imperialist opinions after the fall of the Empire, and has thus given a proud lesson to many notable persons who have forgotten the benefits which they or their parents have received from the Emperor. However, he risked more than they in openly declaring himself to be a supporter of the Empire, for when one is running a business which opens on to the street, one is exposed to having the windows smashed.[3]

Worth expressed his loyalty with a delicate gesture. Eugénie had often carried a bunch of violets when she attended balls or official opening ceremonies. During the Universal Exposition of 1867 Worth had invited his former boss Mr Allenby to Paris, and had presented him to the empress. A few violets had fallen from the bouquet she was carrying, and Worth asked if he might give them to Mr Allenby as a souvenir of the occasion, whereupon the empress gave Allenby the whole bunch. Because of this kindness, Worth began the custom of sending the empress a bouquet of violets every year. Now that she was exiled he made a special point of keeping up this tradition, and he did so until the day he died.

His despair during the events of August and September can be imagined. He had already witnessed the revolution of 1848, and the emperor's coup d'état, and must have hoped that by now France had settled down to a stable regime, yet here he was at forty-five seeing everything on which he depended crashing in ruins about him. As he stood at his salon windows and watched the crowds pouring down the rue de la Paix to the Tuileries, he must have been plunged in grief. He was completely powerless to affect the situation, but the fruits of his twelve years' labour were being squashed underfoot. He would have to begin all over again, but where, and how?

He announced that he would not be bringing out a winter collection that month. One loyal customer, the Marquise de Manzanedo, thereupon declared that she would continue to wear his last spring collection until he could make his next presentation of models, but Worth and Bobergh must have wondered if they would ever bring out a collection again. Otto Bobergh was convinced that

57. True to Worth no matter what – the Marquise de Manzanedo.

this was definitely the end. They had achieved a glorious success but he could see no future without an empire and he asked for the partnership to be dissolved. Taking his share of the profits, Bobergh returned to Sweden, where he bought himself a castle and married the actress Thérèse Björklund. He resumed his first love of painting, and for the remainder of his life he specialized in landscapes. His house in Stockholm became a venue for Swedish artists, his works were acquired by the Nationalmuseum and the Konstakademien, and he died on 29 January 1882.[4]

It was not so easy for Worth to abandon France. Not only were his wife and sons French, but the whole business was French – from the seamstresses, the lace manufacturers, the textile weavers, the button and bead makers, the embroiderers, to the page boys. Only the sales assistants had been English, with one Swede. Worth stood at the top of an enormous pyramid of fashion suppliers and producers, and such a structure simply did not exist on the same scale in other countries. If he moved back to London he would still need a lot of material from France, so what was the point in moving? He resolved to stay on in Paris and see what developed.

Two weeks after the flight of the empress, the Prussian army stood at the gates of the city. An astonished Europe saw Paris, that capital of gaiety and supreme elegance, subjected to a grim and vicious siege. Worth turned his salons into a hospital for troops, and the temple of taste was filled with the wounded and the dying. The Worths had to stay there, for it was not possible to leave Paris for their estate, so they gave what medical help they could, nursing the soldiers of the Third Republic for the sake of Paris and France. The siege dragged on for four months; supplies of food dwindled, disease began to break out, prices shot up, as the Prussians determined to starve them out. The one bright spot in the whole period for the Worths was that they became acquainted with the old painter, Camille Corot, who used to dine with them on whatever food could be obtained. Out of this friendship came the suggestion that Corot should take one of the Worth sons as a pupil. The artist agreed, and of the two boys it was Jean-Philippe, then fourteen, who was considered to be the most gifted artistically. Every Sunday he went to draw and paint under Corot's direction, and so acquired a professional training in art which his father had never had. Obviously Worth wanted to give his sons a better start than he had enjoyed himself. One of the artefacts Jean-Philippe produced at about this time was a plaque of his father in profile, while the guns boomed in the background.

Paris surrendered to the Prussians in January 1871. Once again the downfall of a Napoleon saw German troops parading through the French capital, as they did in 1815. The balance of power had been

58. A new friend in the midst of disasters – the artist Camille Corot, photograph by Nadar.

59. Prussian troops in the gardens of the Palais des Tuileries.

changed and everyone would now have to take note of Berlin. Napoleon III, still a prisoner, later made the prophetic remark that Prussia was now so powerful that the rest of Europe would have to unite to crush her one day, as indeed they did. Apart from tearing off the border provinces, Prussia took the fortresses of Sedan and Metz, and imposed an indemnity of 200,000,000 francs, remaining in partial occupation of France until it was paid off. On the signature of this 'peace' with the republican government, Napoleon III was released in March and allowed to join Empress Eugénie and their son the Prince Imperial in England, where they settled at Camden Place, Chislehurst.

Worth reopened in March 1871. Indeed he had little option but to try to keep in business with a wife, two sons, and 1,200 employees all dependent on his success. The times were by no means secure, however. The attempt by the new republican government to enter Paris was being resisted by the citizen's militia which had been defending the city. A revolutionary Commune was set up, a mixture of old style Jacobins and the new adherents of Karl Marx, and it was determined to resist the republican government, which it condemned as bourgeois. The red flag was hoisted, mobs roamed the streets, and Paris faced an even more serious crisis. Lillie, Mrs Charles Moulton, went to Worth's at this time. She knew there was going to be a peaceful demonstration, led by a young man named Henri de Pène, which intended to march down the rue de la Paix to the Communards' barricades in the Place Vendôme in order to beg for the restoration of order, but the street was still empty when she got there, although the barricade was manned, with cannons in place. She walked across the road to Worth's and had just entered his salon when the sounds of a crowd began to draw nearer. Worth led her to the balcony and together they watched as the demonstration came into view and began to make its way down the street. De Pène, followed by men, women and children with banners appealing for peace, headed the procession. On seeing Worth, de Pène beckoned for him to come down and join them, but Worth shook his head. 'Not I,' he said with a smile, and went back into the salon. Hardly had he done so when there came an enormous roar as the communists fired their cannon against the defenceless crowd. Worth's staff dragged Mrs Moulton off the balcony and back into the salon, as the street outside became a panic-stricken holocaust with the dead and the dying strewn from side to side.

Worth ordered his front doors to be opened, and 300 demonstrators found refuge there, many of them wounded and one dying. Mrs Moulton was so upset by this horrible sight that her one wish was to return home. Worth would not allow her to go out into the rue de la Paix but, as he had no back exit, he sent her next door. One of his women led the way, taking her up through the workrooms to the staff bedrooms at the top of the next house, and so down again to its back door on the rue St Arnaud. From there Mrs Moulton found her way through the frightened crowds to her carriage. This incident was enough; the Moultons packed their bags and went back to the United States. It was enough for Worth, too. Plainly one could not run a business under these conditions and he took his family to Le Havre, ready to flee across the Channel if need be.

It was well he did so, for Paris was now subjected to a second siege, as the republican government attempted to oust the Commune. The next two months saw some of the bloodiest scenes in French history, but by May government troops were beginning to gain ground. The extremists of the Commune would not give in without trying to destroy everything around them. On 23 May one of their leaders, Bergeret, set out to obliterate the empty imperial residence, the Palais des Tuileries, scene of Worth's greatest triumphs. Together with associates, the rebel filled the building with gunpowder and petroleum, and at 9 p.m. he set fire to it. Soon the whole Renaissance palace was engulfed in flames from end to end, and at 1.15 a.m. the central cupola exploded and collapsed. That seat of glory was no more. As if this atrocity were not enough, Bergeret then set fire to the Bibliothèque du Louvre, and thousands of rare books and illuminated manuscripts were destroyed, despite the desperate attempts of scholars to save them. He would then have burned down

60. The burning of the Palais des Tuileries.

the Louvre Museum and Art Gallery (luckily the rarest works had been removed) but Maréchal MacMahon, Duc de Magenta, fortunately arrived with government troops and prevented further senseless destruction.

As the government had now won Paris, the Worths returned in June and one of the first things they did was to walk down their road to the Jardin des Tuileries to see what damage had been done. The sight made them weep, Marie Worth clinging to her husband's arm. Only the palace walls still stood; the roof and the floors, all those golden state rooms, were gone for ever. The destruction of their world was made manifest physically by these blackened, gaping walls. Worth could only groan with despair. What could he hope to rebuild out of this enormous loss?

The Metternichs also returned at this time, and together Worth and the princess sat and lamented the days that were over. The Austrian government wanted the Metternichs to continue in their ambassadorial role, but, in December, President Thiers of the Third Republic ruled that they had been too much associated with the imperial regime and asked Austria to replace them. They left in January 1872, driving past the ruins of the Tuileries to look once more on the remains of the court where they had had such an influence.

The departure of the princess caused Worth even more pain. The two women in French society who had mattered to him most, the empress and the ambassadress, were now both banished. It was not an absolute tragedy, both women could continue to order clothes from abroad, but nothing would be quite the same again. The empress and the princess had both been friends, delighting in his conversation, asking for his opinions, joining him in devising fashions. Their absence left an enormous gap in his life, but it did not diminish his continuing loyalty. Princess von Metternich wrote: 'He has not forgotten for a day that he owed his reputation to me, and he has given me witness on all occasions of his deep and sincere devotion.' Worth created a little tradition to honour the princess as he had done with the empress and, as she was a Catholic, he sent her every Easter a piece of box tree that had been blessed in Sainte Clotilde, the parish in which the Metternichs had lived in Paris.[5]

Nevertheless he had to carry on. He was too much the designer to even consider another career. Bobergh was no longer there to help him, but no matter. He and Marie had run a dress department before and they could do so again. Another manager could be recruited, any other absentees could be replaced. What was the great imponderable was how many customers would come back, and only time would answer that. Worth occupied himself with getting the business going again. A new registration was taken out, and henceforth the firm labels would carry but a single name, copied from the bold signature on his British passport, WORTH.

What he probably only came to realize slowly was that he had also won his independence. Hitherto fashions had always been launched at court, with the dressmaker under the supervision of the committee of ladies-in-waiting, but now here was Worth, a designer of immense prestige throughout the world, suddenly standing on his own, with no one to supervise his innovations except himself. It did not matter if a particular empress disliked his latest idea or not, henceforth Worth alone would decide. Of course he had got his own way with Empress Eugénie in the past, and of course dressmakers had always introduced fashions in their own little establishments, but no fashion was ever as important as that which was launched with full court approval and publicity. In future Worth would have to sound those trumpets himself, and he was the only dressmaker with sufficient reputation to be able to summon the international press, to dictate to the fashion world, and to issue edicts for society to follow. Here was a new phenomenon, a couture house which stood independent of any particular court, and where fashions were launched solely on the command of the designer. It was a pattern which was to be followed by the couture houses of the future, where the only restriction on innovations was the designer's own sense of judgement. It could only happen because of the huge prestige and fame which Worth had built up during the Second Empire, which now gave him sufficient authority to continue in his own right.

Worth was not the only person to worry about the future of the fashion trade in Paris. Several people wondered if the 'gallantry wares' as the Germans called them, the *articles de Paris*, those frivolous and unnecessary goods such as ornaments, artificial flowers, clothing and furniture, would ever recover from the disastrous downfall of the Empire. One individual who had come to Paris to see the destruction was the journalist F. Adolphus of *Blackwood's Magazine*, and in late August 1871 he was wondering about the effect of the war on the most labour-intensive industry in the city, dressmaking:

I would get up the subject, and would write an article for 'Blackwood' on 'The Influence of the Siege of Paris on the Art and Trade of Dressmaking'! I would inaugurate a study of the psychology of women's gowns in their relation to both international and civil war! What an utterly new idea![6]

Whom could he question on such a subject, whom could he expect to have all the facts and figures at his fingertips, whom, but Monsieur

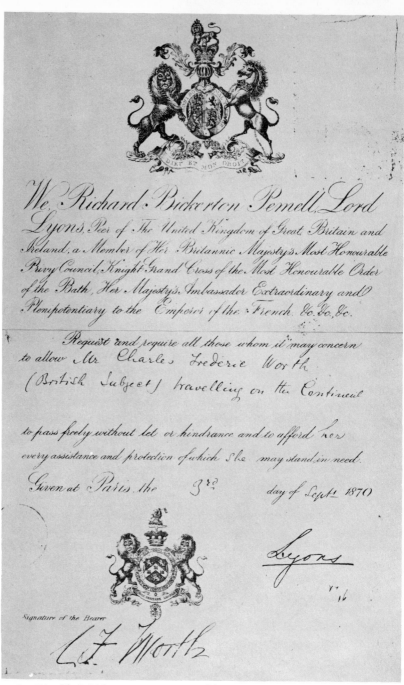

We, Richard Bickerton Pemell Lord Lyons, Peer of The United Kingdom of Great Britain and Ireland, a Member of Her Britannic Majesty's Most Honourable Privy Council, Knight Grand Cross of the Most Honourable Order of the Bath, Her Majesty's Ambassador Extraordinary and Plenipotentiary to the Emperor of the French &c. &c. &c.

Request and require all those whom it may concern to allow *Mr Charles Frederic Worth (British Subject)* travelling on the Continent to pass freely without let or hindrance and to afford *her* every assistance and protection of which *she* may stand in need.

Given at Paris the *3rd* day of *Sept.* 1870

Lyons

Signature of the Bearer

C. F. Worth

61. Worth's British passport – presumably written in a hurry as 'he' becomes 'she' towards the end.

Worth? 'I had been told, it is true, that he was as busy as a Cabinet Minister; that it was more difficult to obtain an audience from him than from a reigning sovereign; and that he was a loftier personage, by far, than any living poet.' But Mr Adolphus determined to try, for he was certain that his novel idea would appeal to the great man. After all, was not Worth a veritable figurehead, a real public man? In his person were combined both the artistic theory and the commercial practice of women's dress, so would not Worth also be erudite in the abstract essence and the hidden meanings of dress? As history had called the Second Empire *'l'époque de Worth'* surely the designer could not refuse to let a humble *reporter* sit at his feet to hear his words of wisdom? Adolphus went to the rue de la Paix and sent in his card; in only five minutes, to his surprise, he was before the great man himself. Worth listened to his request, regarded him rather suspiciously, hesitated for a moment, then came to a decision. Yes he would help Adolphus, but there were seventeen ladies in nine rooms all awaiting his attention that very minute, so he told the journalist to come to dinner next day, dress informal.

Overjoyed with this success, Adolphus next day caught the 6.30 train from the Gare St Lazaire to Suresnes, which took half an hour, and was met on the platform by Gaston Worth, now nearly eighteen, whom the journalist considered very good looking with charming manners. Gaston led him to the great red brick château and they stood on the terrace looking at the view over Paris, and soon afterwards Worth himself came galloping through the gate, splattered with mud, having ridden the distance in a quarter of an hour. Worth was going in to change, but a lady in white appeared on the verandah – Marie Worth. 'Her elegance, her grace, her winningness were such that I stood still in admiration,' Adolphus reported, overawed. Worth introduced them, then went indoors.

With the ease of an accomplished woman of the world, with combined dignity and simplicity, with infinite gentleness of movement, she made two steps towards me, smiling graciously, bowing slightly, welcome on her face. She wore a high but short-sleeved white satin dress, striped with bands of black velvet; a profusion of lace hung over her; long Suède gloves reached almost to her shoulders; two or three bracelets were on her arms; a diamond was half hidden here and there in the lace. Never did white satin appear to me to be so completely absorbed into the person of the wearer; she and her gown were so absolutely one that, for months afterwards, Madame Worth and white satin presented themselves to my thoughts as synonymous, simultaneous, identical, unseverable. I could neither disjoin them, nor conceive one without the other. All other women in white satin appeared to me imposters.

Adolphus had arrived in informal attire, as directed, but Madame Worth was dressed; she *was* dress. More than any other woman in the world she had the right to extreme elegance at any time. Moreover, she was so sympathetically attractive, and with such a grand air, and such charm. Adolphus considered her charm to be Spanish rather than French, for he thought himself an authority on the subject, and would not have been surprised if she were presented as the Marquesa de la Vega de Granada, daughter of the Conde Duque de Valladolid y Burgos. As Marie came from the Auvergne, perhaps her nature was more southern than northern in essence. Certainly she bowled him over. Worth reappeared in a rusty brown jacket and a battered straw hat with the crown missing. Evidently after spending every day surrounded by the most luxurious clothes in the world, Worth liked to dress down when pottering about at home, a very English characteristic, for who but for his accent can tell an English duke from his gardener when off duty?

Dinner was served in an enormous conservatory, full of palms, ferns, and exotic flowers, for winter gardens were all the rage. After the soup, Worth told Adolphus to begin his questions. The journalist was so pleased by his reception that he ventured to expand on his original theme. What did Worth think of the metaphysical aspects of dressmaking, of the influence of dress on the formation of a woman's character, of its effect on national character, and of the moral effects of dress? Worth found this flood of queries all rather perplexing. He had never thought about dress in those terms. As for the war, well it had cost them a year's business, but orders were coming in again fast so he thought that business would pick up. As for the influence of dress on character, Adolphus would have to explain what he was getting at; narrowing his approach the journalist asked:

'With what object do women dress?'

'What a question!' laughed Mr Worth. 'Do you mean to say you don't know? Why, women dress, of course, for two reasons: for the pleasure of making themselves smart, and for the still greater joy of snuffing out the others.'

'And never for their own persons only? Never to frame in and set up their individuality by clothing it in what befits it best? Never to harmonize their essence with their substance, their self with their surroundings?'

'I must say again that I don't quite follow you. If you mean whether they dress to suit their bodies, according to their own ideas of suitability, I should say no at once; because, you see, the women who come to me want to ask for my ideas, not to follow out their own. They deliver themselves to me in confidence, and I decide for them; that makes them happy. If I tell them they are suited, they need no further evidence. My signature to their gown suffices!'

'Do you never find a rebel amongst them? Does no one ever claim the right of personal invention and choice?'

'Choice? Yes, certainly; but only between my various suggestions. And very few do even that; most of them leave it all to me. But as for invention, no. My business is not only to execute but especially to invent. My invention is the secret of my success. I don't want people to invent for themselves; if they did, I should lose half my trade.'

Marie Worth looked at her husband with great affection, and touched her forehead, saying that the secret of his success lay there. Adolphus persisted on the effect of dress on character and, trying to be helpful, Worth spent the next half-hour telling him anecdotes of all the jealousy, envy, hatred and love which went on among his clients, but said frankly that he suspected that he did not know anything about the sort of developments the journalist was asking about. Adolphus found these tales very amusing, but they were personal not analytical, so he moved the conversation round to nationalities. Which of Worth's international customers spent the most? The couturier replied that it did not run in nations, although it was usually a Russian or an American who was the most extravagant, and occasionally a Peruvian or Chilean. On the whole Frenchwomen, the English and the Germans did not lose their heads. Some of the Americans were certainly the greatest spenders, and all the American women he had met seemed to love dress.

'And I like to dress them, for, as I say occasionally, "they have faith, figures, and francs" – faith to believe in me, figures that I can put into shape, francs to pay my bills. Yes, I like to dress Americans.'

Poor Adolphus was beginning to despair, for it was becoming clear that Worth was not a fountainhead of theoretical knowledge. As a last try, Adolphus asked about the revival of trade, for if Paris was the capital of frivolous products surely that could not revive very rapidly. Worth did not agree; why, the very reason people came to Paris was to buy frivolous items, so of course trade would pick up. Ah, said Adolphus, that was a philosophical point and he tried to pursue it, but was rewarded with another half-hour of Worth's entertaining gossip on the energetic pursuit of the unnecessary by his clients. When he raised the question of metaphysics again, he got no further.

135

Obviously Adolphus's definitive analysis of the theory and ideals of dress was not going to be written. He thanked the Worths for their most kind reception, thought them most excellent people, but realized that they belonged to a world other than his.

The encounter was a classic illustration of the yawning gap between the enquiring mind and the creative mind. The former can stand back, survey the field of human activity, and deduce the prevailing movements in it; the latter is far too busy with the invention and the creation to have time to stop and construct theories and explanations. After all, Worth's formal education had ended at the age of eleven; what he had learnt since, he had mostly taught himself, and naturally being a designer he had concentrated on visual subjects. He had no training in the definition and analysis of intellectual concepts. His life was dominated by the need to produce a continual stream of new designs, which took too much mental energy for much to be left for detached theorizing. Adolphus got nowhere with the interview, but all honour to him for trying, and it should have taught him that the doers are not necessarily the thinkers.

What Worth did know about was women and the dress business. Trade did improve with the secure establishment of the Third Republic. The revolutionaries had been defeated, the rich were still rich, and they wanted Worth. Edmond de Goncourt found evidence of this early in 1872:

> 11 January. Nowadays, finding a blockage of stylish carriages in the rue de la Paix, exactly like that during a first night at the Théâtre Français, I was wondering who was the great person whose door was being besieged by so many members of high society, when, rasing my eyes above a porte-cochère, I read: 'Worth'. Paris is still the Paris of the Empire.[7]

The fact that Worth was open was in itself a guarantee that nothing had changed too much. True the presidential circle was elderly and dull, but Parisian society organized its own courts. Madame Thiers did dress with Worth, but she lacked the savoir-faire and glamour of a leader of fashion, apart from being too old for such activities. It was the election of Maréchal MacMahon as president in 1873 which really brought back the glitter and the gaiety. This old soldier had won victories in the Crimea and Italy for Napoleon III, and had been governor-general of Algeria between 1864 and 1870. He was something of a monarchist by sympathy and in this he reflected the true nature of France. Paris might be republican but the provinces were conservative and favoured monarchy. In fact the early years of the Third Republic saw both lines of the Bourbons, and the Bonapartistes, all hopeful of ultimate restoration. Napoleon III was actually planning to stage a coup in March 1873, but his bad state of health prevented it. He had long suffered from stone, and had to be operated on on 2 January and on 6 January, but he died on the 9th. Six years later his heir Louis the Prince Imperial was to be killed while serving with British forces in Zululand, when he was only twenty-three, and that ended any real hope of the return of a Napoleon IV.

During MacMahon's presidency many of those associated with royalty returned to Paris. Princess Mathilde's salon resumed its pre-eminence in the literary world, many of the beauties of the imperial court returned to ornament French society, and Princess von Metternich was able to pay regular visits. The high-spot of the reign of President MacMahon was the exhibition of 1878, which was intended to proclaim France's recovery from the disasters of 1870. It was visited by such royals as the Prince and Princess of Wales, and it was the first time that Alexandra of Wales went to Maison Worth in person. She had a number of ladies-in-waiting with her, who fussed and got in the fitters' way, insisting repeatedly that the girls must not stick pins in HRH. Worth snorted that his staff never stuck pins in customers.

The couture house was as busy as before. Presidential balls, ambassadorial receptions, official visits and celebrations, ensured a healthy picture in Paris, but more significantly foreign custom was expanding rapidly. Worth had thought that foreigners might help him to survive the depression of 1870–71, and he was to be proved right many times over. Foreign courts remained as splendid as ever, and now there was the new aristocracy of American millionaires, eager to break into European high society, and competing with each other in extravagance, and self-exhibition and promotion.

Most welcome was J. Pierpoint Morgan who came to the aid of France with a substantial loan to help her over the acute financial difficulties of the early 1870s. He took his second wife, Frances, to Worth's in 1877, and she was a regular customer thereafter. Pierpoint Morgan had some ideas of his own concerning suitable brocade and lace, so long hours were enjoyed discussing the relative merits of particular designs and colours. He also attended the fittings, something few husbands bothered to do, but he liked to know that everything was going to be perfect to ensure major impact when Mrs Pierpoint Morgan wore that particular creation in New York. Worth and the steel magnate became quite close friends, and it was a relief for visiting Americans to find a dressmaker in Paris who spoke English, so that they could be sure that there would be no misunderstandings or confusions over orders.

Pierpoint Morgan was often in Paris without his family, so on these occasions he would call at Worth's on his own to place orders for gowns he liked, which Worth would make up according to the measurements already on his files, and then send them over to the States by steamer. No matter how rich a client might be, the arrival of a trunk from Maison Worth, full of unseen treasures, was an event which sent the wives and daughters into raptures. Squeals of pleasure, gasps of admiration, delighted surprise, and rushes to the nearest mirror, were typical of these occasions. The elegance and the price commanded the use of superlatives, and the Pierpoint Morgans never questioned the size of a bill.[8] No wonder Worth liked Americans of this sort.

62. Empress Eugénie in exile.

For the Empress Eugénie it was a different story. Now that she was a widow and a lady of mature years she would have to abjure bright clothes for the rest of her life. Mourning had to be worn for at least three years, which was a long established custom. For the first twelve months the widow could only wear black crape, in the second year black silk trimmed with crape, and in the third year half-mourning of lavender or light grey. Moreover, a widow did not accept any social invitations in the first year, or go to public resorts or other popular places. Consequently the empress had to dispense with the gayer items in her wardrobe. She sent some of these to one of her Alba nieces, Louisette Duchess of Montoro:

Camden Place, Chislehurst
28 September 1874

Very dear Louisette,
I'm sending you the muslin tunic and corsage, and in addition a little cloak from Worth *which I have never worn*. I hope you will find it useful. In any case, it is less heavy than the one you had on at Arenenberg.[9]

This was not such a sacrifice for the empress as one might think, for as a Spaniard by birth she had often worn black when off duty, because it was modest and highly respectable. In terms of colour symbolism black represents constancy.

Worth was so famous and so successful at this time, a unique creator beside whom no other dressmaker could be mentioned, that he exercised a fascination over his contemporaries who were agog to learn the latest item of news from that most august establishment, which had survived the downfall of an empire. A faithful member of Princess Mathilde's salon, Edmond de Goncourt, always took an interest in her appearance, and delighted in any gossip which she

63. Nadar – Edmond de Goncourt with his brother, Jules.

brought back from her couturier. There seemed to be no limit to what people were prepared to pay Worth, even in the year of 1872:

> 24 April. A pretty and unusual interior for a novelist, that bedroom of Mme de Girardin's. This bedroom, she had not had decorated, but, as she puts it, dressed in embroidered satin, by Worth, costing 60,000 francs.[10]

Worth also had some of the rooms in his château dressed in satin, so Mme de Girardin may have been following his example. This does not represent a policy decision on the part of Worth to open a department for interior decorating. Nevertheless it does set a precedent for a couturier, and the first *grand couturier* at that, to become involved in interior design. Whilst Poiret must be given the credit for really taking couture into the field of décor design, early in this century, it is interesting to see that Worth had made a couple of steps in this direction forty years before.

Any innovation made by Worth was a topic for conversation in high society. In 1879 Goncourt was much intrigued by the following:

> Friday, 9 May. A pretty detail of elegant Parisian life. Amongst the young models in the salons of Worth, who display and parade the robes of the illustrious couturier upon their svelte bodies, there is a girl, or rather a lady-model, whose speciality is to represent pregnancy in high life.
> Seated all alone, in the half-light of a boudoir, she exhibits before the eyes of lady visitors in an interesting condition, the toilette designed with the greatest of genius for compensating for the ungainly appearance of being with child.[11]

Thus Worth had started a maternity department. He also had a department for mourning wear, and as the century wore on with more and more ladies taking up sports, he started making elegant sportswear such as yachting suits and riding habits, thereby encroaching on the traditional area of the male tailor.

It is noticeable how male observers of Maison Worth such as Count Primoli and Goncourt were intrigued by the thought of the svelte-bodied models. Perhaps the model girl was beginning to replace the seamstress and the shopgirl in the imagination of the predatory male as the sort of girl who was ripe for seduction but not for marriage. Was there perhaps a gathering of males outside the portals of Maison Worth when the models finished work, much as there was at stage doors? It seems quite possible.

By now Maison Worth had introduced all the features that were to be normal in couture houses thereafter – the presentation of spring and autumn collections, the use of live models, the creation of exclusive designs, and the selling of *toiles* and paper patterns. The one thing Worth did not do was to sell scent; that was to be brought in by his sons. Worth had not marked out any definite careers for his boys, beyond having Jean-Philippe taught by Corot, but both of them had spent their whole lives to date among dressmakers and dressmaking.

Their childhood had been spent in the second-floor apartment in the rue de la Paix, over the salons and the workrooms, and they had free run of the establishment behind the scenes. They had grown up among an endless round of distinguished visitors, lavish creations, constant designing, cutting and construction, so it was inevitable that both sons should have developed an interest in what was going on. They were accustomed to hearing their father spoken of as *'le maître'*, *'le créateur'*, and *'le grand couturier'* and they regarded him with considerable awe and admiration. Both young men expressed a wish to work in the firm, and even after the family had moved out to Suresnes, they had still come to the rue de la Paix to do various jobs for their father during their school vacations, so it seemed perfectly natural that their wish should be granted.

In 1874 Worth settled the question: Gaston at twenty-one was to help with management and finance, and Jean-Philippe at eighteen could assist with design – in view of his training. Obviously they were not given any major responsibilities immediately, but it was the start of their full-time work for the House. It cannot be said that Worth had planned to found a dynasty of couturiers. After all, he was the very first one, and there was no guarantee that his pattern would become permanent but, in the event, this is what happened, and the engagement of his sons ensured that his pattern would continue for two generations at least. In fact four generations of Worths were to run that Paris House – an unequalled achievement by any family in the world of haute couture.[12]

The addition of the sons to the firm eventually led to the House pricing code being based on them. It was not desirable that customers should see how Maison Worth arrived at its prices, so when the cost of items in a dress was added up, it was done on this system: from the phrase *'Chers Frères Worth, on gagne Dieu mais avec volonté-reflechissez'*, the first letter of each word was taken to represent a number from one to zero:

c.	f.	w.	o.	g.	d.	m.	a.	v.	r.
1	2	3	4	5	6	7	8	9	0

Thus the costing of a gown could read, embroidery cwr., dress wdrr., that is, embroidery 130 francs, dress 3,600 francs. The phrase also honoured the founder of the House, as the first three letters stood for Charles Frederick Worth. In arriving at the final price of a gown, the cost of the material was doubled, and that of the handwork was trebled. This system was used by the house throughout the remainder of its history.

The fashions which Worth created in the troubled 1870s did not reflect the political situation by showing any signs of penury. After all, they had to appeal to the whole of Western society, so emphasis on the misfortunes of France would have been unwise. The richness was continued as before, and there was no diminishing of Worth's passionate interest in the construction of clothes. On the contrary, he created some of the most sculptured gowns ever seen. He began with simple modifications, for after the recent political shocks he felt the world would not want any fashionable shock as well. Having introduced the *tournure* or bustle in 1869, he experimented with the way fabrics could be arranged over this frame, and in 1873 produced the fan train. This consisted of three deep pleats in the train as it

64. Worth's fan train of 1873 in an evening gown of black Chambéry gauze with gold stripes, over black silk.

started on the bustle, so that the material spread out in a half circle like a fan when it reached the floor, thereby helping to increase the rounded softness which was the current fashionable line. He was still using the high waist, the Josephine, and now complemented it by introducing another effect from the First Empire, the square neckline with cap sleeves, yet another example of his philosophy of modern design through historical inspiration.

He was allowing fashions a life of about five years at a time, so by 1874 he was beginning to think that a change was due in the rounded look with a bustle, and he set a narrowing of the line in motion. This

65. Narrowing the line, Worth's export model sold to Lord & Taylor of New York, 1874.

can be seen very clearly in a black silk dinner or visiting dress, which was sold to Lord & Taylor of New York for reproduction in 1874. Here Worth abolished the tunic top and apron overskirt, lowered the waistline to a more natural level, and lengthened the bodice down to the top of the hips. He was following up the experiments he had done in the early 1860s where he had tried to do away with the seam at the waist (fig. 35), and in the 1874 dress he achieves a fitted waist by means of long darts from the bust down to the hip. He avoided a waistseam by making the skirt separate, but this was a temporary measure, for in the next example, to be examined below, he merged skirt and bodice into one, without a waistseam of any kind. To narrow the 1874 dress, he reduced the skirt to a slim tube, emphasizing the slenderness by binding it with bands of fringe, and pulling the train right back, using much less material in it and forming a limited amount of drapery in two wings on top. The full-blown fashion of 1869–74 was thus slimmed down dramatically.

In 1875 Worth took the slimness even further, with the invention of his Princess line. This was the culmination of his experiments with waistseams, for he created the one-piece dress with a fitted waist but no waistseam – the fit of the gown was achieved by long darts from bust to hip. This simple but very skilful idea was immediately taken up by other dressmakers and became the fundamental method of dress construction for the rest of the decade, and a classic form to be copied time and time again in the future. It symbolized that exactness of fit which was such an outstanding feature of Maison Worth. How the fit was constructed can be seen in an evening dress of 1876, where fan seams keep the bodice narrow at the waist and then radiate out to define the hips, fitting as closely as a corset. The bustle was reduced still further, and Worth was on the way to introducing the cuirass line in which the gown fitted tight from the bust to the knees, a style which reached its ultimate in 1880, when it was so narrow that walking was difficult. He named his Princess line in honour of Princess Alexandra

66. Worth's experiments with the princess line culminated in the princess gown of 1875, the all-in-one construction which was the basic cut for the rest of the decade.

of Wales and, as seen above, it paid off by attracting her to his establishment.

Ever since 1864, Worth had been narrowing the fashionable line by degrees but there was a limit to how far he could go in that direction. A complete tube from neck to hem would have rendered women completely immobile, so by the summer of 1881 Worth thought that this had gone as far as it could go and perhaps he had better try to bring back some bulk. Crinolines were out of the question, for one could not jump from one extreme to another, and he did not like their impracticability in any case. Perhaps there was something else in his armoury which allowed for fuller skirts without causing any inconvenience. His answer was: revive the bustle. That allowed a lot of material to be used, but put round at the back, out of the way. Thus it was that Maison Worth announced in 1881 its crinolette, so named because it was a much smaller version of a crinoline type frame. *Punch* considered such a prospect too much for contemporary taste, and

67. Another way to obtain fit without a waistseam, using sections, in this evening gown of 1876.

145

declared that no English dressmaker would approve it and warned women against it, in rhyme:

TELL me not in honeyed accents Crinoline will come once more,
That my soul must feel the trammels that I felt in days of yore;
Modesty, I own, forbids me to the public to reveal,
All the tortures that I suffered in the days of steel;
Philistine I was then, doubtless, and those days would fain forget;
Why revive the old wire-fencing, though you call it Crinolette?

Who's responsible, I ask you, for this strange portentous birth
Of ancient hideous fashion, and an echo answers 'WORTH',
Stores of steel they hold in Paris, and though maiden hearts may
    droop,
We're to follow where they lead us, and go back to wire and hoop;
Yet a protest comes from England, ROBINS has declared it vile,
And ELISE and WHITE have answered that they think it awful style.

Then again at Fashion's dictates we must give up the fringe of hair,
Which Aesthetic folks have stated is the thing we ought to wear;
Now 'Othello's occupation's gone', as SHAKESPEARE said of old,
And the *modiste* looks for lucre while the British public's sold.
We'll not yield without a struggle, so, fair Ladies, do not fret –
Stick to Fourteenth century fringes, and abjure the Crinolette.[13]

Punch's protest was in vain, as was criticism from the Aesthetic movement; Worth had spoken and bustles were back. On the surface a dressmaker like London's Elise (who was notorious for overworking her seamstresses and was condemned by Karl Marx[14]) might object to the new fashion, but they all took it up very quickly because it was so good for business – every narrow dress in a lady's wardrobe now had to be replaced by dresses with a bustle. It was hard luck for any dressmaker who had just filled her salon with narrow clothes for summer; she should have observed by now that every five or six years Worth made a major change, and where he went everyone else followed. Bustle crinolettes were to reign until 1888.

There was one fashion in the period which did allow for ease, and did not increase a woman's size. This was the tea gown, which could be worn at home when entertaining close friends, a time when corsets could be loosened and the body be allowed to slump a little. Tea gowns were usually confections of silk and lace, very much like the morning gown a lady donned on rising. Strictly speaking tea gowns were only for hen parties; only male relations could be received in such casual dress, but there was one class of women who did not bother about such niceties. Once that so-called 'professional beauty' Lillie Langtry was making large profits out of royal adultery she

THE CHANT OF THE CRINOLETTE.

TELL me not in honeyed accents Crinoline will come once more,
That my soul must feel the trammels that I felt in days of yore;
Modesty, I own, forbids me to the public to reveal,
All the tortures that I suffered in the period of steel;
Philistine I was then, doubtless, and those days would fain forget;
Why revive the old wire-fencing, though you call it Crinolette?

Who's responsible, I ask you, for this strange portentous birth
Of an ancient hideous fashion, and an echo answers "WORTH;"
Stores of steel they hold in Paris, and though maiden hearts may
    droop,
We're to follow where they lead us, and go back to wire and hoop;
Yet a protest comes from England, ROBINS has declared it vile,
And ÉLISE and WHITE have answered that they think it awful
    style.

Then again at Fashion's dictates we must give up fringe of hair,
Which Æsthetic folks have stated is the thing we ought to wear;
Now "Othello's occupation's gone," as SHAKSPEARE said of old,
And the *modiste* looks for lucre while the British public's sold.
We'll not yield without a struggle, so, fair Ladies, do not fret—
Stick to Fourteenth century fringes, and abjure the Crinolette.

68. To the horror of *Punch* Worth brings back the bustle in 1881.

147

dressed *chez* Worth, and wore his nightgowns to receive her admirers, for they saved so much time in undressing.

How much circumstances had changed between 1870 and the dawn of the 1880s. Worth began the decade in a state of despair; he ended it as triumphant as he had ever been. Empires might fall, but Maison Worth continued. In fact Charles Frederick Worth's success was to last longer than the First and Second Napoleonic Empires put together. Fate it seems was kinder to emperors of haute couture.

Notes

1. Frédéric Loliée, *Women of the Second Empire*, trans. Alice M. Ivimy (1907), pp. 332–6.
2. Maurice d'Irisson, Comte d'Hérisson, *Journal d'un Officier d'Ordonnance juillet 1870 – février 1871* (1885), Paul Ollendorff, Paris, pp. 79–137.
3. *Souvenirs de la Princesse Pauline de Metternich 1859–71*, notes by M. Dunan (1922), Librairie Plon, pp. 138–9.
4. *Svenskt Konstnärslexikon* (1952), Allhems Förlag, Malmö.
5. Metternich, op. cit., pp. 138 and 144.
6. F. Adolphus, *Some Memories of Paris* (1895), pp. 178–200.
7. Edmond and Jules de Goncourt, *Journal* (1891), Bibliothèque Charpentier, vol. v.
8. Herbert L. Satterlee, *J. Pierpoint Morgan* (1939), Macmillan, New York, p. 163.
9. *Lettres Familières de l'Impératrice Eugénie, conservées dans les Archives du Palais de Liria et publiées par les soins du Duc d'Albe, avec les concours de F. de LLanos y Torriglia et Pierre Juserand* (1935), vol. II, p. 27, letter no. CXLVIII.
10. Goncourt, op. cit., vol. V.
11. ibid., vol. VI.
12. For the history of the later Worths, *see* Diana de Marly, *The History of Haute Couture 1850–1950* (1980), Batsford.
13. *Punch*, 2 July 1881, vol. LXXX, p. 303.
14. Karl Marx, *Capital*, ed. F. Engels, trans. S. Moore and E. Aveling (1887), Sonnenschein, Lowrey & Co., vol. 1, p. 239.

Chapter 10

A King among Queens

The most outstanding illustration of Worth's achievement in becoming the first haute couturier is shown by his work for all the courts of Europe, which was on a much larger scale than is realized nowadays. While it was inevitable that the dressmaker to the elegant Empress of the French would also receive commissions from other royal ladies, it was unprecedented for any dressmaker to be so sought out by so many queens and princesses. Orders for special gowns had been sent to Parisian dressmakers and tailors for centuries by foreign royalty,[1] but never had one man catered for such a bevy of royal ladies at one time. Once Worth et Bobergh had won its imperial appointment in 1860, the first courts from which the directors must have hoped for some orders were their native ones.

Sweden did acknowledge Bobergh in 1864–5 when King Karl XV ordered several gowns for Queen Lovisa, as a mark of national congratulation but Worth did not have such luck with the British court. In 1861 Queen Victoria was widowed and went into mourning for the remainder of her life, which precluded any orders for gala gowns from the British monarchy. At the end of his life Worth said to Lonergan, with, perhaps, a tinge of regret: We have worked for all the Courts, but never for Queen Victoria. Jean-Philippe later claimed that the firm did supply the queen indirectly, by sending gowns to her dressmakers, but this can only have happened after his father's death, during the years 1895–1901.

But the queen's withdrawal from public life did not prevent the British aristocracy from dressing at Maison Worth, and they flocked there in their dozens. The absence of a lively court in London added to the attractiveness of the court at the Tuileries. If there were no weekly balls at Windsor, then the British ladies wore their Worth court dresses in Paris. These gowns were as sumptuous as Worth could make them – great puffs of tulle, with court trains of heavy velvet lined with lace.

Worth may have come close to a royal British commission at one stage. According to *L'Illustration* in 1895, Worth kept pieces of his most famous gowns at Suresnes: the dress Empress Eugénie did not wear at the 1867 exhibition, part of a gown for Elizabeth of Austria, part of a gown for Carlotta of Mexico, a brocade chosen for Sarah Bernhardt, and a piece of the wedding dress belonging to the Princess of Wales. Her wedding dress? Worth did not make that – or did he?

The engagement of Albert Edward, Prince of Wales, to Alexandra Caroline, Princess of Denmark, caused a great flutter among London and Parisian dressmakers who competed for the honour of winning the commission for the bridal gown. The wedding was booked for 10 March 1863, and as Worth had held his imperial appointment for only three years at this time, his rivals were hoping that this would provide them with an opportunity to steal some of his thunder. Sophisticated opinion judged that the commission ought to go to Paris if the end result was going to be the height of elegance. Queen Victoria's uncle, King Leopold of the Belgians, said that he would order the bridal gown, and commissioned one of Brussels lace. The dress was actually made up, but at the last minute Queen Victoria decided that the gown would have to be British made. The order went to the dressmaker Elise for a gown of silver-tissue and Honiton lace, garlanded with orange blossom, and Princess Alexandra wore this for the ceremony in St George's Chapel, Windsor. As she was still in mourning, the queen watched from a closet, set like a box at the

69. A British rebuttal – Frith, The Marriage of the Prince of Wales to Princess Alexandra of Denmark, 10 March 1863. On the left foreground is the Duchess of Brabant in the old waist-hung style of court train.

theatre. Some of the congregation considered that the bridal gown was rather drowned in greenery, and lacked the sophistication of a Paris original.

But what happened to King Leopold's gown? He had still sent it to England, for it is listed in the catalogue of bridal presentations: 'His Majesty, the King of the Belgians. A dress of beautiful and costly Brussels lace, with scarf and handkerchief to match.'[2] There was no point in wasting it after all, so the scarf and handkerchief were added to convert it to an evening gown. But from whom would King Leopold have ordered such an expensive creation, if not from Monsieur Worth? Newcomer he might be, but all the European courts were talking of the genius of this designer, and the court at Brussels never failed to notice what was happening in Paris. It is more than likely that the king sent his commission to Worth, but this cannot be proved as the king's accounts have not been preserved in either the Cabinet du Roi or the Musée de la Dynastie in Brussels. Nevertheless if Worth kept a piece of the wedding dress of the Princess of Wales, it could only have been from the dress that she did not in the end wear. One of the reasons why Queen Victoria changed her mind about the gown, may have been that she still found the idea of a man-dressmaker too shocking. Ladies' tailors she was used to, but a male milliner was too much. Paris might allow such goings-on but not Windsor.

Worth never had to suffer such treatment from other courts which actively competed for his favour. As reports of the excellent quality of his creations spread, other crowned heads felt that they too were entitled to such marvellous designs. There may have even been an element of imperial competition, for could the Empress of the French, a lady of non-royal origins, be allowed to carry off the reputation for being the most beautiful and best-dressed consort in all Europe? Were those upstart Bonapartes to steal all the glory?

There was another empress in Europe who was celebrated for her beauty, and it was she who gave Worth et Bobergh their most important commission in the 1860s. Elizabeth of Bavaria had married the Emperor Franz Josef of Austria in 1854 when she was seventeen. A lively girl, with dark eyes and waist-long hair, she possessed great charm, but astonished stuffy Austrian courtiers by taking daily gymnastic exercises to keep her figure slim. She was also an enthusiastic horsewoman, and used to visit England frequently for the hunting. The Austrians prided themselves on her loveliness and felt that Elizabeth was a proper empress because she was of royal blood, whereas Empress Eugénie wore her skirts a shade too short and was not completely *comme il faut*.

During this period the Austrian Empire was undergoing

considerable pressure from its Hungarian subjects for equal status with Austrians, and with the increasing power of Prussia to the north, Austria could not very well afford a major disturbance immediately to the east. The Empress Elizabeth herself was a passionate supporter of the Hungarian cause, being a great romantic at heart, and showed her predilections by sometimes wearing Hungarian dress. At last, Franz Josef yielded to Hungarian demands, and the Austrian Empire was converted into the Dual Monarchy, the Austro-Hungarian Empire, although this still left other nationalities in the realm unequal. The new role of Hungary within the empire meant that there would have to be a separate Hungarian coronation, so that the Emperor and Empress of Austria would equally be King and Queen of Hungary. Consequently the empress had to have a second coronation gown.

It can only have been Princess von Metternich who caused Worth to receive this extremely important commission. She was Hungarian on her father's side, which the empress would have approved of, and she was sufficiently important in rank to be able to advise the empress as to who was the best dressmaker in the world. Elizabeth heeded her advice, and the order went to Worth. It was a commission which required considerable tact, for it had a political role to play and must be the sort of design that would delight the Hungarians. Worth consulted Pauline von Metternich and together they came up with the solution: the dress had to be Hungarian. The problem was to create a form of Hungarian dress that would look national yet would be sumptuous enough for a coronation ceremony.

As his starting-point, Worth took the front-laced bodice which was so characteristic of peasant wear for women and created a version in black velvet heavily embroidered with silver, but instead of lacing it with ribbon, he laced it with ropes of perfect pearls, from which larger drop pearls were suspended. The skirt was silver brocade, very simple in shape but embroidered all over with jewels. The neckline was off-the-shoulder, according to the usual requirement for court dress for women. The ensemble was completed by a veil of finest lace, bridal in its proportions, for a coronation is a form of marriage to a state. Empress Elizabeth was absolutely delighted with the result, and Emperor Franz Josef, usually the most reserved of men, was so moved when he saw his wife trying on the costume that he actually embraced her in full view of her attendants. . . . Such is the power of dress. When the empress wore the costume in Buda-Pest in June 1867 at her coronation, the Hungarians went wild with joy. Worth's most important dress to date was a triumph.

So great was the empress's satisfaction with this gown that she became a regular customer of Worth's thereafter, continuing to order her ordinary and riding wear from Viennese dressmakers, but turning to Worth when she wanted something special. She preferred soft colours, such as pearl grey, and pale violet, and the simplicity of many of Worth's designs appealed to her strongly, for she did not like elaborate clothes. Some of the bills the empress received from Worth survive in the archives of her secretariat in Vienna:

1872 for   6,810 francs.
1873 for 34,089 francs,
            1,515 francs.
1874 for   4,475 francs.
1876 for   3,678 francs.[3]

The extra large order in 1873 was probably in preparation for the empress's twentieth wedding anniversary in 1874.

With two empresses patronizing the couture house it was only a matter of time before others did. No less than three czarinas of Russia appointed Worth their principal milliner, which meant that the Russian grand duchesses and princesses also followed suit. The court in St Petersburg, like all the others in Europe, had very strict regulations about correct clothing for ceremonial occasions. At the imperial Winter Palace ladies had to wear hanging sleeves, and long trains, the length of which depended on their status – four metres for czarinas, three metres, seventy-five for grand duchesses, and three metres, fifty for princesses. Before Worth was officially appointed he had to send a sample of his work to the Master of the Robes, so that the officer could evaluate the shoulder-hung court train which Worth had invented. Worth therefore sent a *manteau de cour* of heavy pink velvet profusely embroidered in silver, which the Russians admired so much that it was given the seal of approval as official court wear, replacing the original waist-hung train. Dressing courts meant that Worth had to become a real expert in all their regulations, which varied from kingdom to kingdom.

According to Jean-Philippe, the first czarina to be dressed by Worth was the wife of Alexander I, but as that lady was consort before Worth was born, he has obviously confused her with the wife of Alexander II, Empress Maria Alexandrovna. Russia had been at war with France and Britain in the Crimea, but Alexander II made peace with the allies and this enabled his wife and some Russian ladies to start ordering clothes from the new fashion house in Paris. As we saw in Chapter 8, it was sufficient for a czarina to send Worth a telegram whenever a gown was needed. Her measurements were delivered by an imperial courier, so there was never any need for an empress to make a special trip to Paris just to be fitted, and Worth himself was far too busy to undertake lengthy trips round Europe visiting various courts, except on extraordinary occasions like coronations. Maria

Alexandrovna was not a lavish dresser, but like all Worth's customers she found out that the clothes he sent were perfect both in fit and line.

The empress's need for finery dropped suddenly in 1865. Her marriage had been a love-match, made in 1837 when she was seventeen and Alexander nineteen, but in 1865 at the age of forty-seven her husband transferred his love to the eighteen-year-old Princess Catherine Dolgoruky, to the intense grief of the empress and the cold fury of his five sons. As if that were not sorrow enough, the same year the oldest son, Grand Duke Nicholas, died suddenly of tuberculosis of the spine. Deeply wounded the empress withdrew into a half-life, burying herself in religion, her own health increasingly undermined too by tuberculosis. She no longer had any interest in gowns from Maison Worth, but Worth did not have to worry – the Czar had his mistress dressed there. As soon as the empress died, the Czar married his princess. Not being royal she could not be Czarina but was styled Princess Yurievsky; nevertheless she dressed very well. The family continued to regard her as a vicious schemer – the marriage had taken place before the mourning for their mother was even over. Alexander II was assassinated in 1881, and one of Worth's finest pink négligées was drenched in blood as the princess threw herself upon the bomb-torn body. Her need for couture clothes was over.

The new Czar, Alexander III, resolved to set a better moral example than his father and he remained faithful to his wife for life. She was Princess Dagmar of Denmark, a younger sister of Alexandra, Princess of Wales. Originally she had been engaged to Grand Duke Nicholas, but when he died she dutifully became betrothed to the next-in-line, Alexander – a giant of a man – and took the Russian name of Marie Feodorovna. She positively adored fine clothes, and became a devoted customer of Worth's for the remainder of her life, continuing with his sons after his death in 1895. Unfortunately her husband had a passion for economy; he cut down on palace bills enormously, and expected his own clothes to be patched and repaired until they almost fell to pieces. Consequently there were many occasions when the Czar scolded his lively wife for her extravagance at Maison Worth. This did not stop her from going there, however, and the elegant simplicity of Worth's creations suited her extremely well, although Alexander III did explode over the price of a sable coat. But the Czar did allow splendour on foreign visits and of course at his coronation. The order for the empress's robes went to Worth, thereby giving him his second imperial coronation commission. He described one of the gowns himself:

For the Coronation of the Tsar and Tsaritsa we had to make a

70. Grand Duchess Marie
Feodorovna, with the
husband who objected to
huge dress bills, Grand Duke
Alexander, later Alexander
III, and their son Nicholas,
the ill-fated Nicholas II,
c. 1872.

71. Alexander III crowning
Marie Feodorovna as his
empress in 1883 – another
supreme triumph for Worth.

155

Court train. It was for the Empress, and was covered in magnificent embroidery in real silver. Women were engaged on it night and day for six weeks.[4]

The empress also managed to throw some spectacular parties in St Petersburg and at their home at Gatchina, and Worth would receive telegrams asking for a red ball or a blue ball, each requiring hundreds of gowns in those colours. It was usual for imperial parties to last until dawn, when the peasants were starting work, but by 2 a.m. Alexander III would be looking at his watch and sending the musicians home. Her husband's lack of *joie de vivre*, however, did not stop his wife from being one of Worth's principal means of financial support.

Marie Feodorovna liked to play a game with her sister, Alexandra; although they lived hundreds of miles apart for most of the time, they would arrange to meet occasionally in identical clothes and give people a surprise. This would have been difficult to organize if they had had separate dressmakers, but matters were simplified by sending the orders to Worth, who could then furnish the sisters with identical

72. Princess Alexandra of Hesse in 1894, the year of her betrothal to Grand Duke Nicholas of Russia.

wardrobes without there being any danger of a mistake. Alexandra was never as enthusiastic a customer of Worth's as her sister though, for British insularity insisted that some of her clothes were made in Britain. Instead, she patronized the seamstresses' slavedriver, Elise, of 170 Regent Street, while her ladies' tailor was John Redfern who began business on the Isle of Wight.[5]

At the very end of his life Worth was close to a third imperial coronation commission. Alexander III died in 1894, so preparations began for the coronation of Nicholas II in May 1896, and Maison Worth had started work on the gowns when Worth died in 1895; the order was completed by Jean-Philippe. Marie Feodorovna, now Empress Dowager, needed another court robe, and so did the new Empress 'Alix', Alexandra Feodorovna, the last czarina, as did all the grand duchesses and princesses. Accordingly, work had to be started well in advance of the occasion. When Alix became engaged to Nicholas II in 1894, Marie Feodorovna made her a present of a whole new wardrobe from Worth, but Alix was to be the despair of dressmakers and courtiers, for she had little interest in clothes and insisted on wearing brocade smothered in diamonds when chiffon was all the fashion. Her shyness and lack of style contrasted badly with her lively, elegant mother-in-law, and court life almost ceased. Worth did not survive long enough to witness the fate of the last czarina to patronize his house. He was to miss the downfall of dynasties. In his day the number of monarchies actually grew as the Balkan States expelled the Turks and acquired their own kings; Germany became an Empire and so did Brazil. Worth could not foresee that they would all collapse so suddenly.

Russian imperial custom was extremely important for Worth because it compelled the Russian aristocracy to shop at Maison Worth too, and their orders were always large. Alexander II's sister, the Grand Duchess Marie, was in Paris in 1867 and she bought some of Worth's tunic dresses. She was always accompanied by twelve ladies-in-waiting, and as soon as their mistress indicated that she wanted a particular dress, they all asked for the same model, but in different colours. Thus, when the grand duchess spent an hour and a half with Worth, he could easily sell a hundred dresses in that time, and sometimes more. Princess Bariatinsky was another regular visitor; she was the wife of the Court Marshal in St Petersburg, and they had two daughters for whom the princess would order ball gowns at the rate of one dozen each, together with fifteen dresses and cloaks for herself. When one daughter married, her trousseau from Worth was 15 summer dresses, 15 winter dresses, 30 coats, and 1 *manteau de cour*.[6]

While Alexander III disliked parties and preferred early nights, his grandducal brothers, Vladimir and Alexis, did not share his attitude, indulging in riotous party-going and night-clubbing in St Petersburg and Paris. Thanks to them high society in the capital of Russia flourished, for they were always willing to grace a ball or a masquerade. The long tradition of extravagant expenditure on entertaining, and the taste for heavily bejewelled costumes were both extremely important for Worth. If a degree of restraint was necessary in designing clothes for Western courts, he did not have to apply such considerations to the Russians, and could indulge any fondness for display by composing the most luxurious toilettes imaginable. 'Give him carte blanche, he is daring and splendid in his conception,' said Dickens thinking of those 'generous edifices of brocade, lace, gold, and silver. Richness and costliness characterize his style – velvets embroidered in gold, and covered with lace; sea-green silks loaded with frappant borders of rich colours – a feast to the eye.'[7] This splendour suited Russian taste perfectly, and it was almost a point of honour to appear in as much wealth as one person could carry. Russian grand duchesses and princesses were accustomed to wearing gala gowns so heavy with embroidery, jewels, and rich fabrics that they could hardly move. Indeed there were tales of a lady who, when her pages laid her train on the ground, came to a full stop because she could not tow that solid mass of brocade, lined velvet, and massive embroidery behind her. Weeping with frustration she had to be carried home by her servants. Vanity can be self-defeating! But to Worth such oriental insistence on magnificence was salvation, for it kept him afloat during crises and sustained him thereafter. As far as profits were concerned, the Russians shared the honours with the Americans at Maison Worth.

No matter how far an empire might be from Paris, distance did not stop its inhabitants ordering clothes from Worth. The Mexican empire was so French and Belgian that Paris was its other capital where gowns were concerned. While the United States was locked in civil war, Napoleon III saw in Mexico an opportunity for France to gain a dominant role in Catholic Central and Southern America. If a canal could be built to connect the Atlantic and the Pacific oceans, it would bring France immense profits from the sudden build-up of trade. Deceiving Britain and Spain as to his true intentions – to establish a French puppet state in Mexico – Napoleon III sent in his troops and after initial setbacks they took Mexico City in June 1863.

The country had been an empire, very briefly, in its history, and Napoleon III now determined that it should be so again. As emperor he selected the Archduke Maximilian of Austria, who had married Princess Charlotte of the Belgians at Brussels on 27 July 1857, when he was twenty-five and she seventeen. The couple came to Paris early in 1864 and, since the Mexican empire was a French creation, it followed that the new empress should obtain her wardrobe from the French imperial couturier. When a group of Mexican conservatives formally offered Maximilian and Charlotte the crown, the young empress received them in a Worth court robe of crimson, trimmed with Brussels lace. Suitably laden with trunks and dress cases, the imperial couple sailed for Mexico. During the voyage Maximilian, with typical Hapsburg attention to detail, compiled 600 pages of directions for court etiquette, dress and precedence, for his future state.

They reached their new capital in June 1864, but instead of concentrating on Mexico's enormous internal problems, Maximilian was more concerned with the glorious display of monarchy. He converted the old Spanish fortress of Chapultepec into a mixture of Versailles and Schönbrunn, and started to hold glittering receptions in an attempt to equal the brilliance of the court at the Tuileries. He had Napoleon's Cent-Gardes copied with their uniforms of sky-blue and silver, and the empress, called Carlotta by the Mexicans, gave Monday balls like Empress Eugénie back in France. These were held in the palace ballroom, with the emperor and empress presiding beneath a velvet canopy, but for all the glitter the atmosphere was stiff and dull, and lacked Parisian *élan*.[8] According to her lady-in-waiting, Countess Paula Kollonitz, Empress Carlotta loved showing off:

> . . . Simple as she was in her daily life, her habits and needs, she dearly loved state magnificence on her appearance in public; she herself had a childlike joy in showing herself on great occasions to the astonished multitudes in her diadem and gold embroidered robe, with its long and highly adorned red velvet train hanging from her shoulders.[9]

Of course the shoulder-hung train was a Worth speciality. Some French comtesses and diplomats came to the new court, so Worth gowns were as frequent here as in European courts. Behind the display, however, both private and public life were sour. The new emperor used his position to work his way through the empress's Mexican ladies, and even fathered a bastard on the gardener's teenage wife. The effect on his twenty-four-year-old empress can be left to the imagination. Everyone agreed that she had more intelligence than her husband, so she could not have been deceived as to what was going on.

Outside the court Mexican opposition was increasing. The French had underestimated the strength of Mexican republicanism, and there was growing resentment at this imposition of an Austrian emperor and a Belgian empress by French troops. By 1866 the imperial court found itself hemmed in by republican armies, so in July Carlotta was sent back to Europe to plead for help. She met with a flat refusal from Napoleon III, who would not commit more resources to his own enterprise, and the rest of Europe was too shaken by Prussia's defeat of Austria to have any thoughts for Mexico. Distraught with anxiety, struggling to save a husband who did not deserve her, terrified of the outcome, Carlotta had a mental breakdown and began to suffer from delusions of persecution. She was certified as insane and after being passed round her relations was eventually taken in, without enthusiasm, by her brother Leopold II of the Belgians, who lodged her in the Château de Bouchot in November 1866. She was twenty-six and remained there until her death in 1927 when she was eighty-six. Back in Mexico, Maximilian was captured by the republicans in May 1867 and shot on 19 June. The three-year empire was over – except for Carlotta. When her sister-in-law Empress Elizabeth of Austria called on her in 1875 she was horrified to find her sitting on a mock throne wearing a tinsel crown, but her attendants kept her very elegantly dressed and well groomed.[10] Her Worth finery helped her to remain an empress, if only in her mind.

A much longer lived empire, on the opposite side of the world, also began to hear of Worth. In the reign of Meiji-Tennó, 1867–1912, Japan was reorganized on the European model and old customs began to die: men stopped wearing topknots, and women stopped blacking their teeth, while class distinctions in kimono were abolished in 1868. Westerners had been regarded as smelly barbarians, but now Japan's emperor was taking them as his model, and his empress had to play her part. Worth day clothes were ordered easily enough, for they covered the body in much the same way that the kimono did, but Western evening wear was a problem. Respectable Japanese ladies did not show their shoulders in public, or have low-cut necklines, so Worth was asked to provide evening dresses that were not indecent by Japanese standards. By now, of course, Worth was an expert in coping with the different regulations of individual courts and he solved the problem with ease. It was enough to make evening gowns on the pattern of day dresses, with high necklines, but in richer materials, with large patterns to appeal to Japanese taste, in heavy Lyon silk with flower designs. When the gowns arrived in Tokyo the emperor was entirely satisfied, which serves to show how well Worth understood the nuances in national taste over clothing from one country to another.

Amongst royal houses it was the Bourbons of Spain and the Bragança-Saxe-Coburgs of Portugal who made the use of Maison Worth a regular tradition to be handed down from one queen to the next. The first of the Spaniards was Isabella II, who came to the throne as a baby in 1833. Like a surprising number of monarchs she was not adequately trained for the job, and she developed into a wilful, impulsive intriguer. Clothes were one of her passions – the other was men. The rise of Worth immediately caught her interest, and orders for lavish gowns flowed from Madrid to Paris. Good taste was not her forte, however, and the queen would pile on the ornaments and decorations until the pure elegance of Worth was buried beneath an encrustation like a Spanish altar. Isabella was in Paris in 1867 for Napoleon III's exhibition jamboree, and Worth was summoned to receive her demands – he did not condescend to wait on crowned heads. But Isabella's official custom was brief. In 1868 her army and navy invited her to leave Spain for good, considering her government and private life a national disgrace. So back she went to Paris and settled down to a life of gigolos and pleasure – dressing at Worth's as a private person.

Spain was now faced with the problem of who to put in Isabella's place. Her uncle Don Carlos had opposed her succession all along: Spanish law allowed queens to inherit, but Carlos was claiming his own right under French Salic Law as he was a Bourbon. The Cortes, however, wanted a constitutional monarchy and the throne was granted to the son of the king of Italy, Amedeo of Savoy in 1870. In 1872 Don Carlos attacked, and the new king promptly went home rather than become further involved in Spanish tangles. After a brief interlude as a republic, Spain invited home Isabella II's son, Alfonso XII, then a military student at Sandhurst. He reigned from 1874 to 1885 as he died when he was only twenty-eight. His wife, Maria Cristina of Austria, then became the regent. She dressed with Worth but, being a widow in a deeply religious country, her requirements were for sober clothes in blacks, lavenders and greys, with exceptions only on important ceremonial occasions. Maria Cristina remained regent until 1902, when her son Alfonso XIII was sixteen, so she outlived Worth himself, but Spanish royal custom continued. From 1906 Jean-Philippe and later Worth's grandson Jean-Charles dressed Alfonso XIII's queen, Victoria Eugenia, until the Spanish dynasty went into exile in 1931.

The Portuguese house had four kings between 1853 and 1910 – of the four, one died young and one was assassinated. Luis I reigned the longest from 1861 to 1889 – and was both a model monarch and a Shakespearean scholar. His wife, Maria Pia, Victor Emmanuel's daughter, was a loyal customer of Worth's where she bought her finery, and this Italian connection was another of the couturier's regular royal supports. It was the downfall of these South European monarchies in the twentieth century which was to undermine Maison

Worth in the end, for they had helped Worth's heirs to survive the collapse of the empires.

Outside royalty, some of Worth's most important commissions were for the British Empire in India. Queen Victoria and Princess Alexandra might not be very forthcoming, but there was no hesitation on the part of the British aristocracy to avail themselves of the talent of the great British designer in Paris. As was seen in Chapter 1, the Earl of Lytton first brought his wife, Edith, to Worth's in 1873, when he was secretary at the British Embassy. Edith Lytton became such an admirer of Worth's gowns that she remained a customer for the rest of her life. When the earl was appointed Viceroy of India by Disraeli in 1876, Edith immediately turned to Worth for her vice-regal wardrobe. Trunkloads of evening gowns were essential, as they could also be worn with court trains for ceremonies, and, given the time it took for a ship to reach India, it was advisable to take as many clothes as possible at the start, for orders could not be dispatched as swiftly as in Europe. By far the most important gown Worth had to make for the vicereine came in 1877 for the Delhi Durbar. It was at this great gathering of native princes that the viceroy proclaimed Queen Victoria Empress of India, so the vicereine had to have something special to wear:

> Worth sent me a lovely gown from Paris, of dark blue velvet, and silk let in at the sides and the front, stamped blue velvet on white satin ground, the pattern like Prince of Wales's feathers, and the bonnet to match, Marie Stuart shape, with pearls round and soft blue feathers . . .

she wrote in her dairy.[11] The Marie Stuart bonnet was a typical historic touch by Worth. Lord Lytton resigned his post in 1880 following the defeat of Disraeli's government and criticism from Gladstone, but in December 1887 the earl was appointed British

73. V. Princeps – The Viceroy of India proclaiming Queen Victoria Empress. The vicereine stands a few paces behind her husband on the dais.

Ambassador to France, and the countess was able to continue her patronage on the spot. A visit to Maison Worth was a necessary feature of her existence and even when she was a widow and in her eighties back in England, she still used to pop up to London every year, where Gaston Worth had opened a branch of the House, for her 'little bit of finery' as she called it. Lady Lytton's custom established a precedent and many British vicereines of India – down to the very last one – were to order clothes from Worth and his heirs.

Worth had become established as *the* court couturier for any court, be it imperial, royal or viceregal. From the viceroy's court in Dublin, through the receptions held by governor-generals of dominions, to the ceremonies of Indian princes, no court in the British Empire failed to feature some Worths on its ladies. Indeed a court was hardly worthy of the title if it did not dress at the supreme court couturier, and the ladies of the corps diplomatique found that it was an international rule to wear a Worth before royalty. Nevertheless there might be just one heretic in the corps. When Sir Augustus Paget was appointed British Minister to the King of Italy at Florence in 1867, his wife Walburga, who was German, became acquainted with the Prussian Minister d'Usedom and his Scottish wife, a lady of considerable proportions. 'Her large body was generally adorned, though not confined, by Worth's most *osé* [daring] creations . . .' Madame d'Usedom proved to have a character of similar dimensions, for she . . .

> . . . was a constant source of amusement to me. One day when coming into her room, I found the whole place littered with lace and cherry-coloured bows, whilst she, with a big pair of scissors, was ripping off the trimming from a lovely grey silk dress, which had just arrived from Paris, one of Worth's choicest creations, and she explained to me that she simply did not like it and so she was pulling it to pieces. Anyone who can remember the prestige which surrounded Worth's name at the epoch must respect such independence.[12]

It is a wonder she was not executed for sartorial high treason!

Lady Paget herself did not display such heretical leanings, and always wore a Worth for such occasions as the wedding of her brother, Count Maurice Hohenthal-Hohenpriessnitz, at Oberhofen. The little church was up a steep hill, 'to which we had to *patauger* on our feet, adorned in Mr Worth's best. Mine was pale silvery blue, with wonderful buttons embroidered with little gentlemen and ladies dancing'.[13]

Another lady member of the corps diplomatique, who is an invaluable source of information on the difficulties which could be encountered over court dress, was Lillie Moulton. She and her husband Charles, as seen earlier, returned to the United States in 1871, where Charles died. Lillie subsequently married a Danish diplomat and accompanied him on his postings round Europe, to the courts at Stockholm, Rome, and Berlin, and the republican capitals of Washington and Paris. It was as Madame de Hegermann-Lindencrone that Lillie made her first appearance as an ambassadress, at a reception held in the Palazzo Quirinale in Rome by King Umberto and Queen Margherita of Italy, in January 1881. For such a ceremony, her first presentation to the Italian court, Lillie had to wear a gown that was both stately and attractive, and in keeping with Italian court regulations. Loyal letter writer that she was, she duly told the folks back home all about it:

> . . . about my dress made by Worth. It really is quite lovely – white brocade, with the tulle front – all embroidered with iridescent beads and pearls. The *manteau de cour* is of white satin, trimmed with Valenciennes lace and ruches of chiffon. I wore my diamond tiara, my pearls on my neck, and everything I owned in the way of jewelry pinned on me somewhere.[14]

Trains were required to be $4\frac{1}{2}$ yards long.

The new ambassadress was graciously received, and found the queen superbly elegant, but of course she dressed at Worth too.

> I was quite overcome by the Queen's dazzling beauty and regal presence. She wore a beautiful dress of very pale lemon-colored [*sic*] satin, embroidered in the same color. A red-velvet *manteau de cour* covered with heavy embossed silver embroidery hung from her shoulders.[15]

Which shows that Worth's train was now established at the Italian court too. For a palace ball in February 1881 Queen Margherita wore light blue brocade, trimmed down the front with old Venetian lace. The Queen of Italy was a devoted customer of Maison Worth, so when she paid a state visit to Russia she took a Worth wardrobe with her. She wore a gown of blue satin embroidered with pearls and silver for her first meeting with the Czar, but unfortunately her maid had forgotten to remove the Russian import label from the skirt. Alexander III spotted it, bent down to take a closer look, and declared that the queen was a walking advertisement for Worth, to general amusement.[16] The Czar certainly recognized that name because of his wife.

In 1890 the Hegermann-Lindencrones were appointed to the Swedish court, and Lillie found that there was a diplomatic war going on between the Swedes and the ladies of the corps diplomatique. For her presentation to the Queen of Sweden, Lillie was informed that she must wear a black satin ballgown with *décolleté* neckline, a train four metres long lined with black silk, white kid gloves, and *manches de cour*. Never having heard of such sleeves, she asked what they were and was told that they were puffs of white satin covered with strips of black satin – an echo of the slashed sleeves of Queen Christina's period.

74. Queen Margherita of Italy.

These sleeves were peculiar to the Swedish court, and had been insisted on by Gustav III in the eighteenth century; when the French Marshal Bernadotte became King Karl XIV Johan of Sweden in 1818, his queen Desirée wisely retained the Swedish court sleeves as confirmation of their new national identity. In 1890, however, the *doyenne* of the corps diplomatique notified Lillie that the ladies of the corps refused to wear the Swedish court sleeves because they did not like them. There had been a stalemate until a compromise was reached under which an official presentation at the Royal Palace, Stockholm, was replaced by an informal presentation at the Swedish summer palace at Drottningholm, when the queen would receive diplomatic ladies in *toilettes de ville*. It was now the autumn, however, and Lillie did not want to have to wait until the court went into its summer residence for her presentation. The diplomatic ladies insisted that she should not give in, but Lillie decided, now that she was Danish, to ask her own Queen of Denmark what ought to be done. The queen replied that she herself would obey Swedish court regulations on a visit, and asked Lillie to do the same, so for the sake of Scandinavian solidarity Lillie obeyed. The diplomatic *doyenne* refused to introduce Lillie on the day, pleading a headache, but the presentation went ahead and Lillie was held in great gratitude by the Swedish queen.[17]

The Hegermann-Lindencrones were posted to Berlin between 1902 and 1912, and Worth would have been horrified to hear how rules over court dress were being disregarded after his death. The Kaiser's court required ladies to wear a ballgown with train four metres long, an extremely low *décolletage* like the 1860s, and white kid gloves, even for ceremonies which began at eight o'clock in the morning. Lillie found the long train extremely tiring, and envied Russian ladies who were allowed to wear national Russian court dress, and British ladies who could wear their court of St James's ostrich plumes and white veils. The problem with the German off-the-shoulder neckline was that it was very out of fashion, for evening gowns in 1902 usually had sleeves, and ladies objected to it.

> The ladies of the *Corps Diplomatique* are not always so observant of court rules as they ought to be, and their *décolletage* is not always impeccable. If Worth sends a corsage with the fashionable cut – what do they do? They manage, when they stand on their platform *en vue*, to slip their shoulders out, thereby leaving a tell-tale red mark, only to slip the shoulders in place when royalty has turned its back.[18]

The culprit here was Jean-Philippe Worth and how angry his father would have been at his making such a glaring mistake over court dress. For ladies attending German court events the off-the-shoulder style was compulsory, and Worth would have exploded at his son's sending fashionable dresses. That was a mistake which he himself never made and part of his prestigious reputation rested on his infallibility in this area. No matter how much courts differed from one another in their clothing regulations, Maison Worth should follow the instructions down to the last detail. The clever dress designer should be able to make court dress look magnificent and attractive, even when it contained no fashionable elements, and this was precisely what Worth himself did. And what was the civilized world coming to, when ladies of the diplomatic corps, who should be

75. A. von Menzel – *Im Weissen Saal*, 1888, showing the bare shoulders required by the German court.

experts in polite behaviour, were being so discourteous as to refuse to wear, or try to circumvent, foreign court dress? When Lillie de Hegermann-Lindencrone sent a telegram asking him for a Swedish court dress with *manches de cour*, that is what he sent, correct down to the last black satin strip, and she very correctly wore it. That is how things were done in Worth's day, and how much he would have despised the subsequent drop in standards.

The United States might be a republic but this did not stop its lady citizens from eagerly wearing court dress if the occasion came their way when visiting Europe. If they could not do so as members of the corps diplomatique, the wives of senators or governors could request presentation either through their embassy or through personal acquaintances already presented at court – and here American wives of British aristocrats like Jenny Churchill were useful contacts to have. Typical of such ladies was Mrs Fairchild, wife of the governor of Wisconsin, who visited London in 1870–75. She was permitted to pay her respects to Queen Victoria, and ordered her court costume from Worth, who made it of red velvet. The occasion and the dress evidently meant a lot to Mrs Fairchild, and she kept the costume for years afterwards. It was probably the most expensive gown she had ever bought, and one did not throw such things away. So proud was she of this court dress that she wore it years later at her daughter's wedding in the 1890s. Unfortunately she had put on a lot of weight in the interval, and there was an opening of six inches across the front which had to be filled by stuffing material down the gap. Alas for past glories!

The Second Empire had disappeared down the drain of history, but Maison Worth was sustained by other monarchies flocking to its door. Worth could climb no higher than he was now: the *grand doyen*

76. Mrs Julius Fairchild of Wisconsin in her Worth gown for presentation at the court of St James.

of all couture, the supreme authority for court appearances. His House had come to acquire the position of a shrine, the centre of ultimate expertise, the infallible fount of knowledge on all aspects of dress. No other establishment could boast such experience in catering for courts across the length and breadth of Europe and beyond. Worth's reference library had become a veritable archive of information on court procedure and dress regulations. If a monarchy decided to modify its rules over apparel for a particular occasion, or if there was any alteration in colour or embroidery, where women were concerned, Worth was notified at once. If there was a coronation in the offing, Worth would receive full details of all the requirements for female ceremonial dress, and the latest information on the robes for peeresses. He did not have to ask for such material, because chamberlains and mistresses of the robes sent him copies automatically, in the certain knowledge that Worth would make most of the costumes. No woman in the upper reaches of society who had to attend the most distinguished ceremonies of the day would fail to heed the advice of the supreme dressmaker, and the more the *nouveaux riches* came to visit courts, the more they needed that counsel.

77. The British Court. Madame Tussaud's waxwork display about the time of Queen Victoria's Golden Jubilee in 1887. The firm made a point of obtaining Worth gowns for its royal ladies in order to be as true to life as possible. There are dresses of both the 1870s and the 1880s here.

If Worth had ever wished to place shields about his door, declaring 'By Appointment to Her Imperial Majesty . . .' there was no longer any room for all the insignia that would be needed: the coats-of-arms of the consorts of the Austrian, French, Japanese, Mexican and Russian empires, and those of countless queens and princesses of kingdoms. But what did Worth need of others' coats-of-arms, for was he not a king in his own right?

Notes

1. Diana de Marly, 'Fashionable Suppliers 1660–1700', *The Antiquaries Journal* (1978), vol. 58, ii.
2. *An Historical Record of the Marriage of H.R.H. Albert Edward, Prince of Wales, with H.R.H. Alexandra Caroline, Princess of Denmark; Official Catalogue of Bridal Presentations* (1863), Darton & Hodge, p. 57. The costume made by Elise is now in the Museum of London, but the original lace is missing.
3. *Kaiserin Elizabeth Account Book*, Haus-, Hof-, und Staatsarchiv, Österreichisches Staatsarchiv, Vienna, courtesy of the Director, Professor Dr Richard Blaas.
4. W. F. Lonergan, *Forty Years of Paris* (1907), Fisher Unwin, pp. 199–200.
5. For more on Redfern *see* Diana de Marly, *The History of Haute Couture 1850–1950* (1980), Batsford, ch. 3.
6. J.-P. Worth, *A Century of Fashion* (1928), pp. 210–11.
7. C. Dickens, *All the Year Round*, June–December 1867, vol. XVIII.
8. Sara Yorke Stevenson, *Maximilian in Mexico* (1899), The Century Co., New York, pp. 128 and 223.
9. Countess Paula Kollonitz, *The Court of Mexico*, trans. J. Ollivant (1868), Saunders, Otley & Co., p. 220.
10. R. O'Conner, *The Cactus Throne; the Tragedy of Maximilian and Carlotta* (1971), Allen & Unwin, pp. 344–7.
11. Unpublished MS. diary of Lady Lytton, extract by courtesy of her grand-daughter, Lady Cobbold.
12. Walburga, Lady Paget, *Embassies of Other Days and Further Recollections* (1923), vol. I, p. 237.
13. ibid., vol. II, pp. 302–3.
14. Lillie de Hegermann-Lindencrone, *The Sunny Side of Diplomatic Life, 1875–1912*, p. 93.
15. ibid., p. 94.
16. J.-P. Worth, op. cit., pp. 205–6.
17. L. de Hegermann-Lindencrone, op. cit., p. 205.
18. ibid., pp. 281 and 292.

Chapter 11

Leading Ladies

Worth is so well remembered as an important figure in fashion history that his work in the theatre has been forgotten. His role as a theatrical costumier began as soon as he had been appointed court couturier, for managements and actresses were as eager for his clothes as other customers. In this sphere Worth's love for historical costume and his commanding position were to be very influential in reforming stage dress. There was a long tradition in the theatre, which had started in the seventeenth century when actresses first began to appear regularly on the public stage, and which is by no means dead today, that leading ladies should have the last word over what they were to wear during a performance. Very often the only new clothes in a new production were those of the heroine – the rest of the cast was clothed in assorted pieces from the stock room, and in what they brought along themselves. It was just the same for actors, because the actor-manager system, then in operation, meant that all the expense and attention was lavished on the star performer, the actor-manager himself. With actresses this meant that they insisted on appearing in public dressed in the height of luxurious fashion, regardless of whether they were playing a peasant maid or a mediaeval queen.

Calls for the reform of this situation had been gathering momentum since the mid-eighteenth century. The plumes and trains of grandiose Baroque theatre costume had gradually been discarded in favour of more historically accurate clothes, designed to suit the period of the play. This movement had been greatly assisted by changes in contemporary artistic theory, which was of course part of the same expression. Neo-classicism had made it possible for actors to adopt classical dress when playing Julius Caesar, and the Gothic revival which followed enabled mediaeval costume to be used in drama set in that period.[1] Such reforms, however, did not bring about a marked improvement in every sphere of theatrical costuming, for a lot depended on the attitude of the individual manager and star. Moreover, the impact of contemporary fashion always made it impossible for a production to depart too far from the current understanding of what was considered beautiful.

Actresses in the 1850s would have agreed that the towering wigs of the 1770s were wrong for classical roles, but they would not have dreamed of playing Phaedra or Cleopatra without a crinoline. Even today when there are some actresses who will alter their contemporary appearance in order to perform a historical role – such as shaving their foreheads to play the part of a fifteenth-century woman – they are by no means universal, and the more an actress becomes established as a star the less willing she is to alter her image. This attitude was still strong in Worth's day, when leading ladies insisted on looking glamorous according to the contemporary concept of that ideal, and would not allow any drastic alterations in their appearance.

The fashionable concept of beauty is an image which changes every few years, but young people find it difficult to depart from its rules and actresses wished to look beautiful in contemporary eyes, although this meant that their portraits and photographs rapidly acquired a dated look. That there should have been a change in this attitude as the century developed, with some leading ladies showing a greater willingness to perform in period dress, was due to Worth's sensitive appreciation of the clothes of the past, his ability to create sumptuous reproductions which were so magnificent that they could not be considered dowdy or devoid of beauty, and above all to his tremendous authority over anything to do with dress which even actresses would hesitate to disobey.

Stars went to Worth initially because he was the most famous dressmaker of all. His word was final on what constituted a fashionable appearance, and actresses wished to avail themselves of his wisdom, his experience and his magic, so that they might be the most fashionable performers on the Parisian stage. The Goncourts discovered this when they went to the first dress rehearsal of their play *Henriette Maréchal* in 1865, which starred Mme Plessy in the title role:

> 3rd. December: As audience there was a curious public, and above all Worth and his wife, without whose inspection Mme Plessy never acts, and with them all the world of famous modistes and dressmakers.[2]

In other words Worth's approval of an actress's appearance was considered just as indispensable by thespians as it was by princesses and duchesses. His opinion was so revered that women in the world of entertainment could no more do without it than ladies in the corps diplomatique, or at the court. What couturier since could boast of so universal a monopoly?

The turning to Worth for historical theatre costume was a natural development of his work in masquerades and court amateur theatricals. Stage managers heard reports of the gorgeous gowns involved, and may have seen them at such places as the balls at the Hôtel de Ville. Consequently, they wanted similar splendour for their own productions, and of course they were already buying ordinary Worth gowns when the empress had finished with them. This was now the situation at the Tuileries or at St Cloud where you could see Worth gowns on the court stage and in the audience at the same time, and soon this could be seen in public theatres also. On important first nights both the gowns of the starring actresses and the ladies in the audience were from Maison Worth et Bobergh. This was particularly noticeable at the gala opening of Offenbach's operetta, *La Grande Duchesse de Gerolstein*, during the exhibition of 1867. The Empress Eugénie, attired in a rose pink silk evening gown by Worth, and accompanied by Czar Alexander II, the Kings of Prussia and Spain, the King and Queen of Portugal, the Queen of Holland, the ex-King and King of Bavaria, together with assorted ambassadors and visitors, watched the star Hortense Schneider sing the title role attired in beautiful creations from the imperial couturier. After all,

78. Hortense Schneider in the title role of Offenbach's *La Grande Duchesse de Gerolstein*, 1867.

the operetta was set in a court, and performed in front of monarchs, so who else other than Worth could dress it with appropriate magnificence? For her court appearance the grand duchess had to have a court costume by Worth, the court dressmaker. The dress he made was of white satin covered with coloured embroidery, a feature of his House, and accompanied with his distinctive shoulder-hung court train of glittering satin lined with ermine. Those members of the audience during the operetta's run who did not have the right of entry to court, could see here some of the splendour that lived behind the palace walls.

While some of Worth's gowns for the empress ended up on the public stage, the situation was sometimes reversed. Empress Eugénie was so impressed by one of his costumes for the actress Marie Delaporte that she ordered a copy for herself. Mlle Delaporte played in several of the works of Alexandre Dumas *fils*, and he often accompanied her to Worth's in order to help her choose her wardrobe. Another of Dumas's leading ladies, Eugénie Doch, who had been the first actress to perform the role of Marguerite in his *Dame aux Camélias* in 1852, also went to Worth for her costumes in the 1860s and 70s. The popular playwright, Victorien Sardou, was another dramatist who took actresses to the couture house – in particular Mlle Antoine, star of his *Rabagas* – to discuss the dresses for her latest appearance. She gained a reputation for being well dressed on the stage and off, which she achieved by using Worth for both sets of clothes. Sardou, who is best remembered as the author of *Tosca*, did not always share Mlle Antoine's taste, for on one occasion he was reluctant to agree to a pink dress trimmed with cherry-coloured ribbon which Worth was presenting, but he was overruled by the actress and Worth together. Mme Ristori of the l'Odéon, who had been a great rival to Rachel herself, was another example of an actress who went to Worth for both her theatrical and private wardrobes. Jean-Philippe remembered his father making her an evening wrap – a burnous of gauze and satin all in white.

Most of Worth's theatrical ladies came from the Comédie Française. In addition to Eugénie Doch, there was Maria Favart, famous for her roles in the plays of Emile Augier, Victor Hugo, and Alphonse Daudet's *L'Arlésienne*, who also ordered stage and ordinary wear. Then there was Sarah Bernhardt who gave Worth and the Comédie Française a lot of trouble.

She first arrived at the salon to order one dress for a play. Worth thought this rather odd. Only one dress? Did she not have any changes in the play? he asked. Slowly he found out from her that she actually had five changes of costume, but she planned to order each dress from a different dressmaker. Worth ruled that this was quite unacceptable. If he was going to be responsible for the design of one costume, he should be responsible for all five, so that all the leading lady's clothes were well thought out as a harmonious sequence. He refused to accept the order under any other conditions. After much hesitation and complaining Bernhardt eventually agreed, and placed an order for all five. Work went ahead, the costumes were delivered, but on the opening night Worth discovered that the impossible Sarah had reverted to her original scheme. She wore four gowns by lesser

79. Stormy Sarah Bernhardt in 1867.

dressmakers and only one by Worth. Needless to say the great man took offence at such cavalier treatment, and sent Bernhardt the bill for all his costumes. Sarah refused to pay, whereupon Worth replied that he would require the Comédie Française to deduct the money from her salary. Crackling with rage like a charge of electricity, Sarah was obliged to honour her order, but she vowed that she would never, never, bring her custom to Maison Worth again! We can manage very well without the likes of you, was Worth's lofty response.

Yet this was not the end of the trouble that Sarah caused. In 1880, having broken the company's regulations for some time, she finally stalked out of the Comédie Française for good. This left the theatre management with a crisis on its hands, for Bernhardt was booked to perform the very next night. Sophie Croizette was called upon to take her place, but alas Mlle Croizette was built on generous proportions, while Sarah was downright skinny – none of her costumes would fit! In desperation the Comédie Française appealed to Worth to come to the rescue. With his flair for resolving costume crises, he designed a new wardrobe and, with his team of seamstresses who were ready to work all night, produced two velvet replacements for Mlle Croizette in twenty-four hours, no less splendid than the originals. The theatre expressed its eternal gratitude and preserved those two costumes for some time afterwards, but it does not think that it still has them today.

Among the last actresses from that august national company to dress at Worth's, was the young Marie Louise Marsy. *The Woman's World* magazine, edited by Oscar Wilde, considered Worth's wardrobe for her in June 1888 to be so good that it provided a full description for its British readers:

> The costumes made by that master in the art of design in dress, Worth, for Mlle Marsy in the *rôle* that she is now playing at the Porte Saint Martin, are examples of superior taste to fashion. These exquisite creations are in tender tones of grey, pink, and violet, suggesting the sweetness of pastel colouring.
>
> The first is a Récamier dress of violet Indian cashmere, draped in front with classic simplicity; the skirt is flat at the back, the sleeves are wide, a sash of black watered ribbon is tied behind.
>
> A gown of tender rose-colour, in thick faille, draped in Greek fashion, displays on one side a skirt of cream net; it falls in a train behind; the bodice is gathered in folds at the waist.
>
> Another violet dress of faille. The skirt is flat, striped with interludes of black lace introduced at every breadth. The round cape is trimmed in the same style.
>
> A silvery cashmere draped on one side, and trimmed with heavy silk fringe. The sleeves, collar, and wide white watered silk sash, knotted behind, are all embroidered in silver.[3]

In 1890 Mlle Marsy was asked to play Celimène in Molière's *Le Misanthrope*. Still only twenty, she told Worth that he would have to make her look like an old lady of twenty-eight for the part. The costume he designed certainly had an air of mature grace, and was an interesting combination of styles. Strictly speaking the dress should have been of the fashion of 1666 to be right for the play, but Worth evidently felt that something closer to the fashion of 1890 was really needed to meet with current taste – so he made the costume more appropriate to 1690, giving it a petticoat and gown looped back to form a long train, which had been modish in 1690 and was fashionable again in 1890. The sleeves he kept within contemporary fashion by using the early form of gigot sleeve which was then beginning to become the dominant style in women's dress. Nevertheless he kept to the seventeenth century for the actress's hair, causing it to be dressed upwards in front *en tour*, exactly reproducing the hairstyle of the 1690s. In designing this costume, which was partly

80. Marie Louise Marsy in Molière's *Le Misanthrope*, 1890.

historical and partly contemporary, Worth was illustrating how far a designer is a prisoner of his period. To have used flat sleeves just as large sleeves were all the rage would have resulted in the costume being thought too dowdy. No doubt he would have liked to have made the costume completely accurate, but in the revival of past styles in dress it is the old form of dress which relates in some way to contemporary clothing, which has the best chance of meeting with general public approval, because it does not depart too far from what people are used to. In attempting to reform theatre costume, Worth

177

had to be always aware of this caveat – how far the style would harmonize with contemporary taste.

As with all his other work, the fame of Worth's theatre designs spread to other countries, and actresses began to demand wardrobes from Maison Worth, whether they were appearing in Stockholm or New York. In England, when that horizontal beauty Lillie Langtry took to the stage to earn some money in a vertical position, she demanded that all her gowns should come from Monsieur Worth. She was to appear in a revival of Sheridan's *The School for Scandal* at the Prince's Theatre, in February 1885.

81. Lillie Langtry as Lady Teazle in *The School for Scandal*, 1885.

As the comedy had been written in the eighteenth century it ought to have period costume, and who else could recreate past fashions so well as Worth? He designed all her costumes for the play, and they attracted much attention. The *Queen* magazine published a full spread of Mrs Langtry's wardrobe, and a cartoon appeared revealing the horror of the rest of the cast, for they would all be upstaged by the splendour and beauty of the Worth gowns. This was the inevitable fate of those not in lead parts, for they did not get new clothes. Their costumes in this case were all hired from Nathan's, while the programme proudly proclaimed that Mrs Langtry's were specially commissioned from Worth et Cie, which of course was part of the publicity. A wardrobe from Worth was an added attraction.

Great care was needed in recreating the clothes of 1777, for the high hairstyles and huge mob caps of the period could appear to swamp an actress. Worth therefore used silk gauze for the mob cap and the fichus, which gave them a degree of lightness and softness, avoiding the hardness of cotton. It was important not to hide Mrs Langtry's face, for it was part of her fortune, depicted by Millais, and pursued by Oscar Wilde and the Prince of Wales. Very subtly Worth achieved historical accuracy, while allowing the contemporary ideal of beauty – Langtry's Grecian profile – to show to advantage. Thanks to him she was able to play Lady Teazle without being dwarfed by her period costumes; in fact the clothes gave a better performance than she did. It says much for Worth's success in persuading leading ladies to perform period plays in correct costume, that a woman like Lillie Langtry who would have insisted on wearing highly fashionable clothes if she had been born twenty years earlier, was willing to wear period costume. After all, she had a lot to lose if period dress made her look unattractive, but Worth had the power to give old styles a new beauty.

Worth was equally successful in the sphere of opera. Paramount among the first *prime donne* to come to his door was the great Adelina Patti. Born in Madrid of an Italian family, she made her singing debut in New York, and then conquered London and Paris in rapid succession and was soon established as one of the favourite attractions of the Opéra, in works of Mozart, Rossini and Verdi. Following such phenomenal success, which made her a star of the Second Empire overnight, Patti was soon able to afford the privilege of obtaining her clothes from the most expensive dressmaker in town – Worth. At first she made the common fault of leading ladies in requiring that her costumes were simply fashionable dress, richly ornamented to show that she was the heroine. Thus, in July 1867, she had appeared at the Royal Opera House, Covent Garden, in Gounod's *Romeo and Juliet* wearing an evening gown which was covered with a network of seed pearls. This would have been very suitable for a fashionable salon, but it was not the costume of the early Italian Renaissance in which the opera was set. Gradually by persuasion and illustration Worth drew her away from this thoughtless attitude, and told her that she could look just as important and impressive in a period costume, suitably adorned and elegantly designed. Patti started to dress at Worth more and more, ordering both her stage and private wardrobes from him, and so she came increasingly under his influence, heeded his advice, and allowed herself to be dressed in period dress for period works. Jean-Philippe thought his father was Patti's exclusive dressmaker, but this was not true as two of her theatre costumes in the Museum of London were made by Brossier frères in Paris; nevertheless Worth can be seen as Patti's principal supplier.

82. Adelina Patti as Juliet in *Romeo and Juliet* at Covent Garden, 11 July 1867.

Another star of the Paris Opera in the 1860s and 70s was Emma Albani. She said to Worth, 'You make me look pretty, and I'll take care of the rest.' Such a request was not difficult for him to grant, for Worth possessed an infallible magic touch which was always able to give a woman an aura of beauty, whatever her physical failings – albeit at a price. Mme Albani was assured that her every stage appearance would be breathtaking, but the performance, as she said, was up to her.

A newcomer to operatic fame was Nellie Melba from Australia, who started dressing at Maison Worth in the 1880s. Only a rising star then, she did not qualify for the attention of the great man himself, but was handed over to Jean-Philippe for his consideration. Worth himself she only saw at a distance: '. . . wandering about about the great *salons* of the Rue de la Paix, wearing a black skull-cap and making occasional suggestions to his brilliant son.'[4] She clearly did not converse with Worth himself, for she thought that he came from Manchester and had a broad North Country accent – the last thing to be expected of a man who left Lincolnshire when he was twelve, who was groomed as a smooth salesman in London, and who had been on intimate terms of conversation with European royalty and aristocracy for over thirty years. It was Jean-Philippe as assistant designer who stressed his father's policy to Melba: 'Speaking of Worth, makes me feel that I must pay him some of the debt I owe for the constant help and advice he gave me, in making me realize how important it was to look as well as I sang.'[5]

83. Emma Albani at Covent Garden, April 1872.

What Melba did not appreciate was that anything which Jean-Philippe suggested for her had to be approved by, and if necessary corrected by, his father. Jean-Philippe was being groomed to succeed his parent in design, but he was never given *carte blanche* to do as he liked, and Charles Frederick Worth always kept the reins in his own hands.

Some beautiful clothes came out of this unequal partnership. In May 1888 Melba was to appear at Covent Garden in Verdi's *La*

Traviata, an opera set in the 1850s. Fashionable dress in the 1880s was very square and stiff with the bustle sticking out from a woman's back at a sharp right-angle, but it was only twenty years since the crinoline had been ousted and it was now regarded as an ugly and absurd creation. Therefore, to have dressed Melba in a full 1850s crinoline in 1888 would have been to court disaster, for she would have been laughed off the stage. A sensitive compromise had to be evolved which had all the character of the 1850s without the dress looking too wide for contemporary taste.

The ballgown for Violetta in *La Traviata* which emerged from this analysis and consideration was a beautifully soft creation of green velvet veiled with pink chiffon, trimmed with light fur. It had the most important elements of an evening dress in the 1850s, the off-the-shoulder neckline, the distinctive tiers of frills in the skirt, and Melba had her hair dressed low on the neck, interwoven with flowers at the nape, which was exactly the hairstyle so much associated with Empress Eugénie during that period, but the costume had no crinoline. It was a masterly solution to the problem, and the influence of Worth senior was dominant, for who knew better than he the nature of clothes back in the 1850s? Melba was delighted with it, and all her theatre clothes from Maison Worth enchanted her repeatedly.

> Some of the dresses which Worth made for me were dreams of beauty. In particular, there was an exquisite coat of cloth of gold, hand-painted and sewn with jewels, which I wore in *Lohengrin*. It was so lovely that when I appeared in Russia before the Tsar and Tsaritsa they sent for me after the second act, and one of the first actions of the Tsaritsa was to bend over my cloak and take it in her hands and to stroke it, saying: 'How perfectly lovely this is.'[6]

This was in February 1891 when Melba was on tour with Jean and Edouard de Reszke. That self-same cloak had been dumped on the ground at the frontier station when surly Russian Custom officials had turned out all of Melba's luggage and dress cases before allowing her to proceed to St Petersburg, which was not the sort of treatment to which a *prima donna* or a Worth gown was accustomed. The Czarina who admired the cloak so much was Marie Feodorovna who knew a Worth when she saw one. One wonders if she used the occasion to remind Alexander III that clothes from Maison Worth really were worth the money. What other milliner could have made such luxurious yet such elegant gowns? It will be noticed that there was no lowering of house standards for theatre costume. The best materials were employed, as in masquerade clothes or fashionable wear, not theatrical tat. The silks, the velvets, the jewels, were all real, not imitations or inferior quality. Excellence applied as much here as

84. Nellie Melba as Violetta
in *La Traviata*, 1888.

85. The cloak for Melba to
wear in *Lohengrin* in 1891.

elsewhere, so the heroine wore true silk chiffon and not cheesecloth masquerading as chiffon. Worth's theatrical illusions were just as impressive off stage as on.

Adelina Patti's successor at the Paris Opéra was the American singer Emma Eames, who in July 1894 was invited to Covent Garden to sing the role of the Countess of Longford in Emil Bach's one act opera, *The Lady of Longford*. The period of the piece was the 1630s, so when Mme Eames asked Worth to make the costume he was delighted as the seventeenth century was his favourite period in the history of dress – we have seen him revive its bustle for fashionable clothes in 1869 (fig. 44). What is more, fashion in 1894 was not too remote from

86. Emma Eames as the title role in *The Lady of Longford*, Covent Garden, 21 July 1894.

fashion in 1634, as both decades favoured very large sleeves, and this enabled Worth to create the costume with full historical accuracy – secure in the knowledge that contemporary audiences would not consider large sleeves to be alien and grotesque. Turning to Van Dyck for his inspiration, Worth designed a costume that was as close to period as was possible – with slashed sleeves, falling lace collar, square neckline – and he also persuaded the singer to dress her hair correctly, as he had done with Melba, so that the whole period image was recreated. Thus, when conditions allowed, a Worth theatrical costume could be as accurate as human hands could make it.

Opera singers also gave public recitals, and on these occasions a grand evening gown was essential so that the *prima donna* could impress the audience from the moment she appeared on the platform. Naturally, therefore, concert artistes turned to Worth for something sumptuous. Emma Eames and Patti ordered such gowns, and in the Brooklyn Museum, New York, there is a Worth concert gown for the American singer Mrs Daniel Drew of about 1880. It is of white brocade with a pattern of oak leaves and acorns, the skirt edged with silk fringes and sweeping out into a full train. It is stately and formal, achieving grandeur without being too ornate or heavy, and is a surviving example of the restrained taste exercised by the master when creating semi-theatrical wear.

It became a regular feature of Maison Worth to dress a singer in both her public and her private lives, in the same way that the House did with so many actresses. This applied to Nellie Melba as much as it did to Patti, for no star would have wished to limit the effect of a Worth creation to the inside of theatres, so they rushed to him for clothes that were equally impressive for their social lives. Although Worth himself died before the advent of filmstars, two of his clients were to act on film after the turn of the century: Sarah Bernhardt, and the great actress Eleonora Duse who obtained both her private and theatrical wardrobes from Worth – so the range of his theatrical clientele was wide indeed.

Time of course takes it toll, as Melba noticed:

> I always felt very smart when I came back from Paris with a new collection of Worth dresses, although when I look back at the rather faded photographs of myself in those days I can hardly help laughing at the fantastic fashions which we used to think beautiful.[7]

That was the fundamental problem in reviving any form of dress for the stage, for it is the inevitable fate of any design that the ideal image of one generation will not do for dressing or housing the next. The nearer one is to a style that is just past, the uglier it appears; the further a style recedes, the more attractive it can grow. The problem with recent designs is that one can remember how far the reality of the fashion failed to meet with the idealization, how unsuitable it looked on certain figures and to certain faces, how bizarre were the attempts of contemporaries to mould themselves into the new image, and the fate of that fashion as it became vulgarized. Moreover, some people will stick to a fashion even when it has gone out of date because it was the image of their youth, so that forty years after a mode, one can still find some traces of its clothes and make-up on figures and faces whom it has ceased to flatter. A similar retention can be seen in men's sexual imagery. A man's concept of the desirable woman is conditioned by the fashions of his youth, for that was the time when he first became sexually aware of women, and he can retain this particular image as his ideal of erotic arousal for the rest of his life; which is why some men still drool over thoughts of frilly underwear or black suspenders decades after such items have disappeared from the fashionable lady's wardrobe.

The theatrical costumier has to be aware of all the subtleties involved in attitudes towards clothes of previous years. He has to be conscious of the vision of his own day, and how it will see the different styles of earlier periods: whether it will find them attractive or hideous, according to their similarity or disparity to what was in favour then. Worth showed great ability in being able to reinterpret past styles of dress, and great tact in making the recreation acceptable to modern eyes, while striving to remain as faithful to the original fashion as contemporary attitudes would allow. Worth was a purist when circumstances permitted; when not, he was a reluctant compromiser. Loving art and clothes from earlier periods as he did, his main interest in the theatre was to bring those fashions back to life.

Notes

1. Illustrations of these developments can be seen in Diana de Marly, *A History of European Theatre* (1971), Visual Publications educational filmstrips, pts 6 and 7.
2. Edmond and Jules de Goncourt, *Journal* (1891), Bibliothèque Charpentier, vol. II.
3. *The Woman's World*, ed. O. Wilde, June 1888, p. 382.
4. Dame Nellie Melba, *Melodies and Memories* (1925), Thornton Butterworth, pp. 150–1.
5. ibid.
6. ibid.
7. ibid.

Chapter 12

Le Grand Doyen

In the last decade of his life Worth was revered as no dress designer had ever been before. The names of the tailors and dressmakers who created the great gowns of the distant past are known only to those of us who dig through the archives, but the name of Worth is still remembered today as signifying something special. So august was his position, so unchallenged his command, that he was held in awe. George Sala of the *Daily Telegraph* saw him as combining the qualities of several famous figures from history:

> It is in the Rue de la Paix where the veritable Temple of Fashion is situate, the *sanctum sanctorum* of feminine frivolity, over the more than Eleusinian mysteries of which the great Worth presides in person. The masculine eye has no more chance of penetrating its arcana than those of the Bona Dea; yet reports have from time to time reached me that the hierophant combines the suavity of a Grenville, the diplomatic address of a Metternich, the firmness of a Wellington, and the prompt *coup d'œil* of a Napoleon; and that before him princesses discrown themselves, duchesses tremble, countesses bow their aristocratic heads in mute acquiescence, and citizenesses of the Transatlantic Republic humbly abnegate that self-assertiveness which is one of their most prominent characteristics.[1]

The first couturier went in fear of no one, for he was paramount, an authority whom no one dared to challenge or ignore. Jean-Philippe saw his father as:

> A potentate, adored by his family and his employees, and his slightest word heeded by all women, from queens to commoners. He even had his way with Empress Eugénie herself upon occasion. Therefore it was only natural that in time he came to have no awe of anything, neither of the royalty of birth nor wealth, and to recognize only two higher in authority than himself – God and the Emperor.[2]

The former apprentice at Swan & Edgar, the former shop assistant at Lewis & Allenby, the leading salesman at Gagelin, was telling empresses what to do. He could look a queen in the eye and inform her that her taste in clothes was abysmal and needed his immediate attention. Worth was never arrogant, but he knew his own value and was touchy about receiving due respect. This made life rather difficult for his heir who had to walk a tightrope between introducing his own ideas and not usurping his father's place:

> . . . He was rather jealous of his position and authority, and often I had to step very lightly, particularly in his own special province of design and the development of new materials, in order not to hurt his feelings or seem to usurp. And this, despite the fact that he had trained me zealously to be skilled about such things, and that it was the dearest wish of his heart that I should succeed him.[3]

One senses an air of frustration in Jean-Philippe at this time. Here he was in his forties, educated in design by Corot and by his father,

87. Worth at-home toilette in grey-green damask, with dark green velvet sleeves and brown fur trim, 1890. It was not until 1887 that Worth allowed illustrations of his dresses to appear in magazines on a regular basis, and this was chiefly intended to benefit his customers overseas in the USA.

but unable to launch any innovation without Worth's permission. With his father entering his sixties, Jean-Philippe must have been itching for the day when Worth would retire, but he never did. It was a problem common to dynasties: the crown prince counting the days to the departure of the king. But Gaston was not involved in such impatience. His sphere was administration and finance, and his father had no interest in such mundane subjects. Design was the thing.

The reverence for Worth is shown by the purple prose in magazines which even Oscar Wilde allowed, as editor of *The Woman's World*, and which flooded in lurid colours from journalists' pens, as they ransacked their brains for superlatives. Thus Wilde's Paris reporter Violette enthused:

> Worth brings the same perfect taste to the design of the ball-dresses which emanate from his show-rooms. One of his late designs, in its chromatic scales of colour, its discords and its harmonies excited

88. Worth's afternoon tea gown, Cleopatra, in soft woollen; short jacket of *poult de soie* with crystal cabuchons, seamless bodice, 1891.

and satisfied the eye as he alone understands. It was of maize satin, strewn with delicate rose-buds. The skirt fell in straight folds. It was trimmed with thick flat ruches of tender blue net, and opened over a petticoat of the same net. The petticoat was trimmed with ruches, of yellow-toned chicoré-green, fastened here and there with blue ribbons which was repeated in knots on the bodice.[4]

89. Worth spring costume of cream faille and otter brown velvet, 1891.

During the late 1880s bright colour contrasts were all the rage, and Worth could produce the most startling results for women who could flaunt such clothes, but he never stopped designing extremely simple gowns in restrained taste where that suited the wearer better. In the 1890s Worth sobered colour contrasts down in favour of more subtle combinations. An at-home toilette of 1890 (fig. 87) had grey-green damask in the gown with sleeves of dark green velvet. A gown for afternoon tea in 1891 (fig. 88) was in a less strident tone of yellow which Worth called Cleopatra. Also in that year he created a spring costume in cream faille with otter brown velvet as its contrast, and a summer cape in pale heliotrope with white lace on the shoulders, followed by a winter suit in iron grey cloth with a dark grey velvet collar and ivory satin waistcoat. These were restful harmonies compared with what had gone before; a retreat from excess.

90. Worth summer cape in pale heliotrope cloth, with velvet collar and lapels with white lace overlay. Blouse effect front in silk muslin, July 1891.

91. Worth tailored suit showing late eighteenth-century influence – iron grey cloth, dark grey velvet collar, white ivory satin waistcoat, October 1891.

92. Worth's seamless princess gown in pearl grey cloth with dark blue velvet sleeves, and white crepe puffs at shoulder and collar, October 1891.

The experiments with construction still went on, and the early nineties are important for the work Worth did on seamless dresses. These were not completely devoid of seams altogether but they did strive to omit as many seams as ingenuity would allow. The idea grew out of his invention of the princess line and tried to produce the same effect of a fitted gown while dispensing with the complicated darts and seams needed by the earlier design. Soft wool and elasticated wool were what made such experiments possible, for they could be pulled round the figure in a complete circle. In March 1891 he showed his seamless bodice (fig. 88) and by October was advertising his seamless princess gown, which had a diagonal back fastening. Typical of these wrap-round dresses was a bias-cut seamless gown of 1892, where the wool started at the back of the right shoulder and travelled right round the body to finish on the right hip. Only the bodice and sleeves were constructed with seams. The key to the final shape was the fitted foundation. This remained as rigid as ever, so that the bias-cut wool flowing over it reproduced its firm line and reflected its shape exactly. With that to rely on, the draping of the wool could be as flexible as Worth wished, and the use of the bias was important in

93. Worth's bias cut seamless dress in blue elastic wool, the main section starting at the shoulder and wrapping right round in front to the hip. Sleeves and skirt panel in yellow bias cut, 1892.

193

allowing the fabric to be so fluid, clinging to the figure on the one hand and flaring out into the skirt on the other. This was a major innovation of the period, but few dressmakers dared to follow the technique, so that time has forgotten that such a development took place. It is the 1930s which are usually thought of as the decade of the bias-cut, particularly in the work of Vionnet, but Worth was concentrating on the bias as long ago as 1891. As in so many things he was the pioneer.

94. Worth autumn cloak in light brown wool lined with cream silk, passementerie of many-coloured metal beads across the shoulders, 1891.

The superb quality of his other gowns continued unabated and Worth was now fond of sweeps of undecorated fabric topped off with a sudden explosion of ornament. He used this idea mostly in cloaks, mantles and coats, making them completely plain up to the shoulder or neck, where he would add lace, or fur, or passementerie in a flourish of colour or pattern. As people tend to look at each other's faces first when meeting, he was putting the decoration where it would be noticed most. Worth might have been unable to satisfy

Adolphus's metaphysical demands in 1871, but he was something of a psychologist where subtle visual impact was concerned. Right to the end he was creating clothes that were both original in construction and beautiful in appeal. His was the invention, and after his death Maison Worth never had such genius in devising new methods of dressmaking, new modes of construction. The fashion trade owes Worth a lot more than it appreciates.

95. Worth evening gown of sky blue satin trimmed with black fur and embroidered with beads, 1894.

Typical of his gift for improving dressmaking techniques was his gored skirt. Whereas dressmakers before him had used panels of rectangular shape in the skirt of a dress, and achieved the fit at the waist by gathering the material in, Worth invented panels of fabric which were shaped in themselves to accord with their position in the gown. Thus his panels were wide at the bottom but narrowed towards the top, so that they could all join at the waist in a neat fit, without any bunching of material or gathers or pleats. Time and time again it was the smoothness of a Worth gown which was most striking, for it fitted without any need for elaborate seaming or darting. By making the fundamental parts of a gown the right shape to begin with, Worth ensured that the result was perfection.

Consequently all the best business came to him. The event of the summer of 1888 in Paris was placed entirely in his hands where clothes were concerned: *The Woman's World* reported:

> The wedding which was the event of the season was the marriage of the Duc Decazes with the daughter of the Duchesse de Composeler [*sic*]. The dresses all came from Worth; and as the bride desired to wear mourning as deep for the loss of her step-father, as if she were in mourning for her own father, the costumes designed for her by the supreme artist in dress were symphonies of white, grey, and lilac.
>
> The wedding-dress was of thick white silk, the round train and petticoat very gracefully draped, the front of the skirt cut out in rows of scallops, fringed with orange-blossoms, and edged at the hem with a thick wreath of orange-blossoms, the bodice draped with white crape, fastened with orange-blossoms; a diadem of the same flowers, and a net veil, completed a bridal atttire of rich simplicity.[5]

The wedding was also recorded by the *New York Herald Tribune*, which being American, had more to say on how much money was involved.

> The bride, a beautiful girl of nineteen, with an income of $120,000 a year, wore a superb costume of white peau-de-soie, said to have cost 30,000 fr. It was trimmed with orange blossom and a tulle veil covered her face. The Duchesse de Camposelice wore a pearl gray brocaded silk, the tassels of the same color, and a bonnet of lace and feathers glittering with diamonds. The Duchesse Decazes was radiant in lilac silk, lace and diamonds. The Princesse de Scey-Montbéliard wore pale rose. Princess Philip of Saxe-Coburg-Gotha appeared in pale blue silk, with demi train, trimmed with lace, and a bonnet of lace, pearls, feathers and old rose ribbon. Queen Isabella wore a striped old rose silk, pearls and a Persian mantle.

It will be observed how Worth kept the whole ensemble of bride and female guests in subtle tones which would all blend together. Despite their resounding titles, however, the blood concerned was not of the bluest. The bride was one of Isaac Merritt Singer's few legitimate daughters, and her mother one of Singer's few legitimate wives, who on his death had been left $1·5 million in Singer shares. She had then married the Belgian Duke of Camposelice, a Vatican title. Her eldest daughter Winaretta had married Prince Louis de Scey-Montbéliard in July 1887, but had separated from him in 1889 because he was always pestering her about Singer money. In 1893 Winaretta remarried, this time to one of the most truly blue-blooded families in France: to Prince Edmond de Polignac.[6] Money is the most effective escutcheon there is.

By 1894 another American heiress was begging Maison Worth to clothe her. Consuelo Vanderbilt came out that spring and went to her first ball at the Duc de Gramont's in the Avenue des Champs Elysées to make her début. She wore a white tulle dress from Worth, which had a tightly laced bodice and a flowing skirt. She had a ribbon round her neck and her hair piled up in curls, and white gloves that came almost up to her shoulders. There were two sorts of debutante balls at this period: the white ball where all the girls were debutantes, and the

96. Carolus-Duran – Consuelo Vanderbilt, later Duchess of Marlborough, in 1894.

pink ball where young married ladies were also present. The eighties and nineties were the heyday of the tasteless exchange of well-endowed daughters for European titles which took place between American new wealth and the so-called nobility. Poor Consuelo was to be no exception and was dragooned by her mother into marrying the cold Duke of Marlborough. A future duchess could only obtain her trousseau from one House if she was to be worthy of her position – the trousseau came from Worth. What Consuelo herself would have liked would have been something in tulle or organdie which teenage girls normally wore for evening, but what she received was what

Maison Worth and the duke considered suitable for duchesses, such as an evening dress of sea-blue satin with a long train trimmed with white ostrich feathers, and a pink velvet gown decorated with sables.[7] It was Jean-Philippe who supervised the fittings, for a mere Duchess of Marlborough did not qualify for the individual attentions of the great couturier himself. Only royalty could claim that. The self-styled Upper Ten Thousand might like to consider themselves to be superior to everyone else in existence (a good indication that they were not) but it was Worth who decided whether a lady merited his accolade or no. Entry into the former did not automatically qualify for the latter.

Outside his costume empire, Worth concentrated his attention on his estate at Suresnes. That was where he put his profits, for he remained something of a country man at heart in that he liked to put his money in tangible objects like bricks and mortar. He did not play the money market or invest; it was Gaston who was to set the house on a proper financial basis with investment schemes and pensions for the employees. Worth preferred to turn Suresnes into a fantastic palace. He had acquired the site in 1864, on a hill to the west of Paris, overlooking the bend of the Seine, and across the Bois de Boulogne towards the Arc de Triomphe. The house began as a villa, but Worth added to it over the years until it became a château. He used to commute on horseback to the rue de la Paix, arriving there at ten in the morning and returning at six in the evening, but when he grew older he found this tiring and acquired a house in Paris on the corner of the Champs Elysées and the rue de Berri, near the Protestant Temple, only going to Suresnes at the weekends. The more he spent on enriching his château the more high society clamoured for invitations to see it. Princess von Metternich was a regular visitor but found Worth's passion for building *de trop*.

> Whilst Worth had taste in everything which concerns the toilette, he lacked it, in my opinion, for everything else. The villa at Suresnes which he enlarged and expanded adding a wing here, a wing there, and pavilions and chalets, gave the effect of a confusion of buildings on a site which was much too restricted, all clashing with each other.[8]

L'Illustration considered Suresnes to be a mixture of Gothic, Indian, Old English and Moorish architectural styles. Such a *mélange* was very characteristic of the period, the painter Lord Leighton added Moorish rooms to his English house. In addition to all this, Worth added the ruins of the Palais des Tuileries. The old palace could have been restored because the walls were still standing, but the Third Republic, in its fear of a Napoleonic revival, refused to do anything

97. Worth's château which just grew and grew.

98. The gateway to Worth's château, the only part which remains. As the Napoleonic emperors used the busy bee as their device, Worth adopted the snail – slowly but surely climbing to the top.

which might seem to honour that ousted régime, and so had the palace demolished. Worth was outraged and set about rescuing as many of the sculptures, columns and stones as he could accommodate in his grounds. The saving of these Renaissance pieces was laudable but the result was lamentable, for the scale of the ruins overwhelmed the estate and the château. Nevertheless Worth can be forgiven for trying – his grounds were probably the only place where the ruins were safe from political assault. Once again he was making his loyalty to the Empire perfectly clear.

If the grounds at Suresnes were over-crowded, so were the interiors. Beyond the entrance was a monumental white marble staircase adorned with two crouching lions, worthy of a Venetian Doge. All the apartments were decorated with great richness, and Princess von Metternich declared that she would rather have lived in a room bleached white than in a salon of which Worth was extremely proud, for it dazzled with gold, satin, brocaded velvet, embroideries and gilded furniture. Taking his example from the politican Gambetta, Worth also had a silver bath in the *cabinet de toilette*, while in a secluded corner he had a fountain which flowed incessantly with eau de Cologne.[9] Adolphus had found Suresnes and its inhabitant a strange medley of opposites.

> There was a perplexing mixture of patriarchal simplicity and of the assertiveness of modern money, of thoroughly natural unaffec-tedness and of showy surroundings, of total carelessness in some things and of infinite white satin in others, which was so new to me that, at first, I felt a little bewildered, and wondered whether I was dining with Haroun el Raschid in one of the disguises he so often wore.[10]

An even severer critic was Edmond de Goncourt. Princesse Mathilde was another of Worth's regular visitors, and on Sunday, 9 September 1882 she took Goncourt with her:

> Everywhere on the walls there are plates of every period, and of every country. Mme Worth says there are 25,000 of them, and everywhere, even on the backs of chairs, drops of crystal. It is a delirium of bits of porcelain and carafe stoppers . . . resembling the interior of a kaleidoscope.[11]

As a matter of fact collecting old china was a highly fashionable pursuit in the 1880s; in London Rossetti and the Aesthetes were going for china in a big way, witness du Maurier's cartoons in *Punch*. The trouble with Worth was that he could afford to collect as much as other people put together, hence the excess. Goncourt, however, was not an unbiased observer, for he loathed contemporary taste and considered certain aspects of the eighteenth century to be superior to anything modern. The crowded interiors, the shelves of porcelain, the sumptuous hangings and the ornate furniture which he condemned were the height of contemporary fashion in interior design. Simplicity was out of vogue and Worth was merely following the current mode, only more so. He who preached purity in dress was unable to apply the same vision to décor, and followed furnishing fashion.

If the interiors were overdone, the gardens were much admired. Apart from the vast conservatory with its forest of palm trees and ferns, there were grassy slopes on which grew lilies, irises and gladioli in that very natural English manner. Princess von Metternich was enchanted and had never seen a floral arrangement like it, being more accustomed to formal French gardens and the densely packed flowerbeds of the Second Empire. The informality of Worth's gardens she considered charming. There was nothing wrong with the reception either.

> Whenever one went to visit Suresnes, M. and Mme Worth never failed to serve us with a tasty snack, either in the garden or in the magnificent dining-room. The tea service was in vermeil china; the servants, in kneebreeches and silk stockings, had the air of being at a stately home; in a word, everything was done with remarkably good style.
>
> The master of the house did the honours simply and without affectation. His wife, on the other hand, put on airs and acted the great lady. The sons . . . held themselves modestly apart.

It would be too much to expect a grande dame of the nineteenth century not to find fault with a hostess who began her career as a shop model, but is surprising considering that the princess had never been ashamed to be seen in public with Mme Worth and had launched fashions so often with her.

The British ambassador and his wife had no such qualms. They loved the Worths and often went to Suresnes for tea. Lord Lytton had started doing so back in 1874, before his appointment to India, and resumed the habit on his return to Paris. Lady Paget would have liked to have gone to Suresnes too: 'I did not go to Mr. Worth . . . if you had not spoken against it, I should have done so, as the Lyttons wanted me to go, they say he is such fun.'[12] Her husband, however, had just been appointed Minister to Italy and he was rather stuffy about the idea of his wife taking tea with a dressmaker. Not so everybody else. Worth was such an excellent raconteur that society delighted in his gossipy anecdotes. Those tales which had not satisfied Mr Adolphus were what the aristocracy loved to hear, for they recognized the characters in them. In his couture house Worth was grand as grand could be; at Suresnes he was relaxed, charming and easy-going; a delightful companion and host.

He had other qualities too. Princess von Metternich was quite a wit in her own right but she allowed Worth similar ability:

> Next, what attached me to him was his wit and his admirable good sense. It is impossible to possess a better judgement over men, matters and events than he had. If he had not been led to be a couturier, through the circumstances into which he was born, he would always have made his mark in no matter what sphere. I repeat, it was a pleasure to chat to him.

His flair for judging women was impeccable.

99. Watts – The first Earl of Lytton, 1884.

It was unprecedented for a dressmaker to be treated with such friendliness by princes, and even today a dress designer cannot expect to move in the same circles as all those he clothes.

Worth's other great interest, apart from dress and his château, was his family. Loyalty to the women in his life was a Worth characteristic – to his mother, to his princess, to his empress, and to his wife. They were a devoted couple, and Marie Worth worshipped the man she considered to be a genius. They had long been grandparents for Gaston married early and had his first child, Françoise, in 1873 but, as so often happened in those days, she died while still a baby.

By 1882 the following grandchildren had arrived: Colette, Jean-Charles, Renée and Jacques. Of these Jean-Charles and Jacques were to run the couture house in the twenties and thirties – the third generation of Worths in the business. Jean-Philippe never married but he did manage to acquire a daughter, Andrée, probably through a secret liaison, whom he acknowledged and brought up, subsequently marrying her to the jeweller Louis Cartier in a very appropriate union of luxurious dynasties.

Worth indulged his grandchildren, and when roller-skating became all the rage, as commemorated in 'The Skaters' Waltz', he built the children their own skating rink at Suresnes. The site was so crowded, however, that he had to install this facility on the roof of his stables. The grandchildren of course held their grandfather in some awe, but Worth probably treated them in the same unaffected way that he treated all his guests. Although the family was now thoroughly French, Worth retained his British passport to the very end as an insurance against fate, and he remained a member of the Church of England. His Catholic wife found this very annoying, living as they were in a Catholic country, and repeatedly tried to convert him. But as Worth was obstinate and used to getting his own way, her efforts were always defeated. Marie even tried to force him to eat fish on Fridays, but the great man refused, and eventually she had to be satisfied with a compromise: Worth would eat lobster on Fridays.[13]

His health was never perfect. Princess von Metternich used to become very annoyed if her couturier was taken unwell just when she needed his advice.

> His health left a lot to be desired, and he would be ill at any moment. These indispositions were very tiresome for us, for they always came at an inconvenient moment, and they took the proportions of catastrophes when they coincided with the big *bals costumés* which were given so frequently during the Empire. One day, when we were arriving at the rue de la Paix to try on our costumes for the ball which was to take place that same evening at the Tuileries, we were informed without respect that M. Worth had retired to his apartments, suffering from a frightful migraine!
>
> The consternation was general. What to do? How does one put this on? The staff were like blockheads and could not give us any information; the seamstresses knew no better, for in each workroom they had made different parts. What to do? Taking my courage in both hands I climbed up to Worth who was living on the second floor over the court. I burst into his bedroom, and found him lying on his chaise longue, with compresses over his head and eyes.

The princess informed him that he owed it to the empress to ensure that all her guests were correctly costumed, and Worth agreed to see them. The ladies donned their fancy dress then paraded slowly past the master as he lay on his couch. Worth raised his compress from his eyes and murmured, 'Frightful . . . Ridiculous . . . Appalling', which caused the princesses and duchesses further horror. Pauline von Metternich declared finally that if Worth did not do something that day would mark the start of his downfall, so the poor man had to leap from his couch, fling his compress and bandage aside, and crying 'Forward march!' like a general to troops, lead the ladies down to an hour's inspection and sorting out.

Migraine was only too frequent a problem. Goncourt noted that Worth often went home unable to eat or enjoy his seat at Suresnes, because of the severe headaches brought on by the scents and perfumes of the great ladies he had been dressing all day. The conditions in the salons were very stuffy and crowded, and were not helped by the French fear of opening windows. Worth was absolutely pestered by his clients, for they all queued up for his attention, and of course the staff were wanting his advice at every moment. The place was like a hothouse, and Worth probably rode back to Suresnes on horseback, instead of taking a carriage, in order to clear his head. His success took a large price in terms of nervous strain.

In the last decade of his life Worth began to give himself more holidays, now that he could trust his sons to keep the firm running. In about 1885 he travelled to the Isle of Wight, which Queen Victoria and Lord Tennyson had made a very fashionable resort, to take advantage of its sea air. There he could forget the frenzied pace of Parisian couture, and relax in wonder before the immense sunsets of the Solent. As he was in England, for the first time in forty years, he resolved to pay a special visit to a woman he revered, and crossing to the mainland took train to Farnborough and Empress Eugénie. What an ironical meeting that was. The sovereign who had granted Worth the custom which ensured his success, now encountered the man who had survived her downfall, overcome her ruin, and continued in triumph ever since. He had prospered where she had only survived. Worth addressed her as if she still were a sovereign, for to him she remained precisely that – his empress. This would not have been the last time they met, for Eugénie started visiting Paris again, and Worth would have been among the first to pay his respects on her arrival. They would talk of past glories and of the dead son the empress mourned for. She would stay at the Hôtel Continental, overlooking the Tuileries Gardens, and when people asked how she could bear to contemplate the site of such painful memories she would reply that no pain could equal that which she had suffered already. She was to outlive Worth by twenty-five years – although he had been born in 1825 and she in 1826 – and she survived until 1920, long enough to see Prussia beaten in 1918 and France revenged for the defeat of 1870.

Worth did not revisit Bourne. He supported both his parents financially, but the father who had abandoned wife and son in 1835 was never received by that son again, and had died in 1878 – unforgiven. The shame and the humiliation had left a bitter scar, and the man of success had nothing to say to the man who was a failure. Worth had no wish to see again the scene of his betrayal. But he remained devoted to his mother, and he must have had her to stay with him for long periods at Suresnes. When Adolphus was there in 1871 he noticed that the house was full of Worth's relations. It seems that Worth was not too proud to entertain his own family as well as his wife's, who were also provincial. Indeed he probably took a pride in showing them how well he had overcome the disasters of his childhood.

Worth began to spend the winters in the South of France, following the example of the British aristocracy who made it fashionable to flee from the cold. He did so in 1895, returning to Suresnes in late

100. Empress Eugénie in 1896.

February. It was still far from warm in Paris, and Worth caught a chill taking his grandchildren out for a walk. He developed a temperature so Marie put him to bed, and Worth informed Gaston and Jean-Philippe that he would not be coming to the rue de la Paix next morning and they would have to manage without him. His condition deteriorated rapidly, the chill turned to pneumonia, and he died on Sunday, 10 March, aged sixty-nine.

The news of his death was published in thousands of newspapers across the world. Every little county journal in the United States seemed to carry a paragraph with the news that the great man-milliner was dead. Hundreds of telegrams began to arrive at the rue de la Paix and at his two homes. Foremost among them was one from the Empress Eugénie: 'In my prosperity and in my sorrows he was always my most faithful and devoted friend.' What other empress ever said that of her dressmaker?

There were telegrams too from the Duchess of Alba, Eugénie's relation, from Russian customers like the Princess Wladimir and Princess Alexandra Bariatinsky, from the empress's former ladies-in-waiting, one of whom was the Marquise Alcedo, and from the lady who went on wearing Worth when he was forced to close – the Marquise de Manzanedo. From Sweden came telegrams from Thérèse Bobergh the widow of his former partner, and from Isidor Carlsson, their former *premier commis*. The artist Coëffier who had painted Worth's portrait sent one, and so did some of Worth's theatrical ladies, among them Adelina Patti and Nellie Melba, who was then in Chicago. London society was represented by letters of condolence from Margot Asquith and Lady de Grey. There were telegrams and letters from every European court, and there were some from seamstresses: from Albertine Debechaux, who had joined Worth in his dress department at Gagelin, followed him loyally to Maison Worth et Bobergh, and stayed with him at Maison Worth, and from another seamstress, Annie Chapman from Godalming who had worked for him until 1879. And there were commiserations from the textile trade which was going to miss him so badly, from the Chambre Syndicale des Dentelles et Broderies, and from the Chambre de Commerce at Lyon where Worth had been its principal customer for silks and brocades.

The body was moved from Suresnes to the house on the corner of the rue de Berri and the Champs Elysées, where it lay in state as people came to pay their respects. The funeral service was held in the protestant Temple de l'Etoile, attended by two thousand mourners. The Third Republic did not give him a state funeral, but it came as near to that as high society could make it, what with the Serene Highnesses and the ambassadorial Excellencies who were there

101. Friand – Worth at sixty-seven in 1893; weary brown eyes portray
the fatigue produced by success.

both as customers, friends and representatives. Worth was laid to rest in the family tomb he had constructed on his estate at Suresnes, where he was joined by his wife three years later; but one cannot lay wreaths on that spot any more, for it was destroyed by German bombing in 1940.

102. Marie Worth as a widow in 1895.

How singular it was, remarked *The Times* in its obituary on 12 March, that Worth, and those who were now trying to rival him, should have taken the lead in what was supposed to be a peculiarly French art. An Englishman had conquered fashion and its capital, and held them in his sway for thirty-five years – from 1860 to 1895 – and he did so by transforming that craft into a new entity altogether. As Dickens had said as early as 1863, 'It must be avowed that this Anglais has created a novel art' where precision in dressmaking, where perfection in cut, and expertise in the knowledge of fabrics were all combined. As *L'Illustration* put it, Worth was the first to rescue female costume from the pedestrian bourgeois meanness that was routine, the first to elevate costume into art, and to teach Parisiennes not just to dress themselves but to adorn themselves as the disciples of that art. *Ce singulier Anglais* had held Paris by all her threads, for he was the oracle where fashion was concerned, and from Sacramento to the Steppes of Russia the name of Worth haunted the dreams of young ladies. '*Ah! Combien de fois les robes de "chez Worth" jouèrent le rôle du Paradis!*'

Worth made women chic. This was a new term which he made fashionable, and Valerie Feuillet first heard him use it early in 1860, so she explained what it meant in a letter to her old servant:

> He is very amiable this Worth. You will pleased to know that he pays me many compliments that he very happy to dress me because I have a pretty figure and *du chic*. Chic is a word which you perhaps have never heard. It means personal elegance, elegance having a look.[14]

It was not enough to wear the fashion; women, said Worth, must add something extra special – taste, harmony, style – the application of aesthetic standards in order to create a composition, for, as Worth always insisted, he did not design dresses, he composed them. The total look was what he aimed for, and that was why Worth inspected his customers like a general with his troops, to ensure that the final composition was as pure as he could make it.

Worth changed dressmaking in Paris, just as Napoleon III changed Paris from a town of narrow allies to a city of wide avenues. Worth overwhelmed all the little clothing businesses with one haute couture house which held a monopoly of the greater part of the luxury dressmaking trade, and set the patterns for the middle classes to follow. There have been many fashion dictators and couture houses since, dividing Worth's empire between them, but not one of them has equalled his wide dominion or held it for so long. The Poirets and the Diors are lucky to last a decade or two. From the time of his very first dressmaking department, Worth thought on a larger scale than his female rivals. He was alive to the expansion of trade and industry, and built his business up on the same proportion. He was quick to use the new inventions of his day and they enabled him to expand, both in terms of dress production and in the global range of his activities. He ran what was, behind the golden façade, a factory where 1,200 pairs of hands turned out parts which Worth fitted together. He would have scorned the word factory himself, but that in scale and operation was what it amounted to. He was an artist who thought like an industrialist.

And what did he feel for France, this Englishman who had done so much to reinforce the position of Paris as the capital of international high fashion by inventing haute couture, and upon whom French textile mills, lacemakers, and accessory producers depended? Jean-Philippe quoted him as saying:

> I owe everything to France. She enabled me to express myself, gave me every opportunity to succeed in the work I was fitted for; she has been everything to me. It seems to me only fair that I prove my gratitude to her by doing everything in my power to bring her prosperity.[15]

He declined any honours for his services, refused the Légion d'Honneur, for he felt that his achievement was his reward.

He had his contradictions and would not have been human if he did not. He adored France but remained British; he considered himself an exclusive artist but he mass-produced; he would unnerve lady clients in the salon by his lordly criticisms, but be completely charming to them at Suresnes; he was immensely grand on duty, but casual and unaffected at home. No matter, said Princess von Metternich, his feelings of recognition and loyalty outweighed his failings and his presumption, where a person of her rank was concerned. But what she called presumption, was a talent conscious that it was superior to those who, lacking that ability in themselves, had to come to it for their improvement.

There are few physical signs of Worth's triumph in Paris today. The gateway to his château still stands and there is a road named Worth in Suresnes, but the building itself was demolished by his sons who thought it too impractical. They replaced it with a Swiss style villa which still exists but the marvellous view over Paris was, in 1926, completely blocked out by hospital buildings. There is no statue to Worth in the rue de la Paix, although it surely owes him one, as the first independent grand couturier. The empires he worked for have disappeared; there are not the same number of courts or the same number of ceremonies; the social season no longer dominates city centres; reckless extravagance is no longer a social virtue. Yet the couture industry he founded lasted for a century in his pattern; only since the 1960s has it had to widen its appeal by doing less for the individual rich and more for the even richer masses. He was the first of his kind, and none of his imitators have matched him since. He belongs to the past, but his story will never cease to be a fascinating rise from ignominy to glory. Princess von Metternich was right, he was something of genius, 'ce bon M. Worth'.

Notes

1. G. A. Sala, *Paris Herself Again*, (1880), pp. 327–9.
2. J.-P. Worth, *A Century of Fashion* (1928), pp. 143–4.
3. ibid.
4. *The Woman's World*, June 1888, p. 382.
5. ibid, July 1888, p. 431.
6. Ruth Brandon, *Singer and the Sewing Machine* (1977), pp. 211–16.
7. Consuelo Vanderbilt Balsan, *The Glitter and the Gold* (1952), pp. 33–4 and 68–9.
8. *Souvenirs de la Princesse de Metternich 1859–71*, notes by M. Dunan (1922), Librairie Plon, pp. 142–4.
9. ibid.
10. F. Adolphus, *Some Memories of Paris* (1895), pp. 187–8.
11. Edmond and Jules de Goncourt, *Journal* (1892), Bibliothèque Charpentier, vol. VI, 9 September 1882.
12. Walburga, Lady Paget, *Embassies of Other Days and Further Recollections* (1923), vol. II, p. 289.
13. Verbal information from Maurice Worth.
14. Mme O. Feuillet, *Quelques Années de ma Vie* (1894), pp. 203–4.
15. J.-P. Worth, *A Century of Fashion* (1928), p. 174.

Appendix

Some surviving examples of Worth Gowns

Musée de Costume de la Ville de Paris – (a branch of Musée Carnavalet)
Dark green day dress, Worth et Bobergh, *c.* 1869.
Grey and mauve silk dress, *c.* 1885.
Brocaded satin evening dress, *c.* 1892.
Cream-striped silk day dress, *c.* 1893.
Afternoon gown described by Marcel Proust in *Le Gaulois*, 1894, as 'a gown of pinkish lilac, strewn with orchids, and covered with mauve silk muslin'. The muslin overskirt is now missing.

Musée des Arts Décoratifs
Maroon and beige stamped velvet afternoon gown, *c.* 1895.

Centre d'Enseignement et de Documentation de Costume
Gauze de Chambéry bodice by Worth et Bobergh, *c.* 1869, torn.
Deep violet velvet cape with jet fringes, *c.* 1871.
Dark green evening gown of Princess Galitzine, lined with silk and embroidered in gold and silver, 1890.
Red velvet afternoon gown of Comtesse de Greffulhe, *c.* 1894, with long train.
Black velvet evening gown of Comtesse de Greffulhe, *c.* 1894, embroidered with silver lilies.

LONDON

Museum of London
Gown of soft mauve silk damask, with Tudor effect sleeves and chiffon trimming on the bodice, *c.* 1895. Hon. Mrs Harold Nicolson provenance.
Blond sheepskin cape decorated with sequins (most of which are missing), *c.* 1895.
Opera cloak in green ribbed silk with moiré effect, with appliqué lace on shoulders, collar and front, Watteau pleats in the back, *c.*

1895. Sold in London by Worth's former employer, Lewis & Allenby.

Worth boutique, 50 Grosvenor Street
Black silk mourning dress for large lady, *c.* 1885, with original bill.

Victoria and Albert Museum
Dark green afternoon gown, 1889.

LIVERPOOL

Merseyside County Museums
Dinner gown of turquoise green satin, covered with turquoise green chiffon and net. Boned bodice with separate skirt. The satin is completely covered with the chiffon and net, which are embroidered with pattern of wheat-ears and turquoise green chenille leaves, in cream floss silk, turquoise green sequins, silver bugle beads and green glass beads. Short puffed sleeves of net, embroidered with wheat-ear pattern, diamenté beads and silver braid. Condition very fragile. Presented by the Duchess of Roxburghe. Date *c.* 1893–5.
Dinner gown of pink velvet, with square neckline in front and V-shaped neckline at back, which are swathed with pink velvet. Front of the bodice is decorated with green and diamenté glass beads, gold sequins and silver thread. Gored skirt has a wrap-over panel in front, of pink velvet lined with pink satin and edged with the same decoration as the bodice. Short puff sleeves trimmed with white tulle, *c.* 1893–5. Presented by the Duchess of Roxburghe. Condition good but slightly faded.

EDINBURGH

Royal Scottish Museum
Charles Stewart Collection, one male and one female masquerade costume slashed in sixteenth-century style, *c.* 1893.

USSR LENINGRAD

State Hermitage Museum
Satin dinner gown with floral pattern, *c.* 1880, with dark velvet cuffs and insets around the hem, which is decorated with beadwork, square neckline trimmed with lace, and lace ruffles, short train lined with velvet.
Black satin gown with square neckline and half-length sleeves, *c.* 1890, decorated with dark red glass beads and lace.
Lilac velvet dinner gown, *c.* 1890, with high collar, long sleeves, the skirt draped with panels, trimmed with lace.

New York Historical Society

Worth et Bobergh ballgown of 1860, in turquoise blue moiré faille with matching silk velvet bertha. Matching jacket and little straw hat to convert it to an afternoon ensemble. As such gowns cost so much, a double use could help to alleviate a husband's state of shock. The ballgown version was worn by Mrs Hewitt at the dance at the Academy of Music in honour of the Prince of Wales, October 1860.

Museum of the City of New York

Worth et Bobergh reception gown, *c.* 1868, with bodice and train of flaming pink satin, and paler pink satin skirt. Cuffs and skirt trimmed with bands of bottle green velvet overlaid with blonde Spanish lace.
Reception gown, *c.* 1873, of amber yellow silk faille bodice, back skirt and train, plus a pink *gros de Londres* vest and front skirt panel, trimmed with rosettes and fringes.

The Brooklyn Museum

Afternoon gown, *c.* 1871, in bishop's purple chevron-striped faille, with bodice and skirt panel in plain satin.
Jeune fille summer morning dress, *c.* 1880, in grey green cotton, embroidered with a daisy head pattern in beige thread.
Concert performance gown of Mrs Daniel Drew, *c.* 1880, in white brocade with pattern of acorns and oak leaves, trimmed with white satin and silk fringe, long train, for impressive entries and exits.
Walking gown, *c.* 1881, in off-white fine cotton voile, trimmed with pure white Valenciennes lace and fawn-coloured silk grosgrain bows, worn by Mrs Hewitt.
Debutante ballgown, *c.* 1882, of white slipper satin, the train of alternating bands of tulle and satin. A garland of roses and tulle sweeps round the front of the skirt and up to the left hip.
Visiting dress, *c.* 1886, in amber and russet brown striped moiré silk faille. The skirt is puffed out from below the knee in front, up to the bustle at the back. Pale blue chiffon neck ruffle, with grosgrain ribbon at cuffs and forming the sash, also of pale blue.
Promenade gown for autumn, *c.* 1886, in garnet red satin and velvet panels, trimmed with braid and garnet beads.
Promenade dress, *c.* 1888, consisting of a redingote, vest, and skirt. The coat of twelve sections, is of deep brown faille with a pattern of satin sunbursts, the vest and skirt are of beige satin. An ensemble of sculptural simplicity in the outward effect; very complicated beneath.

Opera cape, c. 1892, in raven black satin, with large pattern of parrot tulips in bright pink, yellow and green, resembling embroidery, which is in fact part of the weave. A piece of this satin is also held by the Musée des Tissus at Lyon.

Evening gown, c. 1893, of pale pink brocaded satin with striped feather pattern in deeper pink, the sleeves and corsage of chartreuse silk velvet. Bands of pearl embroidery across the bodice, on the sleeves, and down the front of the skirt.

Artistic dinner gown with Empire waist and Renaissance sleeves, c. 1895, in ice blue and pale mauve silk with feather pattern. Front panel of blue satin trimmed with lace, and matching satin bows on the sleeves. Two wires help to hold out each sleeve

All these gowns were in the Brooklyn Museum's 1962 exhibition, 'The House of Worth', which also included clothes from the period after Charles Frederick.

The Costume Institute, The Metropolitan Museum of Art

Worth et Bobergh evening gown, c. 1869, in peacock blue silk faille, trimmed with embroidered ivory satin bands and multicoloured silks.

Afternoon gown, c. 1874, in dark blue-grey silk faille with turquoise accents. Bustle and train with tablier trim at the sides.

Day dress of cut and uncut brown velvet with a motif of flower and bow knot on a cream satin ground, 1880s.

Dress of brown satin with large brocade rose, c. 1883, which has been altered.

Ballgown, c. 1887, in pale green and white satin, embroidered with sunburst pattern of silver and gold beads, trimmed with chiffon ruffles in pastel shades.

Ballgown, c. 1887, of light golden yellow satin with butterfly pattern, embroidered false lapels on bodice. The skirt is opened down the centre front and edged with embroidery, with underskirt panel in same material.

Ballgown, c. 1887–90, of off-white brocaded satin. V-shaped neckline decorated with crystal and gold embroidery.

Evening gown, c. 1888, of yellow satin.

Evening gown, c. 1887–9.

Evening gown, c. 1889.

Bodice of ivory satin trimmed with matching net and beads, late 1880s or early 1890s.

Wedding ensemble, c. 1891–3. Dress with Medici-style wired collar of beads, and apron front on skirt of net and beads. Matching shoes and handkerchief.

Evening gown, early 1890s.

Evening gown, c. 1892.

Evening gown, *c.* 1892–4.

Ballgown, *c.* 1892.

Silk dress, *c.* 1892–3.

Ballgown, *c.* 1893.

Ballgown, *c.* 1893–4, of oyster white satin, with foliate and floral pattern woven in tones of green with touches of salmon-pink and golden yellow. Olive green satin ribbon trimming on shoulders and round waist.

Ballgown, *c.* 1893–4, of ivory satin strewn with silver sequins, and handpainted blue cornflowers which are veiled by ivory gauze appliqué.

BOSTON (Massachusetts)

Museum of Fine Arts

Purple velvet dress and blue velvet dress which formed part of the trousseau of Sarah Choate (Mrs Montgomery) Sears of Boston in 1877.

Wedding dress of brocaded white and silver silk, worn by Helen Bessie Brown on marriage to Emile Kipper at Adams, Massachusetts, 29 December 1880.

Evening dress, *c.* 1880, of pale green-yellow silk and velvet, worn by Mrs Thomas A. Scott of Boston.

Browny red tulip figured satin dress, gray bengaline dress, and cream bengaline dress, *c.* 1880, worn by Mrs Sears.

Pink ribbed silk evening dress, *c.* 1880–5.

Evening dress *c.* 1880–5, of pale blue satin and figured satin.

Evening dress *c.* 1880–5, of white figured satin.

Evening dress *c.* 1880–5, of pink figured ribbed silk.

Evening dress *c.* 1880–5, of white satin with polychrome embroidery.

Evening dress *c.* 1880–5, of white figured satin

Dress, *c.* 1885, of purple-red tulip figured silk.

Evening dress, *c.* 1885–90, of lavender-figured satin and ribbed silk, worn by Fanny Crowninshield (Mrs John Quincy) Adams of Boston.

Dress, *c.* 1885–6, of brocaded red satin, worn by Mrs Alpheus Holmes Hardy of Cambridge, Massachusetts.

Dress, *c.* 1890, of black moiré silk, worn by Mrs Adams of Boston.

Dress, *c.* 1891, of purple leaf figured satin, worn by Mrs Alexander G. Cumnock of Lowell, Massachusetts, attributed to Worth and sold through M. A. Driscoll of Boston.

Dress, *c.* 1895, of cream bengaline, worn by Mrs Scott.

Dress, *c.* 1895, of gold satin, and evening dress of yellow-green brocaded satin, worn by Mrs Sears.

MADISON (Wisconsin)

State Historical Society of Wisconsin
British-style, red velvet court dress belonging to Governor Fairchild's wife, 1878.

Index

Adolphus, F., journalist, 131–6, 200
Aesthetic dress, 114–16
Albani, Emma, singer, 180
Albert Edward, Prince of Wales, 49, 58, 150
Alexander II of Russia, 48–9, 154
Alexander III of Russia, 154–7, 182
Alexandra Feodorovna, Empress, 157
Alexandra, Princess of Wales, 137, 144, 150, 156
Allenby, Mr, textile buyer, 4, 7, 10, 12, 124

Bariatinsky, Princess, 157, 206
Bernhardt, Sarah, actress, 174–6
Bicknell, Anna, governess, 46
Bobergh, Otto, Worth's partner, 31, 37, 101, 125–6
Bobergh, Thérèse, 126, 206
Bonaparte, Princess Mathilde, 16, 21, 51, 52, 65, 137
Bustles, 93, 145–6

Carette, Mme, lady-in-waiting, 44–5, 64, 80, 112, 122
Carlotta, Empress of Mexico, 158–60
Carlsson, Isidor, salesman, 104, 206
Castiglione, Comtesse de, 67–8
Chapman, Annie, seamstress, 206
Chasseloup-Laubat, Marquis and Marquise de, 60, 70
Corot, Camille, artist, 126
Court dress, female, 47–50
Court dress, male, 46–7
Cowley, Lady, ambassadress, 100
Creed, Henry, tailor, 5, 35, 45
Crinolettes, 145–7
Crinolines, 75–83, 91, 145–6

Debechaux, Albertine, seamstress, 32, 206
Dickens, Charles, 41, 90–91, 99, 158
Doch, Eugénie, actress, 174

Drew, Mrs Daniel, singer, 185
Dumas, Alexandre, *fils*, 174
Dupin, Procurator General, 80–83

Eames, Emma, singer, 184–5
Elise, dressmaker, 146, 150, 157
Elizabeth, Empress of Austria, 113, 151–3
Eugénie, Empress of the French, *character*, 21; *marriage*, 19–20; *first Worth commission*, 38–40; *requirements over dress*, 44–5; *her court wear*, 47–50; *her masquerade wardrobe*, 61–7; *adopts crinoline*, 76–7; *orders new walking skirt*, 86–7; *regent in 1870*, 122–3; *flight to England*, 123; *love of violets*, 124; *widowhood*, 138–9; *Worth visits her*, 204; *death*, 205

Fairchild, Mrs Julius, of Wisconsin, 167–8
Fashions, from Worth, 75–95, 142–7, 189–95
Feuillet, Octave, novelist, 34, 64
Feuillet, Mme Valérie, 34, 62, 209
Franz Josef of Austria, 48, 152

Gagelin, silk mercers, 12, 14–15, 20, 23–9, 30, 96
Goncourt, Edmond de, 136, 139–40, 200–201, 204
Goncourt, Jules de, 172
Great Exhibition of 1851, 26–7
Guizot, François, Minister, 18

Haute Couture, 26, 140–41, 209
Hegermann-Lindencrone, Lillie de, ambassadress, 164–7 (*see also* Moulton, Mrs Charles)

Irrison, Maurice d', Comte d'Hérisson, 123–4
Isabella II of Spain, 161, 196

Langtry, Lillie, 146–8, 178–9

Lewis & Allenby, mercers, 4, 6–8, 101
Lewis, Arthur James, 7–8, 10, 14
Lewis, Stephen I, 6–7
Lewis, Stephen II, 7
Lonergan, W. F., 4, 149
Louis, Prince Imperial, 77, 137
Louis-Philippe, King, 15–16
Lytton, Edith, Countess of, Vicereine of
    India, 162–3, 201
Lytton, Robert, first Earl of, Viceroy of
    India, 10, 162, 201

MacMahon, Marshal, Duke of Magenta,
    President, 130, 136–7
Mannequins, 23, 103–4, 140
Margherita, Queen of Italy, 164
Maria Alexandrovna, Empress, 153–4
Marie, Grand Duchess, 157
Marie Feodorovna, Empress, 154–7, 182
Marsy, Marie Louise, actress, 176–7
Maximilian, Emperor of Mexico,
    158–60
Meiji Tenno, Emperor of Japan, 160
Melba, Dame Nellie, 181–2, 185
Merryfield, Mary, writer, 102, 116
Metternich, Princess Pauline von,
    ambassadress, *marriage*, 35; *character*,
    36; *agrees to help Worth*, 37–8; *her
    number of dresses for one week at court*, 52;
    her masquerade and ridotto dress, 62–3;
    launches fashions for Worth, 89–91;
    shocked at what Worth charged, 100;
    considers Worth a master, 108, 202; *leaves
    Paris*, 130; *her opinion of Worth's château*,
    198–201; *view of Worth's health*, 203;
    summary of Worth, 210
Metternich, Prince von, ambassador, 35,
    63, 64, 130
Morgan, J. Pierpoint, 137–8
Morny, Duc de, 60, 64
Morny, Duchesse de, 56, 64, 112
Mouchy, Duc de, *marriage*, 56
Moulton, Mrs Charles (*see also*
    Hegermann-Lindencrone), 22, 48,
    54–5, 68–9, 128–9

Napoleon I, 16, 19
Napoleon II, 17
Napoleon III, *rise to power*, 16–17;
    marriage, 20; *tells empress to patronize
    Worth*, 40; *dislikes masquerade dress*,
    63–4; *his mistress*, 67–8; *his downfall*,
    121–2, 128; *death*, 136–7

Paget, Sir Augustus, 163, 201
Paget, Lady Walburga, 42, 73, 163, 201
Palmyre, Mme, dressmaker, 20, 46
Patti, Adelina, singer, 179–80
Plessy, Mme, actress, 172
Political toilettes, 40, 49
Pourtalès, Melanie, Comtesse de, 72–3,
    94, 121
Princess Line, 84–5, 144

Rimsky Korsakov, Mme, 57, 64–7,
    112–13
Rodger, Mme, dressmaker, 24–5

Sala, George Augustus, journalist, 21,
    187
Sardou, Victorien, playwright, 174
Sargent, John Singer, painter, 114
Schneider, Hortense, singer, 173
Seamstresses, 32, 101–2, 206
Senior, Professor William Nassau, 100
Sewing machines, 102
Singer, Isaac Merritt, 102, 196
Swan & Edgar, 4–6

Taine, Hippolyte, 99, 107, 116–17
Transport, improvements in, 29, 119

Valenciennes, furrier, 124
Vanderbilt, Consuelo, 197–8
Victoria, Queen and Empress, 149–51,
    162
Vignon, Mme, dressmaker, 20, 46

Walewska, Comtesse Anne-Marie, 61, 64
Walewski, Comte Colonna, 19, 61, 70
Whitehurst, Felix, 1, 56, 58, 60, 96
Wilde, Oscar, 179, 189
Winterhalter, painter, 112–13
Worth, Charles Frederick, *childhood*, 1–3;
    apprenticeship, 4–6; *discovers fine art*,
    8–9; *moves to Paris*, 10–14; *at Gagelin*,
    14, 20, 23–30; *wins international prizes*,
    27–9; *own house with Bobergh*, 30–2;
    approaches Princess von Metternich, 37–8;
    saved by Napoleon III, 40; *court work*,
    45–58; *library*, 61–2; *masquerade work*,
    62–74; *his fashions*, 75–95, 142–7,
    189–95; *his couture house*, 98–108;
    considers himself an artist, 110–19; *closure
    in 1870 and 1871*, 124–9; *interview with
    Adolphus*, 131–6; *interior design*, 140;
    maternity department, 140; *price code*,

Worth, Charles Frederick—*cont.*
141; *work for foreign courts*, 149–69;
theatre work, 171–84; *a dictator*, 187–8;
his estate at Suresnes, 101, 198–201;
health, 203–4; *death*, 206; *achievement*,
206–10
Worth, Gaston, 30, 133, 141, 198, 202
Worth, Jean-Charles, 161, 203
Worth, Jean-Philippe, 2, 4, 26, 30, 34,
78, 126, 153, 187–9, 203
Worth, Marie Augustine, *née* Vernet,
background, 23; *as a mannequin*, 23–4,
105; *marriage*, 26; *children*, 30; *sent to see
Princess von Metternich*, 37; *the first to
launch Worth fashions*, 85–90; *a vision in
white satin*, 133–4; *considers Worth a
genius*, 135; *assists Worth at theatre*, 172;
*Princess von Metternich's unkind opinion
of*, 201; *fails to convert Worth to
Catholicism*, 203; *death*, 208
Worth, Mary *née* Quincey, 2–4, 10, 205
Worth, William, I, 1–2
Worth, William II, 2–3, 14, 101, 205
Worth, William III, 2–3, 10